THE BULLDOZER AND THE BIG TENT

BLIND REPUBLICANS, LAME DEMOCRATS, AND THE RECOVERY OF AMERICAN IDEALS

Todd Gitlin

John Wiley & Sons, Inc.

Published by John Wiley & Sons, Inc., Hoboken, New Jersey
Published simultaneously in Canada

Wiley Bicentennial Logo: Richard J. Pacifico

For general information about our other products and services, please contact our Customer Care Department within the United States at (800) 762–2974, outside the United States at (317) 572–3993 or fax (317) 572–4002.

Wiley also publishes its books in a variety of electronic formats. Some content that appears in print may not be available in electronic books. For more information about Wiley products, visit our web site at www.wiley.com.

Library of Congress Cataloging-in-Publication Data:
Gitlin, Todd.
    The bulldozer and the big tent: blind republicans, lame democrats, and the recovery of American ideals / Todd Gitlin.
          p.   cm.
    Includes index.
    ISBN 978-0-471-74853-3 (cloth)
1. United States—Politics and government. 2. Bush, George W. (George Walker), 1946–3. Conservatism—United States. 4. Republican Party (U.S.: 1854–) 5. Right and left (Political science) I. Title.
    JK21.G58 2007
    320.51′30973—dc22   2007001703

Printed in the United States of America
10 9 8 7 6 5 4 3 2 1

Again to Laurel, in love, the biggest tent

CONTENTS

Part Three   Emergence: The Tent and the Principles

Introduction: The Bulldozer Stays Its Course

The second inauguration of George W. Bush overflowed with Shakespearean potential. After a bitterly contested campaign, the president of the United States got what he wished for: uninterrupted power, renewed and rewarded. On November 2, 2004, the most powerful man in the most powerful nation in the world passed through what he called his "accountability moment"[1] and strode victorious through a battlefield littered with ruined enemies. Abroad, Saddam Hussein was his prisoner; at home, John Kerry and Tom Daschle lay at his feet. For months and years to come, congressional majorities, legislative successes, and judicial appointments were seemingly guaranteed to Bush and the vigorous Republican Party he had escorted into the twenty-first century.

Bush was nothing if not ready to claim mandates. On taking office the first time, in 2001, he had unblushingly claimed a mandate from a *minority* popular vote and a dubious victory in Florida, a state whose governing apparatus was commanded by his brother, after an incomprehensible court decision orchestrated by his political allies. Now, with a three-million-vote popular margin

1

on top of an electoral college victory, he could claim a full-bodied majority and press his advantage without limits. He could, in effect, eviscerate the legislature by issuing "signing statements" in which he declared that a portion of the law he had just signed was unconstitutional and therefore he had no intention of following it.[2] (Bush's statements objected to some eight hundred provisions in more than one hundred laws.) He could arrange for leaks and the plugging of leaks as he liked, preside over whispering campaigns, and issue secret and executive orders to deflect counterbalancing pressures within the government. From his pinnacle of power he could behold the next range of peaks, accessible in turn. "Now comes the revolution," declared the conservative direct-mail pioneer Richard Viguerie the day after the votes were counted.[3] Surely, the Republican Party, and in particular its conservative base, owned the American future. Surely, unswerving leadership paid off. How the mighty had risen!

To hubris, apparently. At precisely the moment when Bush stood so splendidly vindicated, the radical right-wing ascendancy had actually peaked. As I write, President George W. Bush's approval ratings bob around below 40 percent, where they have slumped for more than twelve months in a row[4]—even scraping as low as 28 percent, a territory previously reserved for the second-term Harry Truman, the Watergate-battered Richard Nixon, and the inflation- and hostage-ridden Jimmy Carter. Bush lost his iron grip on his own party, so much so as to require compromise on immigration and, even more gravely, recourse to a veto for the first time in his presidency because eighteen Republican senators (including the majority leader, Dr. Bill Frist, and his predecessor, Trent Lott) voted against his hard-and-fast position stopping stem cell research.[5] It was no longer true that the White House automatically controlled the House by the simple expedient of requiring that all legislation be approved by a majority of the Republican majority.[6]

A flood of undeniable facts washed away the Republican reputation. Governing from the right was no longer smart politics. Having consolidated itself into a party of top-down discipline, Bush's Republicans could not shield themselves from the rot at the top. The midterm election turned into a referendum on Bush.

I started counting blessings midafternoon on Election Day 2006, four counties due north of Manhattan, sitting behind a table in the volunteer firehouse—the trophies mounted in front of the rear brick wall—in the hamlet of Stockport, New York, population 2,933. This was an election district where Republicans outnumbered Democrats almost four to one. I had volunteered as a poll watcher and was charged with keeping tabs on Democratic voters so that late-in-the-day get-out-the-vote calls could be made to remind latecomers to turn out before 9 p.m. I was vigilant, also, in case any vote-suppressing hanky-panky materialized. None did.[7]

I sat, yellow marking pen in hand, chatting amiably with my Republican counterpart, a trailer-park resident named Sue who was in her sixties and who wore a substantial cross around her neck. She warmed as she spoke of the recent baptism of her thirteenth grandchild. In front of me were two copies of a list of all the registered Democrats in the election district, 239 of them, supplemented by the names of 32 other voters identified as likely to vote Democratic that year. As our people voted, I crossed off their names. Later, an emissary would whisk the list off to another Democratic volunteer who would call the remaining prospects.

After canvassing in the area, I'd been recruited all of sixty hours before the polls opened. The Monday night before the election, watchers were still trouble-shooting by conference call, getting shunted from one election district to another, receiving instructions from the Democrats' lawyer in the course of a conversation rife with interruption. This unruly, seat-of-the-pants operation was the Democrats' counterweight to the notoriously efficient and fearful Republican get-out-the-vote operation.

Still, the Democratic volunteers did volunteer, the assignments were made, and the information got out. Came Election Day, whiling away the hours, I started keeping count and realized that Democrats were turning out in higher percentages than Republicans. I counted afresh every couple of hours, afraid that my wish might be proving stronger than my accuracy. The Democrats' percentages were not vastly higher, but sufficiently so, and consistently, to win if this kept up. It did.

The state legislature had carved New York's Twentieth Congressional District out of rural areas ranging from the Hudson Valley south of Albany to the Adirondacks north of Albany while skirting the capital city. The incumbent, Republican John Sweeney, had won reelection in 2004 with 66 percent of the vote. Sweeney, a top state Republican operative since the early nineties, had a 10 percent approval rating from the National Abortion Rights Action League, 15 percent from the League of Conservation Voters, 18 percent from the National Education Association, 27 percent from the American Civil Liberties Union, and 69 percent from the Christian Coalition.[8] He was best known to his enemies for shouting "Shut it down!" to a Republican mob in Miami the day before Thanksgiving 2000, in what the *Wall Street Journal* columnist Paul Gigot celebrated as a "bourgeois riot."[9] The mob proceeded to bang on the doors of the electoral commission, stopping cold the recount of Miami-Dade ballots. Sweeney called the commissioners "thugs." His heroics made him a national Republican hero; earned him a coveted nickname from President Bush, "Congressman Kickass"; and won him a seat on the House Appropriations Committee, a premium perch from which to bring home local bacon.[10]

As usual, the district bristled with local factors. Sweeney had a history of boozing. On January 23, 2001, not long after being sworn in for his second term and fresh from a visit to a local bar, he drove his car into a utility pole in his district, knocking out power for eight hours. The state trooper summoned to the scene did not administer a sobriety test, ask the congressman whether he had been drinking, charge him, or ticket him.[11] Now, on Halloween 2006, one week before the election, Sweeney was revealed by the *Albany Times-Union* to have "knocked" his wife "around" (her words to a police dispatcher) the previous December.[12] If any more diagrams needed to be drawn depicting the abyss separating Republican declarations of moral fervor and documented illustrations of their moral turpitude, here was another one.

In this classically gerrymandered district, which went for George Bush by 54 percent in 2004, this time, when the votes were counted, Kirsten Gillibrand, a well-connected Democratic lawyer and first-time political candidate, had left Sweeney in the dust, reversing the vote and winning 53 percent, a margin of 13,642 votes.

So it went in dozens of congressional districts on November 7. How did the Democrats reverse the Republican juggernaut? The short answer is: the Democrats were on fire. So were disillusioned Republicans. Together they burned to curtail, contain, and punish Bush. They hated Bush more intensely than Bush's minority of admirers burned to reward him.

Hatred of Bush—of his no-way-out war, his criminal negligence, his useless moralism, his fiscal recklessness, his corruption and all-around malfeasance—all this amounted to an impressive negativity, and surely it was this negativity that ignited victory on November 7. Sheer, shared hatred set off a backfire that sealed off the largely solid Confederacy—the peculiar region that Karl Rove and Bush had believed was the base of their base, the core of their dreamed-for, enduring Republican majority. On November 8, their dream smelled like ash.

The Republicans had run in 2002, 2004, and 2006 as the party of fear. *Vote for us or evildoers will blow up your cities*—that was their bumper sticker. They presented themselves as Paul Reveres, but at the same time they were themselves the orchestrators of fear, fearsome themselves, demanding subservience from anyone who would differ from them about how to protect the nation.

This looked like a winner. After all, almost five hundred years ago, hadn't Machiavelli written the book on George Bush and his Republican Party? "It is much safer to be feared than loved, when, of the two, either must be dispensed with." But perhaps when Karl Rove underlined his edition of *The Prince*, he got so excited at this point that he skipped the following paragraph, which begins, "Nevertheless a prince ought to inspire fear in such a way that, if he does not win love, he avoids hatred."[13]

Seemingly indifferent to the hatred he courted, Bush gave the opposition a heck of a raison d'être. When my wife and I canvassed upstate, we found amid many indifferent voters several who wanted to talk about how awful things—and Republicans—were *in general*. When I made get-out-the-vote calls to various states for MoveOn, and (as the script requested) asked pro-Democratic voters which issues weighed with them, they insisted to the last woman and man that there was no *particular* issue—it was "everything." When I asked one woman the boilerplate question "Do you think the country's on the right track?" her eloquent response was an extended throaty laugh. These people had had enough.

So the midterm election was a national vote of no-confidence—and more. What with Bush's overreaching and underperforming, the Democrats willy-nilly became the big-tent party. Since 2004, they had been taking measurements, laying out canvas, and putting up poles. Fueled by both the netroots and a party apparatus coming to life, they availed themselves (teeth-grittingly, at times) of all the anti-Bush currents in American life. *All* of them—the liberal (progressive, if you like), the conservative (in the rock-ribbed fiscal sense), the keep-government-out-of-the-bedroom types along with the keep-government-hands-off-my-gun types, all the frowners who couldn't be happy-talked out of the evidence of their senses.

This did not add up to a liberal majority—let alone a lock on 2008—but rather, it was a mighty embarrassment for those who thought they were relentlessly building an irreversible majority on the right. As Salon.com's Tim Grieve noted, there was not one state or district in the country where voters evicted an incumbent "in favor of someone more conservative." All kinds of Democrats won (and lost). Regardless of their views on the culture wars, more of the newcomers would be economic progressives than procorporate hacks—even in Virginia and Montana. The United States of America is not a left-wing country, but it would no longer have twenty-eight Republican governors. It would now have twenty-eight *Democratic* governors. As for the state legislatures where leaders learn the ropes and try out policies and (not least) redistricting happens, according to the nonpartisan National Conference of State Legislatures: "Before the election, Republicans controlled 20 state legislatures; Democrats 19 and 10 were split." Now the Democrats would "control both houses of the legislature in 23 states; Republicans in 16 and 10 are split."

Why Bush's epoch-making triumph should have melted away so rapidly is an interesting question to which the answer is by no means self-evident. The prevalent theory is that Bush finally fell afoul of reality—dire events he could neither control nor conceal—as the logic of his commitment to the fantastical, and his consequent malfeasance, played out. Chill winds came up one after the other, as they were bound to, and his purported new clothes proved unimpressive. Even sycophants could see that the man was covered in goose bumps. Catastrophes arrived in biblical proportions: calamities in Iraq, deluges on the Gulf Coast. Cronyism, corruption, and criminality were evoked by Republican household names: DeLay, Abramoff, "Brownie," Libby, Rove, Cunningham, Foley. The past master of events was repeatedly confounded by events he could not master. As he floundered, he dwindled into a less implacable force. He struck less fear in the hearts of his enemies—even in the hearts of his friends—and more contempt. His initiatives began to fail: Social Security privatization, the Dubai port deal. His far-right culture-war grandstanding—gay marriage, Terri Schiavo, intelligent design—did not succeed in impressing a public whose priorities ran to more mundane travails. The press, which for years had been bending over backward to honor his majesty, became (at least fitfully) rambunctious and disrespectful. Although Bush could claim some second-term victories—placing two conservatives on the Supreme Court, for example—he found himself looking like a liability to many Republicans who had never before doubted that he was their asset in chief. Republican politicians found themselves avoiding photo ops, calling themselves "independents," and dashing madly around their states in order to avoid side-by-side appearances with their titular leader. In the midterm elections, Bush, in a refreshing resort to plain talk, acknowledged that his presidency took a "thumpin'."

Bush's declining fortunes after March 2003 surely followed in no small part from the sinking popularity of the Iraq venture. Professor John Mueller, a reigning expert on presidents and public opinion in wartime, has argued that in Iraq, as in Korea and Vietnam, public support started off robust and proceeded to fall off steeply—even faster in Iraq than in the previous two big wars—and that once it declined, it might level off or fall off at a declining rate, but it never returned to the heady levels with which the war began.[14] It didn't matter whether the war was accompanied by a fierce, steady antiwar movement (Vietnam, but neither Korea nor Iraq), or drenched in television coverage (Vietnam and Iraq, but not Korea), including pictures of American coffins (Vietnam, but neither Korea nor Iraq), or whether the opposition party was vague about its proposed remedy (all three). When hundreds or thousands of American soldiers fell in a dead-ended war, or what was perceived to be a dead-ended war, the news all by itself undermined the president's standing.

Whatever the precise causes of Bush's decline, the outcome is clear. Power in decomposition is not a pretty sight. The beneficiaries of power could no longer assume that uncomplicated loyalty to George W. Bush solved their political problems. Problems hitherto regarded as solved turned out not to be solved at all. About success there is always an aura that radiates downward, and about unsuccess, the same is equally true.

Consequently, from Congress to the Pentagon, and among pundits who for years had lined up to display loyalty to the leader, conservatives loosened their tongues, scoured their résumés, and sharpened their long knives—this time for one another. Brassy trumpet calls recorded Bush's decline and fall, even heralded the possibility that it was deserved—because Bush had hijacked conservatism and betrayed it, rather than escorting it to triumph. Respectable opinion began to ask whether Bush's popularity was irretrievable and the long opprobrium of history irreversible.

As Bush's popularity slid, so did the prospects of the master coalition that the president once seemed, to friends and enemies alike, to represent. Not so long ago, Republican strategists crowed that they had engineered a massive turn in America's political center of gravity. With the old Confederacy, its borders, most of the mountain states, and the Great Plains in their pockets, with a well-oiled (I confess that the double entendre is intentional) machine at their disposal, they were well along in the massive project of building a lasting majority. Having fused the energies (and money) of a mass social movement—the Christian right—with the commitments (and money) of pro-business conservatives, they had perfected a governing machine, exploited a submissive and credulous press corps, and reduced a feckless opposition to scattered whimpers of protest from the wings.

They seemed, in other words, to have solved the master problem of contemporary politics: how to channel the energies of a passionate movement into the power apparatus of a skillful and well-led party. They were not only different ideologically from the Democrats—the distinction was dramatically clear from the moment George W. Bush stepped into the White House—but they were a different *kind* of party, with a different orientation toward politics. They were a bulldozer. They brooked no opposition.

Dissent did not slow them. Their machine not only won elections but, once in power, furthered their ability to win again and again while ruling from the right. While Democrats and liberals wandered since the 1960s in a wilderness of their own making, searching for themselves, complaining about each other, stuck with each other in a bad marriage—can't live with 'em, can't live without 'em—Republicans and conservatives pooled their energies, shared their rewards, lived with their differences, and laughed all the way to the White House and Capitol Hill, to church and bank, alike.

But Bush proved a disaster—not least because his character and worldview ill-equipped him to "preserve, protect, and defend the Constitution of the United States," which was intended, after all, "to form a more perfect Union, establish Justice, insure domestic Tranquility, provide for the common defense, promote the general Welfare, and secure the Blessings of Liberty to ourselves and our Posterity." Whatever his slogans—"compassionate conservatism," "ownership society," "war on terror"—Bush was innocent of any thoughtful conception of "Justice" or "the general Welfare," and his reputation for tending to "the common defense" was spectacularly overrated. His blunders were gifts to satirists, possibly the only occupational group besides oilmen and military contractors to thrive on his presidency. "He likes to be underestimated," said one of the epigones of his governing method, euphemistically known (in an America that wants to be reassured that its affairs are being managed) as his "management style."[15] But if there were any more underestimation, Bush would be a pitiful, helpless cipher.

To see Bush as high-handed, limited, irrational, uninformed, inept, mendacious, reckless, feckless, vicious, and dangerous, and to bash him accordingly, is far easier than to explain how a man so high-handed, limited, irrational, uninformed, inept, mendacious, reckless, vicious, and dangerous succeeded in rising to power as the adored hero of a victorious political party and political movement—"Mr. Right," as the Christian conservative leader Ralph Reed called him in a 1999 cover story in *National Review*,[16] or "The Right Man," as his erstwhile speechwriter David Frum called him later. Reed wrote:

> His charisma is Reaganesque, and his stump skills are already legendary. The strongest case for Bush is based on his conservatism, not his viability. . . . As president, Bush would prod Congress to move on his priorities: cutting taxes, modernizing entitlements, and restoring values. . . . And most refreshingly, Bush has shown a willingness to engage his liberal foes. . . . This aggressiveness [in tort reform and opposition to trial lawyers], as much as his stands on the issues, is vital to the future of conservatism. . . . Bush believes what conservatives believe, and he will give conservatism a smile again.

As many moderates and some conservatives eventually danced away from Bush's embrace, at least temporarily, those who had supported him at the outset but at some point discovered his policies to be mistaken or even disastrous were not particularly interested in asking the questions: Did he change between the time they had heralded him as a conservative hero and the time they threw up their hands over his betrayal of conservative values? Was his stupendous ineptitude a sign, perhaps, that they had missed something essential in his nature way back in the glory days when they had welcomed him unquestioningly into their hearts? And even: was his nature itself a fitting expression of the core of the movement they swore by?

For Bush did not drop out of the blue onto the center stage of American—and therefore world—history. He was, like almost all successful politicians in even feebly democratic societies, the voice of a crowd, and his ascendancy resulted from a social collaboration.

A critical mass of supporters recognized him as *theirs*—a sort of delegate, even an emanation of their identity, a mirror in which they could recognize themselves. His usurpation of power, his abuse of presidential authority, his ignorant deployment of national force abroad, his imperviousness to dissent were not departures from the main line of conservative opinion but an expression of its main logic—the movement party as bulldozer. Bush was not just an ideologue, not just the defender of one particular set of policies over another. He was chosen to lead the United States of America not only because the voting public preferred his views, pragmatically, to the alternatives—not only because of what he thought but because of who he was, or seemed to be; because of his style, which they took to disclose his true character. If he was the decider, it was because, in some part of their selves, they were willing to be—they *wanted* to be—the decided.[17]

In other words, when voters cast their ballots in 2004, they were making an existential choice, declaring how they felt about George W. Bush. The question they were answering was, Which side are you on? A little political science will clarify. Despite the pack-journalism predilection for a postelection story line attributing Bush's victory to his dominance among so-called values voters, the gay marriage bans that grassroots conservatives placed on swing-state ballots seem not to have been a major factor—except possibly in Ohio.[18] Nationally, far more important was the fear of terrorism and the support that Bush gained from his partisans who translated the fear of terrorism into support for his war in Iraq.[19]

Moreover, Bush benefited from a deep partisan divide over the value of the Iraq war. Even though Democratic and Republican voters did not diverge in their overall beliefs about foreign policy, and a sizable majority (59 percent) thought that "the Iraq war was not worth it," Bush won 94 percent of the prowar minority, while Kerry won only 78 percent of the majority.[20] How to explain this discrepancy? Why were so many voters inclined to support Bush while disagreeing with him on such a central issue? The voters diverged in their attitudes toward . . . the character of George W. Bush.[21] Was he "moral"? Did he "provide strong leadership"? "Really care about people like you"? Was he "knowledgeable"?

"Intelligent"? "Dishonest"?[22] Although al-Qaeda committed the September 11 massacres on Bush's watch, after months of Bush ignoring ample and urgent warnings cropping up throughout the intelligence services, Bush's supporters gave him a pass. In their eyes, he was the man who could do no wrong.

Talk about an investor class: Bush's truest believers invested him, or some idealized version of him they carried in their hearts, with their powers of judgment. The president was not only their president but their shaman, their designated teller of truth. He spoke to them, for them, with them so certainly and with such panache as to cancel out the retrograde stuff of "discernible reality," to use a Bush adviser's contemptuous term for the merely empirical. Because Bush spent months maintaining that Saddam Hussein harbored weapons of mass destruction in the run-up to war, his most devoted followers were not only prepared to maintain that Saddam had had them, they were inclined to think that they had been found—even though Bush had long since abandoned any such claim.

If this seems outlandish, consider some statistics on what Americans of different parties believed about facts on the ground in Iraq. In 2005, two years after the American invasion, 79 percent of Republicans (and 37 percent of Democrats) still believed that Saddam Hussein's Iraq possessed weapons of mass destruction when the war began. In March 2006, 30 percent of Republicans believed that "clear evidence of weapons of mass destruction" had actually been found in Iraq. Thirty-two percent of Republicans with some postcollege education believed it, while none of the Democrats with equivalent education did so. Two-thirds of Republicans (as against some 26 percent of Democrats and 40 percent of independents) believed that clear evidence that Saddam had supported al-Qaeda had also been found. The *best*-educated Republicans, those holding more than a college degree, were more likely to believe this than were the *least*-educated Democrats, those with high school degrees or less.[23] If the words *willful* and *delusional* are not suitable for describing such beliefs, when are they suitable? We are in the presence of nothing less than a will to believe. Not incidentally, thanks to talk radio, cable television, and the other communication circuits of the Christian right, people possessed of this will to believe could breathe the recycled air of a self-enclosed ideological universe.

If Bush's base was made up significantly of fervent Christian soldiers, Bush was their fervent Christian general: their leader as deputy, representing a spirit, a mood, an approach to life that—to use the word in vogue—*resonated*. He was an impresario—a conductor of popular currents. If he governed "with his gut," that was how *they*, in the secret or not-so-secret recesses of their hearts, wished to govern—and be governed. If he arranged to be surrounded by yes men, rigging the advice he was getting, dismissing contrary facts and views, blithely discarding inconvenient experts, refusing to step outside a charmed circle of sycophants, they not only liked the outcomes, they trusted him to lead them that way because, with his use of insider phrases as signals of common membership among the elect, he flattered them that they were among the chosen few worth listening to. Where war, environmental despoliation, constitutional integrity, and economic policy were concerned, he may have had a penchant for the phantasmagorical, but when it came to politics Bush was a realist. However limited his life experience, however modest his capacity for persuasion, this modern Prince had a feeling for his constituency—what it craved and what it feared. It was not lost on him that his persona, the happy combination of his dynastic position and his Christian rebirth, warmed the hearts of millions. Their fervent support was his art form. What he believed, others believed. What he didn't know, others didn't know—or didn't need to know. What he refused to know, they refused to know, too.

One of the most challenging of intellectual and perceptual tasks is to regain the capacity to be surprised by reality. If you have a working nervous system, you should jump up, startled, when lightning strikes. This is what Proust meant when he wrote, "The real voyage of discovery consists not in seeking new landscapes, but in having new eyes." Lose that capacity and your mind is muffled. You succumb to the ho-hum sluggishness or, better, the pleasant buzz of everyday life. To avoid this muffling and flatness, you need to see through the sheen of normality to the downright *strangeness* of what exists—a president who openly expresses contempt for law, for science, for journalists, for uncongenial opinions, and for the findings of his own Central Intelligence Agency; who recognizes no limit to his executive power, launches a war amid the Arab world without any coherent purpose, appoints as head of the Federal Emergency Management Administration a man with no experience whatever in managing emergencies, and flies in the face of his own experts to deny that colossal climate change has human origins.

We need to recover our astonishment, not for its own sake or for the grim pleasure of frightening ourselves, but to ignite curiosity as to the origins of this calamity. We must overcome our intellectual numbness and cease to treat Bush as an ordinary president who came to office in the ordinary way and operates in an ordinary manner. We begin to discern a pattern and a lineage in this strangeness.

This is what I attempt in part one of this book: to make as plain in general contour as I know how, and in a voice I hope to be adequate to the immensity of this collective breakdown of decent government, the starkness and strangeness of the Bush years, the conditions for his emergence, and the roots, logic, and meanings of this baleful and harrowing episode in our collective history. I go to the trouble of reviewing this history not because it gives me any pleasure to rehash the awfulness or because there is anything much to be gained by claiming once more just how ruinous these years have been or because many of the facts to come in part one are new to the light of day: to the contrary, I am deeply and gratefully dependent on the reporting of many writers over many years. But I hope to illuminate the larger meaning of Bush and his movement and, further, to make a useful argument about what can be learned toward the prospect of recovery.

To my disappointment, and perhaps that of most readers, part one will not, however, serve as prelude to a triumphal conclusion— not quite, not yet. For the political forces that might usher in that triumphal conclusion are late, confused, bedraggled, and disarrayed. While the Republicans were creating a unified power machine driven by the energy of a relatively simple alliance of movements directed against a single enemy—liberals—the Democrats were collecting a loose assemblage of fragments lacking the coherence and force to move the nation in a common direction.

While the Republicans were establishing their entitlement to rule, in fervent belief that the natural order *required* them to rule in the name of a truth that they brandished, in the conviction that this truth by which they ruled was self-evident, the Democrats were often searching for truth rather than brandishing it. While the Republicans were rising to the heights of their collective ambition, summoning leaders who thrilled their base and personified (not least in their appearance) their ideals, men who ratified their identity, talked their talk, and (at least some of the time) walked their walk, expressing in their demeanor their fancies, their boldness, their sense of mission, the Democrats frequently resorted to leaders who, for the most part, personified their failures—their fecklessness and their disconnection from the drive and confidence of popular movements.

Today, there are progressive movements but, at this writing, not enough of a progressive *movement*. There are Democrats galore, but not enough consistency in the reasons that anyone else should be convinced to join the ranks. The relation between the Democrats and the liberals (whether they brand themselves as progressives or not) is tormented. Still, there are serious prospects for not only short-term but long-term revival. Conspicuous among the Democrats in the Bush years are a growing number of activists who see the party as the new movement—as a phalanx overcoming differences to unite commitment and common principle. Bush in decline might prove to be the ignition for a lasting revival of the liberal project. In part two, I try to assay the roots of the Democratic discontents and the dynamics of movement and party that have shaped liberal history and will shape the liberal fate. In part three, I assess the prospects for a lasting renewal.

Should it turn out that Bush's slippage is irreversible, as seems likely at this writing, and his ability to pile more disasters on top of those already committed dwindles further, the catastrophe of his presidency will not vanish. Should he be succeeded by a prince among men or a princess among women, a Lincoln to his Buchanan or an FDR to his Hoover, salvation will not be nigh and the disaster will long outlast the disaster maker in the form of negligent government, sweeping corruption, fiscal absurdity, and the surplus fear and loathing that accrue toward the United States almost everywhere in the world. For a long time to come it will be essential for both intellectual and practical reasons to understand how Bush and his inner circle arrived at a position to do the damage they did. Not only did they lay their hands on history to propel the nation into a momentous and catastrophic war, but they threaten to do more of the same until the sun sets on their last day in office. They established a reign of secrecy, deception, lawlessness, and unreason unrivaled in living memory—very possibly in all the history of the republic. They invited private interests to devise public policy to a degree drastically understated by the word *corruption*. They took startling risks with the physical underpinnings of planet Earth. They loaded unprecedented debt onto the nation's economy. They denied scientific evidence on life-and-death questions. So the rise of this power elite proved to be—and will continue to be—momentous for the history of the world.

The core of their rule is a bulldozer approach to reality— belligerence as an all-purpose style, whether facing domestic critics or the rest of the world. This was true already in the months through September 10, 2001, when they promoted missile defense, abrogated the ABM treaty, renounced the Kyoto agreement, and confronted China. But then, they were a war clique scuttling in circles for lack of a war. Al-Qaeda gave them a demonstrable enemy. After the terror attacks of September 11, 2001, those in the Bush circle came into their own as war fighters, though the practicalities of war—its diplomacy, its justifications, its strategy, and its planning—were all beyond them. They were idealists of war: that is, they took the idea of war more seriously than the on-the-ground requirements of war. War was their defining mystique. But the mystique of war—the calling to war, the spirit of combat, and the aura of "mission accomplished"—engaged them more than did the raw, ugly, and difficult practice. All the great strategists have known that in order to succeed, war must be a rational activity, tailoring appropriate means to attainable ends. Bush's inner circle, the commanders of policy, floated too far off the ground to be real masters of war. However impressive the technical means at their disposal, they were too detached from reality to command intelligently. They were mastered by war.

Therefore, outside the dwindling ranks of their truest believers, abroad and at home, they forfeited trust. As the war in Iraq continued, new waves of jihadis in Europe, the Middle East, Southeast Asia, and elsewhere found in this American expedition a precise confirmation of their most Manichean scenarios. American credibility, as a result, is rubble. Meanwhile, the Bush budget deficits will tie the hands of administrations for decades (perhaps, like Reagan's, one of their purposes).

The power triad—Bush himself, along with Dick Cheney and (through 2006) Donald Rumsfeld, with a shifting cast of subordinate insiders, presiding over small staffs of trusted advisers—did not accomplish all these feats by dint of sheer force of will, though force of will they share in abundance.[24] They did so by presiding over a party and a political base that shared their purposes, methods, and mentality. They were consolidators of power in behalf of a movement with demonological fervor and absolutist pretensions, a movement that, with everything at stake, saw no reason that the power of government should be limited as long as it was *their* government, for the strength of the righteous brooked no justified dissent and the power of the righteous could not, by definition, be abused. They could succeed in acquiring executive power and consolidating it only by mobilizing a reliable and enthusiastic base—and the base could only realize its passions by submitting to righteous leadership, or, if principle caused any qualms about Bush's closed and deceptive habits, agreeing to overlook their standard-bearer's weaknesses and close ranks.

Power of this degree and scope is not built up in a day. "Building a movement," as the conservative base-builders Richard Viguerie and David Franke wrote, "requires decades."[25] Into its fifth decade now, the Republican movement-as-party is a blended coalition of interests and passions fused at its crowning moments by a supreme hero—first Barry Goldwater, then Ronald Reagan, then George W. Bush. Never underestimate the significance of the leader. Without Reagan, there was no Reaganism. But without a conservative movement, there was no Reagan and consequently no President George W. Bush.

The United States is, to put it mildly, a sprawling and complicated society, so any American party that hopes to be national must blend and represent multiple interests. But the Republican Party that holds power is a *focused* coalition with two, and only two, major components—the low-tax, love-business, hate-government enthusiasts and the God-save-us moral crusaders. In the first instance, they are the voice of plutocracy. With the Republicans in power, the chief beneficiaries of the private economy never lack for friends in high places. A Republican government can be relied on to deregulate, cut taxes (primarily at the top), and subsidize. It blithely spins off governmental functions into corporate hands. It rewards wealth over work and great wealth over lesser wealth. Republican government believes in rewarding these corporations on the premise that what's good for them is good for the entire American people. Even if the income of much of the population stagnates, on the strength of their belligerent posture in the world and their reputation for protecting the nation despite their malfeasance through September 11, 2001, the Republican Party has succeeded in winning the votes of the white working class, especially of men. In a pinch, they can appeal to these voters, the erstwhile Reagan Democrats, on moralist ("value") grounds, inviting them to overlook their own economic travails.

Second, the Republican Party is the voice of a particular version of militant faith—largely Christian, largely evangelical. The party speaks for the impassioned and embattled who, even as they lay claim to Christian values, carry—indeed, brandish—the scars of persecution by secular powers: their redeemer God banished from the public square, from Hollywood, from the textbooks and classrooms, their "culture of life" and conception of decency mocked daily by feminists, homosexuals, secular humanists, and the activist judges who protect them. With a passion born of moral certitude and an intense longing for the millennium when all that was wrong will be set right, they pile up proofs of the surrounding iniquity, proofs that enable them to see themselves as moral exemplars marooned in the Devil's decadent world, one becoming more

Satanic with every passing day and therefore—paradoxically— looming ever closer to salvation. The nature of this faith is such that events both positive and negative can only confirm it. The road to heaven is paved with tribulation.

The Republicans also encompass pockets of libertarians and old-school moderates, and various niche groups are helpful additions— Karl Rove for years proved adept at adding them[26]—but these two large populations are essential. So a leader who honors the Republicans' two major constituencies is the right-wing ideal. Thus Reagan, thus George W. Bush.

And here is one crucial advantage that Republicans hold over Democrats: it goes without saying that it is far easier to blend two constituencies than the Democrats' roughly eight: labor, African Americans, Hispanics, feminists, gays, environmentalists, members of the helping professions (teachers, social workers, nurses), and the militantly liberal, especially antiwar denizens of avant-garde cultural zones such as university towns, the Upper West Side of Manhattan, and so on. (The categories obviously overlap some-what.) This structural advantage also holds for the leader him- or herself: it is easier to rise to party leadership if you personify a two-component coalition—if you are a God-fearing (though, like Reagan, church-avoiding) businessman—than if you are, say, a black lesbian nurse or a Latino wind-energy entrepreneur. It is also easier to coax one of two ideological tendencies (usually the Christian right) to compromise for the greater good of conservatism than it is to persuade an identity-based group (feminists, gays, African Americans) to make concessions on what is, after all, their identity as they see it.[27]

Tribulation is now the lot of Republicans into the foreseeable future. Their success, after all, rested significantly on their reputation for success. In the great game of opportunism, which is the essence of practical political life, they borrowed heavily from their aura of inevitability. As their power peeled away, Republicans tangled on Iraq, immigration, torture—precisely the questions that their base cared passionately about.

Still, the party's immediate travails should not be permitted to obscure the immensity of its achievement and the endurance of its machinery. For years now, the debates that have seized the country have chiefly been the debates that the Republican Party sparked: about tax cuts, preventive war, abortion bans, and immigration restrictions. Republicans' terminology (*tax relief, death tax, war on terror, partial-birth abortion*) became the prevailing terminology. Their slash-and-burn style became standard, their symbolic winks, smears, and dirty tricks drowning contrary facts and passing so many electoral tests—all the way back to Reagan launching his 1980 campaign with a speech defending "states' rights" in Philadelphia, Mississippi, the city where three civil-rights workers happened to have been murdered by local authorities in 1964; then continued in the playing of the Willie Horton card by the president's father in 1988—as to have become predictable elements of the Republicans' campaign arsenal (even when the enemies were other Republicans, as John McCain discovered in the 2000 South Carolina primary).

A heedless, lawless, incompetent presidency; an interminable war; a profoundly corrupted ruling party; a deep disdain for reason—these are among the breathtaking achievements of the conservative movement in power. Antigovernment rhetoric is the haze behind which the movement's leaders abuse power while undercutting the government's ability to conduct itself efficaciously, not to mention constitutionally. No matter how much rhetoric flows forth about the virtues of limited government, the movement party has not hesitated to avail itself of the apparatus of rule, dismantling regulations, awarding favors to its bankrollers, installing unqualified partisans to important positions, sabotaging competent civil servants, concealing government operations behind a curtain of secrecy, and above all pursuing a militant and military approach to the larger world. As anomalous as George W. Bush appears, his style of rule is not exactly original. The right espies a hazy glow emanating from the Reagan years, the better to invent a tradition it can rest comfortably in. Liberals sometimes nod, since from a present-day vantage point nothing seems to them comparable in malfeasance to the Bush fiasco. But in manifold ways Bush's government enlarges upon central themes—and methods—of Reagan's administration, which also taxed work above wealth, encouraged economic inequality, bent and broke unions, cut back voting rights, turned public resources over to extractive industry, devalued diplomacy, imposed a simplistic model of foreign relations upon weak nations, warped its intelligence, and blithely deceived the public.

The movement conservatives' bullying, authoritarian spirit, benefiting from the party's built-in advantages, outlasted the bravado, corruption, and criminality of Richard Nixon's and Ronald Reagan's presidencies. And despite its internal tensions, the Republican apparatus is unlikely to crumble into oblivion. Very likely the fixtures of conservative life will outlast the careers of George W. Bush and Tom DeLay as well, for three reasons: the bulldozer mentality of Bush, Cheney, DeLay, and company was not invented by them; their adoring base persists in its will to believe; and the executive government that succeeds Bush, whether Democratic or Republican, is unlikely to be strong and clear-headed enough to pulverize the Bush coalition—to defeat it so thoroughly as to thwart its ability to linger at the edge of a comeback. So it is a matter of more than historical interest to take the full measure of the conservatives' (and therefore Republicans') tensile strength and the liberals' (and therefore Democrats') weakness. This is why understanding the rise of George W. Bush is no antiquarian pursuit, and neither is studying his approach to politics, his rejection of reason, and the nature of his base and its will to believe.

PART ONE

Emergency: The Long Anti-Sixties

> The frontiersman was impatient of
> restraints. . . . He had little patience with
> finely drawn distinctions or scruples of method.
> If the thing was one proper to be done,
> then the most immediate, rough and
> ready, effective way was the
> best way.
> —Frederick Jackson Turner, *The Frontier in
> American History* (1920)

> "What if you'd missed?"
> "Never occurred to me."
> —Ethan Edwards (John Wayne) to Martin Pauley
> (Jeffrey Hunter) in John Ford's
> *The Searchers* (1956)

> In Texas we don't do nuance.
> —George W. Bush (1998)

1

The Conquerors

S ince November 7, 2006, it has been comforting to recall Karl
Rove's many and vivid earlier prophecies of ongoing, epochal
Republican rule. That midterm election evening, as Democrats
popped corks for the first time since 2000 and effervescent binges
of gloating—born of delight, vengefulness, relief, and a certain
surprise—erupted throughout the land, many liberals reflected that
the binges might be premature, but the drought had been long and
the penalties awful. Still, schadenfreude, like intoxication, is fun,
but it is neither an analysis, nor a morality, nor a politics. How did a
ruinous Republican Party win so much, march so far, and flatten so
much opposition for so long, and just how dead is it now?

From 2001 through 2006, the Republican Party controlled all
the command posts of national government: the presidency, both
houses of Congress, and the Supreme Court. This power was not
born yesterday, and despite big losses in the 2006 elections, it is not
going to wash away in the blink of an eye. In the ten presidential
elections going back to 1968, Republicans captured the White
House seven times.[1] They controlled the House and the Senate
together almost continuously from 1995 through 2006. The Republicans had not accomplished the feat of commanding the White
House and both houses of Congress at once for so long since 1930,
when their previous reign ran aground in the Great Depression.[2]

Moreover, of the 162 active judges who sit in the federal Courts of Appeals, at this writing, 94 of them, or 58 percent, were appointed by Republican presidents.[3] As the 2000 decision in *Bush v. Gore* made ringingly clear, control of the Supreme Court is readily convertible to the coin of executive power.

In 2006, the party controlled twenty-eight of the fifty governorships—an advantage that, as Jeb Bush demonstrated in Florida in 2000, could easily be translated into the more or less indirect suppression of minority votes.[4] (Other state Republican officials, such as the Ohio secretary of state and right-wing activist Kenneth Blackwell, availed themselves of similar opportunities to tip the electoral battlefield in their favor.)[5] State legislators were almost exactly half Republican, half Democratic, but the Republicans had risen from 32 percent in 1972 to the 50 percent they numbered in 2006. The Republicans, who controlled only thirteen legislatures in 1974, controlled thirty-three in 2006. Before 1994, the last time the Republicans had controlled a majority of state legislatures was 1954.[6] If the states are the laboratories of democracy, the Republicans were running the experiments. The party that forswore no opportunity to express its hostility to government—that affected to cherish "the people" and sneered at that alien place it likes to call "Washington, D.C."—again and again proved adept at winning control of government.

This does not mean that the Republicans represented the nation in any simple sense. Democrats, after all, won the popular vote in three out of the last four presidential elections, going back to 1992 (2004 was the exception). Opinion polls, as we shall see, cast doubt on the conservative claim to dominate on many (though hardly all) issues. But, over recent decades, the Republicans became a party quite different from the Democrats: a bulldozer, not a debating society; a loyalty machine, not a loose coalition; a political army for the conduct of war by other means, not a coalition of overlapping believers. The Republican Party became simultaneously a right-wing steamroller and an apparatus of power. It existed to rule.

Republicans didn't always get what they wanted, but they had the initiative. The agenda of government was largely their agenda. When they determined to go to war, the country turned toward war. When they wished to distribute more wealth to the wealthy, they did so. The views they considered morally self-evident were the views that Congress, the elected representatives of the American people, debated. The positions they embraced were the positions that had to be heard—in opinion columns, on cable television, on radio. Even on public radio, their ostensibly liberal nemesis, and even on subjects that are only awkwardly stuffed into partisan slots, talk-show bookers were mindful: "We have to have a conservative." So their echo chamber resounded. They dragged the center in their direction, while what used to be called the left dwindled to the vanishing point.

Yet as I write, the right has paid a steep price for overreaching. Power not only corrupts, it ruptures. With power sustained comes the sense of entitlement, and with the sense of entitlement comes the scramble for benefits, and with that scramble comes the cutting of corners and the easy recourse to criminality. As power centers consolidate themselves, cronies gather round to engorge themselves. As cronyism multiplies, so do overt scandals—abuses of power, dereliction of duty, personal aggrandizement, cover-ups, crimes petty and not so petty. Luck goes bad. Blunders occur. This would not be the first time that a political machine flush with success succumbed to grandiosity and stumbled. It happened to Franklin D. Roosevelt during his second term, when on the strength of his landslide second victory he tried to remake the Supreme Court in order to stop it from obstructing the New Deal. It happened to Richard Nixon during *his* second term, when a surfeit of paranoia and criminality withered the fruits of victory with amazing speed, as in time-lapse photography. It happened to Ronald Reagan during *his* second term, when the illegal foreign policy schemes that linked Iran and the contras ran afoul of the law and the press, whose sleeping watchdogs do awaken every so often. Prosecutors, courts, and investigating committees came to life. The history of political triumph is the history of hubris.

But before the decline came the ascendancy, and the ascendancy should not be dismissed lightly because it overreached. How did the right accumulate such power? By wanting it badly enough, by fielding and financing an army to get it and hold it, by recruiting leaders accordingly, and by making (until 2006) realistic appraisals of the battlefield. The right harnessed the energy of a movement, fierce, devoted, and unbridled, to the apparatus of a party, which delivers rewards to supporters, punishes enemies, and makes careers. The machinery bears the bright shine of the victor—always an enticement to the opportunists who crowd politics as they do all other human pursuits. But to create the machinery, there first had to be a hunger to win—the conviction that the decisive test of virtue in politics is effectiveness.

The entrepreneurs of the contemporary right have never—at least not since 1964, their foundational moment—doubted their will to win power. Richard A. Viguerie may lately have become disillusioned with George W. Bush, but first he wrote emphatically (with coauthor David A. Franke) on the importance of "keeping the movement on the straight path to power."[7] Morton Blackwell, Barry Goldwater's youngest 1964 convention delegate and later the executive director of the College Republicans, said, "After 1964, conservatives got tired of losing and decided that perhaps being 'right' in the sense of being correct was not sufficient to win. Conservatives came to the understanding that we owe it to our philosophy to study how to win; that we had to become proficient in campaigns, and in recruiting candidates, and we had to be active in party structures."[8] These are not freelance pontificators. Viguerie pioneered systematic direct mail for political purposes. Blackwell went on in 1979 to found the Leadership Institute, training budding conservatives how to conduct political campaigns and appear presentably in public.[9] Talk about forging links between theory and practice.

Lacking no certainty that they are morally right, prominent intellectuals of the right frequently express their commitment to make morality pay off in the coin of victory. They are as practical as they are enterprising. While they avail themselves of apocalyptic passions in abundance, they only infrequently despair of modern society in general or Americans in particular. (At least, they do not despair for long. During the Clinton impeachment campaign, William Bennett did deplore "the death of outrage" on the part of a public too accepting of the president's immorality, and just afterward, Paul Weyrich, the head of the Free Congress Foundation and the onetime founder of the Heritage Foundation, proclaimed, "I do not believe a majority of Americans share our values," and said it was time for conservatives to retreat into a world they could control—their own families, where they could carry on home schooling. The conservative columnist Cal Thomas supported him.)[10] Such grim moments soon dissolve into mandatory buoyancy. More typical on the right is the confidence of the neoconservative godfather, Irving Kristol, that history is going his way: "I had no patience with the old conservatism that confronted the tides of history by shouting 'stop!' I could not summon up any admiration for Herbert Hoover or Alf Landon, and I did not regard Franklin D. Roosevelt as the devil incarnate. My political instincts were always inclined to the proactive rather than the reactive, to work with reality, not against it."[11]

Kristol's idealism is activist. He has not been a theorist but a distiller of theories—both in the world and of it. What made him a central figure in the conservative juggernaut is that he was an institution builder: magazine editor, book editor, connection maker, dispenser of money, and counselor to the dispensers of more money. Looking back over his considerable career, Kristol expressed his activist impulse in this fashion:

> In one of my essays in the *Wall Street Journal*, I had urged [conservative] foundations to stop moaning about the welfare state, the "road to serfdom," the death of free enterprise by "statism," and the iniquities of the income tax, and address the realities of the conservative situation. . . . I struck a responsive chord. At least a few of those conservative foundations felt the desirability of breaking out of their self-imposed ghettos.[12]

Kristol's zeal to break out of ghettos stretched even farther. He was forcefully—and typically—committed to conservative unity. A Jewish intellectual of no great religious commitment was willing to make common cause with fundamentalist Christians in behalf of "traditional values." So were Wall Street and corporate backers who cared little (or vigorously disagreed) about abortion, homo-sexuality, and other hot-button issues of the religious right. They were team players.

Will and buoyancy, unity and pragmatism, certitude and dis-cipline, entitlement and militancy, entrepreneurship and institu-tional stamina—these are the elements of the conservative surge.

Now, as a national power, the Republicans start with mighty advantages that there is no point in obscuring, advantages that go some considerable distance to explain why the country's elected representatives so often veer to the right of public opinion. To begin with, the country's electoral architecture tilts their way. The electoral college, that peculiarly original feature of an eighteenth-century compromise that tempered the democratic impulse in order to produce a Constitution that would bottle up the popular will, gives disproportionate weight to thinly populated states, which trend Republican. The eleven states of the old Confederacy control 153 electoral votes all by themselves, and thus, with a virtual Republican lock dating from 1968, when they deserted the Demo-crats en masse to flee from civil rights, any candidate they prefer needs only 117 more votes in order to win election. (Throw in Kentucky, West Virginia, and Oklahoma, and you get 20 more Republican votes, for a shortfall of only 97.) Only the Southern governors Jimmy Carter, in 1976, and Bill Clinton, in 1992 and 1996, were able to pick the lock.

The Senate, of course, carries the same bias for the same reason—the overrepresentation of low-population, disproportionately rural states—but if anything more glaringly. An institution designed for the equal representation of states, not citizens, has become pro-gressively, or rather regressively, less representative of the citizens even after the Constitution was amended (in 1913) to require direct election of senators. As Professor Matthew Shugart of the Uni-versity of California, San Diego, wrote in 2005, "When the Foun-ders agreed that the Senate would have two members from each state, the ratio of largest to smallest state was 12:1. Today it is 70:1."[13] In part as a result, Shugart continued, "The current 100 senators were elected in 2000, 2002 or 2004. In those elections . . .

Republican candidates obtained 46.8 percent. . . . The Democrats obtained 48.4 percent." Yet that year the Republicans controlled the Senate with fifty-five votes to the Democrats' forty-four (and one independent).[14] "In 2000," wrote Jacob S. Hacker and Paul Pierson, "Bush lost the popular vote but carried 30 states."[15]

The House of Representatives is less obviously skewed, but it is still skewed against urban—that is, disproportionately Democratic—voters. In the words of Steven Hill, an opponent of winner-take-all voting, "When the two sides are tied nationally, the Republicans end up winning about 50 more House districts than the Democrats. . . . Even though Al Gore won a half million more votes nationwide than George Bush did in 2000, Bush beat Gore in 47 more of the 2002 congressional districts."[16] Likewise, in 2004, Bush beat John Kerry in 58.6 percent of congressional districts at a time when he won only 50.7 percent of the popular vote.[17] In 2006, the Democrats netted thirty House seats with a national swing of 5.5 points over their 2004 tally, whereas when Republicans picked up 6 points in the popular vote of 1994, that translated into a pickup of fifty-two seats.[18] The rule that the winner takes the whole prize in congressional districts and electoral college votes benefits the Republicans.

So do redistricting schemes promoted by the Republicans with the collaboration of African Americans: in several Southern states, districts containing significant minorities of blacks and previously represented by moderate white Democrats were redrawn so that the black votes were concentrated to guarantee them majorities in a small number of districts. Meanwhile, white voters were grouped in such a way as to permit white Republicans to outnumber moderate whites in the remaining seats, resulting in a net gain for the GOP.[19] The Republicans also resorted to mid-decade redistricting coups.[20] In 2004, the Texas redistricting scheme forced through the state legislature at the behest of Tom DeLay (and largely ratified by the U.S. Supreme Court in 2006) resulted in a net Republican gain of three seats, whereas without it, the Democrats would have been the party that netted three seats.

Such biases are engraved into the political system so deeply as to be fundamental. The mechanics of amending the Constitution are so arduous that a virtual revolution would be required to transform the voting system in a more democratic direction; in order for Congress and the state legislatures or the constitutional conventions to incline to do so, so much else would have to change that the country would be unrecognizable. Yet even after the debacle of 2000, there was no detectable upsurge in either the general public or the political class in favor of revamping the Constitution to reform the absurdities of the electoral college. The issue does not rank high enough on the popular thermometer. Incumbent politicians, for obvious reasons, are disinclined to fight fiercely to overhaul the system that put them in office and keeps them there. Why would senators elected from small states ever support a reform that would annul their decided advantage? So the Constitution's conservative bias is not trivial, but it is, under foreseeable circumstances, impervious to remedy. The disposition of this book is to toughen the mind and steel the will for the good that can be achieved on the earthly side of the millennium, and so I refrain from dwelling further on the weight of ineradicable history. People of an activist disposition should not pick battles with brick walls.[21]

The political system's foundation is tilted, then, and upon it something formidable has been built. Operationally, bottom to top and top to bottom, the Republican Party belongs to its right wing—that is, to the Bush White House and its ideological allies. This does not mean that all Republican voters are committed know-nothings, or even that all Republican legislators veer consistently rightward, or that all the judges the party appoints can be counted on to toe the party line. (In the eyes of social conservatives, they fail infuriatingly often.) It certainly does not mean that American public opinion lines up with the power apparatus—frequently, it does not. But the center of gravity of American politics has swung so far to the right as to have defined a new normality. When push comes to shove, as in the Florida confrontation of 2000, the Supreme Court falls into line, a band of reliable lieutenants. The big surprise would have been if things had turned out otherwise.

The party's key outposts are held by a federation of fundamentalists. Unity is one of the chief attributes of successful coalitions, and the Republicans have a talent for unity. This is partly because they believe that virtue requires standing together. Authority is also a positive value. Much of their discipline derives from agreement on who their enemies are. They practice ideology on a bumper sticker. Their principles are clear and simple, and they rhyme. Viewed generously, they converge around Ronald Reagan's formula: "Government is not the solution. Government is the problem."

Viewed more closely, the bumper sticker reveals its rips and creases: whenever it comes to national security, sex, and crime, conservatives certainly do not regard government as "the problem." When it is convenient, they transform the otherwise oppressive state into a shield, or a shovel for funds. For this, liberals charge them with highly selective reasoning: the sin of hypocrisy. The accusation is fair enough, as a matter of logic. But illogic also has its appeals and its reasons. In the actual world where people piece together their operating beliefs, they do not proceed like logicians. For most people, political ideology is ragged and unruly. It works by impressions, auras, first approximations. Meanwhile, for believers, the main line of conservative ideology assumes a coherent shape. Conservatives like to see themselves as what the Republican power broker Grover Norquist calls "the 'leave us alone' coalition." "The guy who wants to be left alone to practice his faith, the guy who wants to make money, the guy who wants to spend money without paying taxes, the guy who wants to fondle his gun—they all have a lot in common," says Norquist. "They all want the government to go away. That is what holds together the conservative movement."[22]

But, of course, many, perhaps most, Republicans do not want the government to go away at subsidy or abortion time. There is method to their hypocrisy. It is not that the right wants the *government* to go away, but that it wants a particular governing class to go away. This class—largely coastal, often intellectual, and identified with cultural brokers and attention-getters, a sort of Harvard-Hollywood axis of white-wine sippers and Volvo drivers—has gone by different names over the last forty years: "pointy-headed bureaucrats," "effete snobs," "the cultural elite," "counterculture McGoverniks," "Defeatocrats." They are an ensemble of the limp-wristed, the flabby, and the hateful. The right's ability to function over the decades as a unified phalanx depends on this common enemy: for them, liberal elitists are the root of all evil. Even worse (or, for demonization purposes, better), liberals are allied to minorities, becoming a sort of Harvard-Hollywood-Harlem axis as personified by Jesse Jackson and Al Sharpton. Rolling back all these forces of evil was the hallmark of the Goldwater campaign, the Nixon vindictiveness, and the Reagan reign, which then reached some sort of triumphal climax (for a while) in the juggernaut presidency of George W. Bush.

Of course, ideas by themselves do not explain the triumph of the people who proclaim them. Not all simplicities prevail at all times. Republicans embraced these particular simplicities for years without prevailing. Conditions matter. So does the state of the opposition. So one can easily overstate the significance of Republican claims for the coherence of their ideas and the policies that purportedly flow from them. Still, to understand their triumph, we must also comprehend their bulldozer relentlessness, wherein their methods match their worldview.

On America's position in the world, members of the inner Republican circle belligerently insist that they can remake the world in accordance with their designs. Even before they declared a "global war on terror," they strove to usurp the legitimate powers of Congress, the judiciary, civil servants, their own experts, and a public that at times wished to exercise its right to know. On economic and environmental policy, the Republican powers are market fundamentalists: believing that the good of the country is inextricably tied to the good of the grand corporations and their commanders, they permit lobbyists to write the regulations by which they themselves are to be regulated. Indeed, in many areas the lobbyists *are* the administration.[23]

Accordingly, under Republican rule, the channels of corruption have overflowed with swill. Plutocrats—especially from the extractive industries—ride high, serving with heaping tax benefits and deregulatory favors. The dominance of the moneyed interests is not a new story, of course, under either Republicans or Democrats. But the congressional Republicans perfected the game as they consolidated control over the money that drives Washington policies. Having no contrary commitments (in contrast to the divided

Democrats), the ruling party gave generously to corporate interests. Kicking back vast funds into the party apparatus, the plutocrats were integral to Republican power. Lobbyists, the lubricants
of the process, poured into Washington, doubling in number between 2000 and mid-2005, capitalizing on new tax benefits, deregulation, military and security appropriations, and other facets of
the unacknowledged institutional base of Republican power: big
government. The *Washington Post*'s Jeffrey H. Birnbaum wrote in
mid-2005:

> The number of registered lobbyists in Washington has more
> than doubled since 2000 to more than 34,750. . . . [W]ith
> pro-business officials running the executive and legislative
> branches, companies are . . . hiring well-placed lobbyists to
> go on the offensive and find ways to profit from the many
> tax breaks, loosened regulations and other government
> goodies that increasingly are available. . . . The Republicans
> in charge aren't just pro-business, they are also pro-govern-
> ment. Federal outlays increased nearly 30 percent from 2000
> to 2004, to $2.29 trillion. And despite the budget deficit,
> federal spending is set to increase again this year, especially
> in programs that are prime lobbying targets such as defense,
> homeland security and medical coverage.[24]

The movements and ideologies of what has come to be called
"the base" of either party amount to the fuel that drives the engine
of power. The task of the engine is to exploit the loyalty of the base
without cutting off the energy supply. It accomplishes this partly
with palpable results, partly with smoke and mirrors. For political
loyalty is not, whatever the "rational choice" school of political
scientists may think, a matter of logical preferences. Politics collects
passions. As long as enough favors are distributed and enough
ideals respected, the base stokes the engine. While old-fashioned
conservatives were heard to grumble from time to time about
government deficits, swollen contracts and payrolls, and the pay-
offs that followed, the party's small-government fervor was not
substantially dampened by its policies in power.

Why? Because for the right, unity was a cardinal rule of virtue.
Loyalty was imposed by the magnitude of what was at stake:

self-evident Truth. For two generations, the right's passionate warriors have harbored no doubt that they represent the good in a war against evil—not the just against the unjust or the practical against the impractical, but the righteous against the unclean, the normal against the deviant, the natural against the unnatural. Deference to authority is in their natural order of things.

This Republican custom of deference serves the party's activists well, enabling them—during good times—to iron out or override the seams in their alliance. Toward this end, the religious zeal of much of their base is crucial. The party accommodates, even arouses, the religious right and its allies with an amalgam of sex-body-control concerns—abortion and contraception; gay rights and lately, in particular, gay marriage; euthanasia—that its partisans have taken to calling "the culture of life." Overall, "movement conservatives," some of them fundamentalists and others belonging to mainline Protestant and Catholic churches, are galvanized to defend what they see as embattled Christian traditions, and toward this end they propose to enlist the government to enforce their morality.

Religious zeal is the high octane in the Republican base. Their political leadership's ability to fire up a furor is a mighty advantage for them, and obviously the zealous George W. Bush has served them well. Bush, with his unabashed religiosity, his Bible study groups and conversion story, was a perfect choice for this base—and the absence of an obviously compelling heir appears to be a significant problem for the Republican base in the future. But the church-avoiding Ronald Reagan demonstrated that even a suitable simulation of piety from the leadership might satisfy the pious.

The importance of the right's religious base has been commented on so frequently that one might be inclined to downplay it for variety's sake. That would be a mistake. People in this religious base have been the troops of the Republican conquest. They matter so greatly not because their views necessarily express majority opinion but because they care so passionately as to vote their passion, thus leveraging their strength in the Republican Party. During the epochal off-year congressional elections of 1994, the political scientist John C. Green, a prominent student of religion and politics, looked closely at forty-five competitive contests where the Christian right was most heavily involved. "The movement-backed candidate prevailed two-thirds of the time, or in thirty races," he wrote later. "While the impact of the movement should not be overstated, these thirty seats were more than twice the size of the GOP margin of control (thirteen seats). The movement probably had a similar impact on the twenty U.S. Senate races and fifteen gubernatorial campaigns."[25]

In 2004, according to Green and Stephen Waldman of belief net.com, well more than half of Bush's votes—a total of 57 percent—came from the combination of three religious populations: what they call the Religious Right, Heartland Culture Warriors, and Moderate Evangelicals. Among voters of the hard-core Religious Right, Bush boosted his turnout from 62 percent in 2000 to 69 percent in 2004. Green and Waldman wrote:

> But where Bush showed the most improvement was among the "Heartland Culture Warriors," mainline Protestants and Catholics with traditional beliefs and practices. In 2000, Bush won 66% of the Heartland vote; in 2004 he won 72%. Turnout was also up for this group. The Heartland Culture Warriors viewed social issues as the most important. In other words, Bush's positions on gay marriage and abortion likely helped him even more with this group than [with] the Religious Right.[26]

In a society that ranked politics somewhere around gang-banging in moral authority, the Republican leadership connected to a passion. George W. Bush was beloved of a base. Even as his approval ratings sank, he retained the loyalty of one-third to two-fifths of the population. He was the embodiment of an ideal. They looked at him and they ceased to see politics as a dirty, disreputable, and futile enterprise. They saw *their man*—their collective soul militant. Voting Republican, to this base, felt (and is likely to continue to feel) like an extension—even the completion—of their religious mission. No surprise that in 2004, with the help of a far-flung religious apparatus, complete with rallies and broadcasts, Bush turned them out in unprecedented numbers to vote.

In the words of the Barna Group, a Christian survey organization:

> Most of President Bush's supporters did at least two things
> during the first week of November: they voted to re-elect the
> President and they went to church. . . . Overall, born again
> Christians supported President George W. Bush by a 62% to
> 38% margin. In contrast, non–born again voters supported
> Senator John Kerry by an almost identical 59% to 39% divi-
> sion. The difference was in the rates of turnout of each seg-
> ment. Although the born again population constitutes just
> 38% of the national population, it represented 53% of the
> vote cast in the election. . . . 61% of the people who regularly
> attend religious services voted for [Bush], compared to just
> 30% of the vote among unchurched adults.[27]

What these voters saw, according to Barna, was an ideal—their
passion personified:

> Bush backers were most likely to identify the President's char-
> acter (33%) or his views on national security as their impetus
> for support. . . . [T]hey were more interested in the character
> of the candidate and the worldview that forms the basis of his
> decision-making than they were in specific issues. In fact,
> relatively few voters seemed to be driven by issues, regardless
> of which candidate they embraced. This election was more of a
> statement about people's feelings toward George W. Bush as a
> leader and as a person than it was about a particular issue.

What these voters meant by "character" was no doubt intimately
connected to their passion. They knew that when push came to
shove, Bush preferred their passion to mundane law. He represented their zeal, while judges, even if appointed by him, represented a
lesser faculty: brains (or worse, activism). After the 2004 election,
the party leadership was so mindful of its religious base that it
summoned Congress into special session on March 20, 2005, to
declare that the fate of the brain-dead Terri Schiavo was a matter of
compelling federal concern. No matter that the decision these
partisans of "judicial restraint" strived to overrule was that of a
conservative, church-going Republican.[28] Meanwhile, signaling to
his base either his disrespect for science or his incomprehension of

it, and thus his reliability even on subjects remote from his constitutional powers, Bush thumped the bully pulpit to endorse the teaching of "intelligent design" alongside evolution, as if the two— one a scientific theory, the other a pseudoscientific substitute for a theory convincingly refuted almost a century and a half ago by Charles Darwin—were equivalent. "I think that part of education is to expose people to different schools of thought," this sworn foe of moral relativism told a group of reporters. "You're asking me whether or not people ought to be exposed to different ideas, the answer is yes."[29] The judge in question, who decided against the pro–"intelligent design" school board in Dover, Pennsylvania, was Bush's own appointee.

Bush's zeal at such moments only pointed out a built-in conservative vulnerability. In the eyes of the Republican base, Bush's reputation for reliability and probity depended on his ability to ride out divisions in his ranks—to deliver the goods. But as the nation's palpable troubles mounted, his on-message buoyancy failed to work. Since the Democrats did not hold power in any branch of the national government, it was, to say the least, a formidable public relations challenge to blame failures of public policy on the minority party. The persistence of al-Qaeda, the nonstop horrors in Iraq, Hurricane Katrina on the Gulf Coast, and the scandals that brought down Tom DeLay, Jack Abramoff, and Republican members of Congress caught in the Mark Foley page scandal— the Republicans could try to blame all these, respectively, on Bill Clinton and Bill Clinton again, on Louisiana's Democratic governor Kathleen Babineaux Blanco, on New Orleans mayor Ray Nagin, on vengeful judges, on corrupt Democrats, and on bloggers.

But as Republican failures of policy and morality piled higher, the party leadership ceased to look magical. After years in undisputed power, the Republican machine stood all too visible. Nothing failed like failure. And this is where the Republican pyramid of power exhibited weakness. Evident policy failures led to policy conflicts. Personal careers resumed their individualistic paths. The self-seeking nature of political life reasserted itself. Republicans in Congress and in the states started straying from Bush. The command structure shuddered.

2

Centralizing the Apparatus

The Republicans had weathered defeats, scandals, and leadership convulsions before. They had recovered from Barry Goldwater's landslide loss, from the impeachment and resignation of Richard Nixon, from the betrayal (in their eyes) and defeat of George H. W. Bush, from Newt Gingrich's failure to shut down the government, from the misfiring of their effort to convict Bill Clinton of high crimes and misdemeanors, from Gingrich's collapse, and from the implosion of Speaker-to-be Robert Livingston. Like a bulldozer, they never stopped long for obstructions.

Only cloistered intellectuals think that policy ideas are, by themselves, the essence of political life. Despite the massive erosion in Bush's authority, the true measure of Republican domination extends far beyond the overt policies that the party's right wing stands for, even beyond the values that radiate through its rhetoric. There is a distinct and unifying style and climate to its politics. The means by which it pursues its goals; the métier of its procedures; its spirit, tone, and temper; all are distinctive. Rhetoric and method are the music of politics, and the music is never incidental.

To fathom the Republican temper of our time, it is hard to avoid some clichés: leadership and character. Through all its upsets, the

Republican leadership of recent decades is committed to extremity, bullying, and unreason—or what its defenders consider resolve, creativity, and steadfastness. From Newt Gingrich's take-no-prisoners crusade at the head of his "Republican revolution" of 1994, to the House Republicans' wild, doomed impeachment campaign against President Clinton in 1998–1999, to the Bush campaign's militant seizure of the Florida vote in 2000, to the unilateralist zeal that torpedoed the Kyoto treaty, to the repudiation of the scientific consensus on global warming, to the slashing of taxes on the wealthiest, to the cooking of intelligence to launch the Iraq war, to the effort to demolish the fundamentals of Social Security, the Republican leadership has been nothing if not high-handed. It has a hell-bent—make that heaven-bent—faith in its own inerrancy. Such belief in a righteous entitlement to rule goes beyond arrogance—it bespeaks a sense of superiority that justifies all means because it never doubts that its end is sacrosanct.

George W. Bush brought a crescendo to decades of Republican momentum, stamping his personal command model on what was already an ideological disposition toward the firm hand—the president over the law and the party, the party over its elected representatives, and the country over its allies, not to mention the rest of the world. Ronald Reagan may have been too relaxed—or inattentive—to impose unity upon his cabinet officers, but Bush learned from that slackness. Under Bush, the marching orders came from the top. Discipline was hierarchical and impressive—especially in contrast to the Democrats. When, in 1993, Bill Clinton tried to take advantage of Democratic control of both houses of Congress and pass a liberal spending program—the so-called stimulus package—he was met with a solid, filibustering bloc of Republican opposition, but he could not rope the majority Democrats into line.[1] His tangled health-care program was undermined from both ends, with the party's left preferring a single-payer program and its right something less than universal coverage. Even when Clinton prevailed—as in his deficit-reducing budget of 1993—it was without the benefit of a single Republican vote in either chamber.[2]

Imperiousness and the claim of inerrancy are not just incidental quirks of Bush's style but a theory of government and a method of rule brought to a high gloss in an imposingly rigid White House. Enemies must be punished, apostates tossed out. As with those designated "enemy combatants," the very fact that they are suspected of being enemies constitutes justification for punishment. Loyalty must be absolute. Never mind what is, for public consumption, a laissez-faire attitude toward business practices and government financing ("it's your money, not the government's money"), imperious policy dovetails perfectly with today's Republican style of organization, which is hierarchical, intensely coordinated, and, when paranoia is useful for enforcing loyalty, paranoid. This is true of the Bush White House, of the Republican Party, of Republican congressional caucuses, and of the party's national campaigns, fund-raising, and lobbying. These are vertical, not horizontal, organizations; tight, not loose; fierce, not gentle; rugged, not weak. Bush is himself the personification of this martial style. *Newsweek*'s Evan Thomas, compiling the inside version of the magazine's 2004 campaign coverage, wrote somewhat discreetly of Bush as

> a zealot for order. The hard-drinking frat boy had long since found the cleansing joy of discipline. He demanded a tightly wound, top-down, on-time-to-the-minute operation. His advisers, some of them martinets, gave him what he wanted. At Bush-Cheney 2004 headquarters in Arlington, Va., the dress code was corporate and the atmosphere vaguely martial.[3]

The authoritative Republican voice speaks ex cathedra, not conversationally. Its mode is proclamation, not give-and-take. While previous Republican machines did not rival the Bush team in efficiency, they evolved toward the how-dare-you-challenge-me style that Bush perfected, if teasingly at times. When the high political command articulated the line of the day, its talking point phrases—often verbatim—rang out across the right's formal and informal media circuits, through punditry, talk radio, and the Internet. In the speeches of President Bush, the appearances of his press secretary, the political grand vizier Karl Rove, and the Republican National Committee chairman, among other officials, the apparatus blared forth its limited repertory of slogans in a manner so relentlessly, unswervingly "on-message" as to smother dispute or, indeed, colloquy. Action is what counted, and speech mattered when it was a blunt instrument. But speech could not perform that function if it descended to the contemptible level of "nuance." (Thus the significance—discussed later in this chapter—of Bush telling Bob Woodward, "I don't feel like I owe anybody an explanation.") Colloquy went with uncertainty, and uncertainty meant weakness—the brand of troubling weakness that if Bush were a reflective man he would detect in himself.

As uncertainty must be vanquished in oneself, it must also be vanquished in subordinates, for doubt distracts from the mission. As Freud well understood, the psychological power of submission flows from the way in which it relieves followers of their anxiety. If the leader appears to be untroubled by inner frictions, then, by extension, so do followers feel they have transcended themselves. By the same token, only those who have been found loyal to the leader truly testify (in his eyes) to the leader's leadership qualities. So subordinates must be tested by one supreme standard: loyalty. Because loyalty is central, cronyism is the administration's method for making major appointments. All presidents prize the loyalty of their subordinates but also expect them to be good democratic centralists—lieutenants who will argue about policy up to the point where the leader makes decisions, after which time they agreeably fall into line. Bush short-circuited the argument phase. Nonconformity was a sign of weakness.

The Bush White House required fealty, but just as stringently, in return, the president reciprocated. Fealty was the outward sign of self-mastery, the transcendence of all that is unruly in the self. In the inner circle, by all accounts, a fierce loyalty cemented the elect—"good men" and "good women" all, their moral staunchness overriding, at times, even some tests of ideological purity. (Bush chastised movement conservatives for accusing his friend Alberto Gonzales—the former White House counsel turned attorney general—of lapses from right-wing doctrine during his tenure as a Texas judge.)[4] People in Bush's inner circle despised the Clinton White House because it was lax—this laxness (most conspicuously with respect to sex) amounting, in their minds, to the slovenly sixties

personified, the let-it-all-hang-out stylistic liberalism of what Newt
Gingrich in 1995 called "counterculture McGoverniks" in action.[5]
Discipline was less doctrinal than personal, a style of rectitude
manifest, for example, in the dress code imposed upon visitors to
the Oval Office. Doctrine might come and go—indeed, in such
matters as the justification of war, declarations of purpose had short
shelf lives—but in the modus operandi of the ultra-right, not least its
admiring pundits, inconsistency of argument was trivial, beneath
notice.

For the White House, it was self-mastery and self-regulation, not
consistency, that attested to moral excellence: thus the importance
of physical exercise, a strenuous regimen that Bush demanded of
himself under any and all circumstances and that he seemed to prefer
among insiders, for it attested to their seriousness. (In Scotland in
July 2004, with limited time to meet with the seven other leaders of
the world's industrial powers, Bush still made time for an hour-long
bicycle sprint. And he asked at least one interviewee for his first
Supreme Court nomination, Judge J. Harvie Wilkinson III, what his
exercise program was.)[6] It was probably more admirable, then, for
Bush to have quit alcohol without benefit of therapy, self-help
groups, or rehabilitation centers than never to have drunk at all.

The fraternal circle of the "good," fervent in purpose, pure
in spirit, strong of will, mutually reliant, is reminiscent of the
seventeenth-century Puritan saints who, according to Michael
Walzer, originated the "idea that specially designated and organized bands of men might play a creative part in the political
world."[7] The good are the bands of the saved, saved for a reason:
they have the opportunity to move history because they have been
called to do so in times of tribulation. As the historian of religion
William G. McLoughlin described this mentality: "Life is a con-
stant struggle with Satan, both in the life of the individual and
among groups of people, and only by the most intense effort, self-
discipline, and self-control can man hope to keep Satan at bay;
church ritual is of no help in this, but the mutual support of
other saints is."[8] McLoughlin was writing of seventeenth-century
Calvinists-cum-Puritans, but recent culture affords ample opportunities to renew the struggle. You confirm your toughness among

the striving by being born again. You may have skipped out on military service despite your professed belief in the nobility of the martial cause, you may have fallen (into pain-killer addiction or gambling), but you attest to your virtue in other works—in athletics, say, or business. Good works in good company confirm predestination for glory. Of the elect, much is expected, but much may also be forgiven. In ever-renewed battle with evildoers, the good are always tested, always on call.

The battle-hardened army of the "good men" must always be battle-ready. When this army goes into battle—and once the latest battle is over, it is time to prepare for the next—deviations from discipline cannot be tolerated. Potential dissenters, beware: neither Bush nor Rove nor their erstwhile House partner in central command, Tom DeLay, hesitated to promote rival candidates against dissident Republicans. (The practice was so common in DeLay's orbit as to have acquired the status of a verb, "to primary.")[9] Smears of the enemy were standard procedure, as in Bush's campaigns for governor in 1994 (against incumbent Ann Richards, accused of harboring lesbians); for president in 2000 (against primary opponent John McCain, accused of fathering a black child in South Carolina, among other offenses to racist voters) and 2004 (against Democratic opponent John Kerry, accused of wartime lies); in congressional races such as that of Saxby Chambliss for a Georgia Senate seat in 2002, linking the incumbent, triple-amputee army veteran Max Cleland, to Osama bin Laden; or in ad hoc slash-and-burn campaigns to discredit Joseph C. Wilson IV and other professionals who made so bold as to permit their professionalism to contradict the administration line.

Republican national campaigns are command performances, run from the hub. *Newsweek*'s Thomas wrote of "the strict, top-down command structure [imposed] on the volunteer army in the field."[10] Republicans are more skilled than Democrats in welding together the separate elements of their power apparatus, organizing networks, and collecting information centrally, channeling authority downward. They are more experienced making the effort and more adept at making it pay off. During the last third of the twentieth century and the beginning of the twenty-first, they have had the double knack of logistics and generalship.

This is only partly a matter of technique. The conservatives are ruthless about winning. In the highest circles, principle is fine, but the power brokers know that in the heat of battle, principle can be finessed, hedged, postponed. The journalist John Cassidy, who profiled the pivotal Washington power broker Grover Norquist for the *New Yorker*, observed that to Norquist, "the Democrats are the enemy, and politics is warfare. He often uses military terms when he is talking. He says things like, 'If Rome is the walled city, march on Constantinople.'"[11] From attitude, methods follow. The techniques of amassing power both inside and outside Washington, then focusing it against the opposition's weaknesses, flow to those who value the arts of political warfare and invest in them. The insiders know how to make use of the outsiders, who in turn trust the insiders.

As the longtime Democratic operative Harold Ickes told me, the Republicans "exercise more control on their party apparatus. A lot of discipline flows from the White House, and they've held it a lot. I think there's more cooperation and coordination among their big allied groups, the Gary Bauers of the world, than among our allied groups."[12] For politics, in the view of the right, takes place over a span of decades. The late sixties left may have talked up what the German new leftist Rudi Dutschke called "the long march through the institutions," but it is the right that accomplished it. For the moralist right, what is at stake is the entirety of an embattled civilization. So, of course, discipline and persistence are fundamental. That much-used buzzword *infrastructure* is one result. In the seventies, the Olin, Bradley, and other right-wing foundations made long-term grants to ideological havens that one could rightly call think tanks if one believed that they contributed thought more than propaganda and lobbying, but in any event, they committed funds for the long haul, not just project by project. They understood the difference between the campaign of the moment and the ideology of the epoch.

By contrast, after 2004's disappointments, the two largest contributors to liberals' soft-money electoral efforts (the so-called 527 groups, named for the section of the campaign finance law that permitted them) decided to unplug, whereupon the organizations they funded, Americans Coming Together and the Media Fund, collapsed.[13] The billionaire philanthropist George Soros, who by himself donated at least $27 million to left-of-center 527 groups in 2004, gave less than one-tenth that amount in 2006. The five largest liberal contributors in 2004, who donated $86 million that year, in 2006 gave less than $9 million.[14] True, there were legitimate reasons to question massive support for 527s. Under the campaign finance laws, the 527s were prohibited from coordinating directly with the Democratic campaigns. They were thus unable to target money when and where it was needed—for example, at the time of the Swift Boat Veterans for Truth smears. As a result, some of their expenditures were arguably redundant or squandered. But overall, despite all the Democrats' buzz about infrastructure, their funders were as mired in short-term thinking as the corporations they scorned for becoming obsessed with quarterly profits.

Ickes was once Bill Clinton's deputy chief of staff. As he said, control of the White House matters immensely. Consider the career of the aforementioned Norquist, once the executive director of the College Republicans, the deviser of the no-tax-increase pledge that pinioned George H. W. Bush, and in recent years the coordinator of weekly conservative meetings where tax-bashers; conservative moralists; neoconservatives; White House retainers; congressional movers, shakers, and staffers; and movement outsiders all mix and coordinate. Norquist has excellent outsider credentials, ferocious energy, and organizational talent—"Grover admired the iron dedication of Lenin, whose dictum, 'Probe with bayonets, looking for weakness' he often quoted, and whose majestic portrait hung in Grover's Washington living room," wrote his onetime admirer David Brock[15]—but he was boosted to power by the most inside of insiders. It is not inconsequential that some of his earliest Washington positions were atop groups set up by the Reagan White House—first, Americans for the Reagan Agenda, then, in 1985, Americans for Tax Reform, which he still heads at this writing. Norquist went on to attach himself to another outsider who brilliantly maneuvered his way into the inner precincts of power: Newt Gingrich.[16]

Ickes, a lean sixty-six-year-old with thinning hair and a contemplative manner, credits the Republicans and the conservative movement with enviable prowess in organizational intelligence. Although he professes not to consider Karl Rove the flawless genius of modern politics, his eyes gleam and twinkle when he talks about Rove. The son of one of FDR's most important progressive political allies, Ickes is himself a veteran of political campaigns from Eugene McCarthy through the Clintons. In 2004, he led the Media Fund, a technically independent 527 soft-money operation funded in part by George Soros, and the next year he ran for the chairmanship of the Democratic National Committee, withdrawing in favor of Howard Dean. Ickes's positions over the decades display a continuity that Democrats have not so commonly shown.

Ickes knows that political prowess requires more than the habit of command. It requires the ability to learn from the best initiatives emerging from the totality of one's networks, then to generalize them, bulldozing through obstacles, overcoming the clamor of rival egos. One pivotal case that Ickes cites is the right's pioneering use of direct mail, its acquisition and consolidation of mailing lists. "The Republicans, starting in 1974, when the Campaign Finance Act was first enacted, understood fairly quickly the implications, and started developing lists. Richard Viguerie, who was the godfather of their fundraising, understood the importance of small donor fundraising, and for decades they outraised us, outdid us on small donor fundraising."[17]

On such logistical fronts, the Republican continuity is impressive. Viguerie traces his systematic deployment of direct mail to amalgamate, mobilize, and fund the conservative movement to the 1964 Goldwater campaign. Viguerie does not content himself with a modest conception of his role: "As the 'Funding Father of the Conservative Movement,'" his book jacket flap proclaims, "Viguerie is our era's equivalent of Tom Paine, using a direct mail letter rather than a pamphlet to deliver his call to arms."[18] He boasts that he "first comprehended the true political potential of direct mail and used it to create the conservative mass movement."[19] Disdaining understatement, Viguerie declares, "In the years between 1964 and 1980, direct mail was the rainfall that filled ever-more-substantial tributaries—organizations, campaigns, issues—that in turn, by 1980, had created the Mississippi River of American politics: conservatism."[20]

Viguerie's taste for metaphor is not austere, but his pioneering is not in dispute. He tells a story of acumen and initiative, but also of centralization. "Of all the problems that I had in [my] first years as a direct mail fundraiser," he writes, "number one was the lack of identified conservatives on mailing lists. Today I have, in my desk, a book-size file of several hundred conservative mailing lists. . . . And lists are the *lifeblood* of direct marketing." Further indulging his penchant for extravagant metaphor, Viguerie describes how, starting with a list of Goldwater donors, he convinced the proprietors of distinct organizations that they needed to consolidate their separate lists, playing "the role of a mad political dentist, pulling teeth one at a time as I worked to convince these organizations that list exchanges and rentals not only were not suicidal, but they were the way to create an ever-larger movement and enrich everyone's organizations."[21] Viguerie arranged to retain all the donor names,

> which was critical in expanding the base of the conservative movement. . . . By centralizing access to many conservative supporters, conservative organizations were able to prospect at less expense, not to mention faster and with greater precision. It made the movement—which consisted of multiple leaders and organizations—more efficient as well, because it was easier to target supporters who were shown to be predisposed to conservative issues.[22]

By 1980, according to the *Economist* chroniclers John Micklethwait and Adrian Woolbridge, "Viguerie's computers held the names of about 15 million contributors."[23] After "pretty much [having] the [conservative direct mail] field to myself from 1965 to 1978," Viguerie writes, the Republican Party hired away one of his executives, copied his methods, and built up its own mailing list "from around 25,000 names in 1977 to about 2 million by November 1980," this list playing "a significant role in Reagan's landslide election and the GOP's capture of the Senate."[24]

So the Republicans understood early that information was power. Taking lists seriously before anyone coined the term *database* was instrumental to mobilizing their troops. By contrast, the national Democrats were slow and clueless. (A kinder analytical term would be *decentralized*.) According to Richard Parker, a liberal writer-activist with business acumen who was one of the first to appreciate what the conservatives were accomplishing with direct mail, the Democratic National Committee under Robert Strauss refused to accept a list of 600,000 names offered them by the McGovern campaign after 1972.[25] In such infrastructural matters the Democrats lagged for decades.

Meanwhile, the Republicans went on modernizing their lead. Harold Ickes says of them:

> They understood the importance of voter mobilization. I think that starting ten years ago, maybe even fifteen [that is, around 1990], they came to understand that the electorate was getting more and more closely divided, that television was, although important, playing less of a role. The younger political operatives in the Republican Party, of which Karl Rove is their prince . . . came to understand, I think, that voter mobilization, voter contact, modeling the right voters and then figuring out what messages can move the voters that they modeled, reaching them by way of mail, phone, some door-to-door, cable, discrete and focused radio and increasingly Internet, was a way to really get their vote out.[26]

Republican strides in technique were focused on the eventual payoff that counted: Election Day turnout. Then there was research. "They've outpaced us on research," Ickes goes on with the practiced, slightly weary, slightly admiring manner of a man who has long studied the reasons why his team is number two. "[The late RNC chairman Lee] Atwater understood the importance of negative research, and they still have a bigger research team over at the RNC than we do." If that was not enough,

> They've had a national database for ten years called the Voter Vault. They have every registered voter in the country on their database. These are sort of the grubby and technical aspects, if

you will, of winning elections. I mean, it's stunning to think that the Democratic National Committee did not have a national voter database until about a year and a half ago [that is, in late 2003]. Didn't have one. We didn't understand.[27]

Trying to understand why the Democrats didn't understand will help us understand why the Republicans *did* understand. Ickes tells me:

When Terry McAuliffe came in [as DNC chairman, in February 2001], he didn't even know what a database was, and he was persuaded that we really had to do this. [Democratic operative] Laura Quinn did a very thorough investigation, wrote a report on it, and it was at that point, I think, that it was really hammered home to us against the backdrop of the 2000 presidential. A handful of voters and a handful of states, ultimately five members of the United States Supreme Court, decided that election. I think that was a stunning wakeup call for us. . . . And Terry, to his credit, put several million dollars into the development of a national database.

Ickes is skeptical of the notion that the Democrats' failures can be explained by their candidates. "We're great finger-pointers. Our candidates were flawed, especially juxtaposed to theirs." But he finds a deeper deficiency in the Democrats' technology of politics, and this in turn is intimately related to an organizational flaw. "Our consultant class loves media," he says. It has even been argued that one reason for this affection is that Democratic consultants habitually collect 15 percent agency fees from the candidates.[28] Ickes is blunt about the improvisational—indeed, ramshackle—nature of Democratic campaigns, which spring up around particular candidates and melt away when they do. "The direct mail people were all independent contractors. There's no centralization. I think that Rove and Company brought a centralization and a focus to those technical aspects."

What this means technically is a centralization of data, Ickes explains. "They understood the importance of going to all the campaigns of any importance and getting the information that has been collected by those campaigns in the last election and shoving it into their database so that it enriches the database." By contrast:

> We were totally out to lunch. The state parties didn't have their own database. It was all a bunch of goddamned contractors that you paid through the nose for. One didn't speak to the others. And even in our campaigns today, you got a bunch of mail vendors, you've got phone vendors, you've got media people, and they often don't even speak to each other, even in the same campaign. So I think that the Republicans are disciplined both from prosecution of issues, development of language, and the use of that language, and the urging of the allied groups to understand the importance of language, and the party discipline within their party ranks, and the coordination between the party and the Gary Bauers—I'm just using him as an e.g. You know, it's a better, more focused operation.[29]

Here, in significant microcosm, is Republican discipline at work—one more instance of what the political scientists Jacob S. Hacker and Paul Pierson have observed: "The extent of coordination among Republican political elites, imperfect as it may be, is unprecedented in modern American history."[30] The Democrats did impose a tighter coordination than usual in 2006, but the game they were playing was catch-up.

The juggernaut of the Republican right also controlled both houses of Congress from 1995 through 2007, with the exception of the nineteen months between May 2001 and December 2002, when it drove Senator James Jeffords of Vermont out of the party and lost its majority by a hair. Ingeniously, the Republican leadership was able to rule the legislature without having to represent public opinion.

After decades of Democratic control, the House of Representatives operated under the take-no-prisoners reign of the majority leader, Tom DeLay, a master of institution-building whose achievement outlasts his own tenure. Centralization and corruption were his means, the latter lubricating the former. Fund-raising and distribution were centralized; so were propaganda, reward, and punishment; so, as a result, was party loyalty.[31] Like Lyndon B. Johnson during his House and then Senate heyday, DeLay made a career of becoming his party's indispensable man, raising millions of dollars in cash to bankroll his party-mates' campaigns, thus smoothing his rise to power from unpromising beginnings.[32] DeLay, once he clambered to the top party position, also resembled Johnson in having brought together the reins of power, short-circuiting the prerogatives of lesser legislators, making them dependent on his authority for committee assignments and other plums.

As House czar, DeLay stood squarely on the shoulders of Newt Gingrich, who during his four years as speaker, 1995–1998, succeeded in centralizing power into his own hands by achieving a six-year limit for House committee chairs. Though the over-reaching Gingrich was outfoxed by the wilier Bill Clinton and lost his grip on power, he bequeathed his changes to DeLay and his entourage of successors. Republicans have adroitly passed their baton along even as their lead runners have stumbled.

While the Republicans controlled Congress mercilessly, they were able to consolidate the party's virtual merger with corporate wealth.[33] One watershed was the so-called K Street Project, beginning in 1995—the first year of the Gingrich House—when the incoming majority whip, Tom DeLay (aka Tom DeReg), summoned a meeting of corporate lobbyists, showed them a list of their contributions to both parties, told them to reallocate their contributions, and threatened to cut off their access to the House leadership if they refused. (Defenders of this new dispensation maintained that the Republicans were only rectifying a previous Democratic imbalance—but in fact, in 1993–1994, for example, big industrial political action committees favored the Republicans by a margin of roughly 55 to 45.[34]) Soon, lobbyists and the Republican caucus came close to merging.[35] DeLay ushered Republican lobbyists from oil and gas, timber, pharmaceuticals, and insurance interests into his office to write legislation. The K Street Project, organized with the ubiquitous Norquist, forced big lobbying firms and trade associations to work on Republican bills, to pump up their contributions to the Republicans—indeed, to hire more Republicans—offering them, in return, so much access to Republican legislators they might have shared toothbrushes.

When DeLay arrived in Washington from the suburbs of Houston in 1985, committee chairmen were petty barons, secured by seniority, hedging the power of the House leadership. During the DeLay years, Republicans in committee voted routinely en bloc to scotch amendments and cut off debate. The House as a whole met for two days a week, where the majority would—in the words of the Texas journalists Lou Dubose and Jan Reid—

> dispose of legislation in rolling votes, in which long lines of unrelated bills are rolled out for up or down votes with [supreme] efficiency. . . . Bills are also brought to the floor under closed rules, or amended closed rules, which allow no amendments and only an up or down vote. The committee system, floor debate, bipartisan collaboration, social relations across party lines—all are as dated as the brass spittoons that once graced the members' lounges.[36]

Bills without the support of a majority *of Republicans* went nowhere, regardless of whether a majority might be compounded from a Republican fraction voting with Democrats.

Furthermore, DeLay masterminded and bankrolled a 2002 Republican victory in the Texas legislature, which in turn opened the way for congressional redistricting in Texas in 2003, rather than permitting the legislature to wait until the next census in 2010—a rupture with tradition (by politicians who call themselves conservative) that no state had attempted in half a century. DeLay used federal PAC funds he raised to stampede the Texas legislature to accomplish this mission and, when some Democratic state legislators bridled and fled to Oklahoma in order to keep a quorum from forming, enlisted the Department of Homeland Security to find them, arrest them, and bring them home to force a vote on the bill.[37] Such cavalier violation of the principle of states' rights, long glorified by Republicans and their Dixiecrat forebears, resembled the enlistment of the Supreme Court to overpower Florida law in November–December 2000.

On issue after issue, against the most meager dissent, House Republican policies veered toward the jagged far-right edge of public opinion. Yet members of Congress who went to extremes were returned to Washington again and again to represent a public that disdained their extremity.[38] How did the apparatus manage this feat? The Republicans offered what Jacob S. Hacker and Paul Pierson called "backlash insurance" to reassure "skittish moderates," in four forms:

1. *The apparatus controlled the congressional agenda*, preventing "issues that would subject 'moderates' to significant cross pressures— . . . the minimum wage, unemployment benefits, or a patients' bill of rights— . . . from coming up for serious consideration at all."

2. *The apparatus rigged the legislative process.* Closed rules in the House kept moderate amendments out of consideration, thus protecting Republicans from having to vote on them. Senate-House conference committees were controlled by the leadership, with Democrats virtually excluded, resulting in extreme measures that, in the end, even Republicans who initially opposed them would have to support. But they could tell their constituents that they had voted against the original bills.

3. To an unprecedented degree, *the apparatus obscured the most extreme aspects of bills behind benign disguises*, disguises that the press failed to penetrate. Even if the press had lifted the curtain on these maneuvers, only a shrinking part of the public was paying attention.

4. In a pinch, the apparatus could be counted upon to offer *mountainous financing to loyal Republicans*. Few districts were competitive at all.[39]

After years in charge, DeLay received his comeuppance, brought low by his fast and loose ways with ethics, indicted for conspiring to violate campaign finance laws, and forced to resign his leadership and his seat in 2006. The Abramoff exposés pushed lobbyist corruption over the embarrassment threshold.[40] As lobbyists anticipated a Democratic congressional revival, the K Street Project eroded.[41] DeLay's successor as majority leader, John Boehner

(R-OH), a congressman who had once passed out tobacco company checks on the House floor while members debated ending a tobacco subsidy (he later apologized for it), pledged to reform such practices as K Street favoritism, though once in office, he tried watering down reform legislation wherever possible.[42]

But turns in the political weather did not erase DeLay's achievement. Speaker Denny Hastert continued to restrict the House floor's attention to bills that won a majority of Republican supporters—Democrats be hanged. He left the Democrats burdened by his redistricting coups. When he was gone, the Republicans did not cease to overreach. Having gotten away with so many rule changes, tidy financial arrangements, and redistricting successes, they could not believe they could fail to sustain their power indefinitely. Only as the House leadership was tainted in subsequent scandals did their in-house quarrels reach a high pitch. Then, one long night of the knives followed another. There were limits to loyalty, after all.

But the House was only one pillar of Republican strength. No one can speak of Republican power and discipline without special attention to the commander in chief. In a presidential system, one of a party's chief functions is to choose its presidential candidate. It chooses him (or, someday, her) because it thinks he can win—and also because it thinks he can preside over the country in a manner that the party will approve. So even the leader's style is, in part, an expression of what his political base expects of him. If he did not begin his political life as such, he becomes the incarnation of the base. This is especially so for the Republicans, who as the party of hierarchy are more respectful of their leadership's pecking order than the more rambunctious Democrats are. So the Republican Party is factually, and morally, responsible for its leader. It gives itself up to him or, at the least, acquiesces. But the relationship is reciprocal—he shapes the base, selecting from among its several attributes some to accentuate and others to mute. In short, the tenor and the meaning of Republican rule as it has evolved over recent decades are incomprehensible without a closer look at the character and the method of George W. Bush and his inmost circle.

3

The Faithful and
the Willful

When the younger Bush strode into the Oval Office, many liberals assumed that he was, if not an entirely empty suit, an
amiable figurehead in cowboy boots, and that the country would
actually be governed, for better or worse, by the knowledgeable,
experienced, systematically conservative Dick Cheney. There is
certainly a division of labor between them, and Cheney stands taller
than any other vice president in U.S. history. But the preponderance
of available evidence supports the idea that Bush is actually, as he
has said, "the decider."[1] To speak of the administration's approach
is, in the end, to speak of him.

To call the younger Bush "faith-based," or to say that he "thinks
with his gut," is not simply to shower him with insults (or, if you're
on his side, tributes). The label "faith-based" makes sense of available evidence. But even "faith-based" does not wholly capture the
arbitrariness and recklessness (literally, absence of reckoning) in his
method.

It was the reporter Ron Suskind who famously wrote before
the 2004 election that Bush "has created the faith-based presidency." Suskind meant several different things by this label. He
plausibly maintained that "the faith-based presidency is a with-us-
or-against-us model that has been enormously effective at, among

other things, keeping the workings of the Bush White House a kind of state secret." He concluded:

> The president has demanded unquestioning faith from his followers, his staff, his senior aides and his kindred in the Republican Party. Once he makes a decision—often swiftly, based on a creed or moral position—he expects complete faith in its rightness. . . . A writ of infallibility—a premise beneath the powerful Bushian certainty that has, in many ways, moved mountains—is not just for public consumption: it has guided the inner life of the White House.[2]

It guided that inner life into war. It was able to slide into that mode with ease because it was *already* at war—against liberals.

Suskind also used "faith-based" to suggest, among other things, that Bush wished his judgments to be taken *on* faith, as, apparently, *he* took them. Outsiders were not to question what he did or how he did it, either before or after the fact. Now, all presidents prize the loyalty of their subordinates while also expecting them to serve as good democratic centralists—lieutenants who will argue about policy up to the point where the leader makes a decision, after which they fall into line. But as best as one can judge, Bush's bargain with his lieutenants stretched further—it extended to the very process by which the president arrived at a judgment in the first place.[3]

In Bush's inner circle, argument over substance was not welcome. Neither was dissent—from either insiders or outsiders. Outsiders were pariahs from the start. "The best way to get the news is from objective sources," Bush said in 2003 in the course of explaining why he didn't need to read newspapers. "And the most objective sources I have are people on my staff who tell me what's happening in the world."[4] But to speak of Bush as trapped in a "bubble" misses the point. Higher-ups often lose access to unofficial opinion. Insulation is well-known as a price of power. But Bush *chose* insulation. That is to say, he chose ignorance.

As for insiders, part of their "objectivity," as Bush saw it, was that they did not dispute the party line. This was what Colin Powell's former chief of staff, the retired Colonel Lawrence Wilkerson, meant when he referred to key foreign policy decisions being made by "a cabal between the vice president of the United States, Richard Cheney, and the secretary of defense, Donald Rumsfeld, on critical issues," excluding the normal gathering of opinion from within the national security bureaucracy.[5] Insiders marched in lockstep.

But where does Cheney end and Bush begin anyway? A word is in order here about what Joan Didion deliciously called "the blackout zone that is the Vice President and his office."[6] Cheney is widely said to be Bush's éminence grise, unprecedented in his presence and influence, unprecedented also in the secrecy of his operations (to such a degree that the names of members of his staff are classified)— the secrecy, of course, making it impossible to establish just how eminent he actually is.[7] Joseph Lelyveld has astutely said that Cheney "turned the vice-presidency into something approaching a prime ministership."[8] Ron Suskind reports that Bush and Cheney worked out a division of labor wherein Cheney—with Bush's approval—hordes information so that Bush can claim "plausible deniability."[9] Whatever the details of Bush's relationship with Cheney—details that will be extremely hard to unearth in the near run, perhaps ever—it is plain that Cheney is singularly influential. Indeed, Bush's supporters have long seen Cheney that way— affirmatively. When I published an article during the 2000 campaign casting doubt on Bush's intellectual competence, a major theme in the hundreds of protests I received was precisely that Bush, conceded to be limited in experience at the least, would have the benefit of Cheney and Powell by his side.[10]

Cheney is not Bush. Bush may claim to be "the decider"— protesting almost too much—but Cheney is a master of the executive apparatus. Unlike Bush, he has vast experience in the national government, from Gerald Ford's White House to a high Republican position in Congress to the Pentagon, then back to the White House. As the well-known story of his selective prewar deployment of tactically useful intelligence from the CIA and other agencies illustrates, Cheney knows how to navigate through the vast reaches of the executive branch. Unlike Bush, he has presided over a large corporation. Cheney does not claim a deep religious commitment like Bush's. His ideas about the world are grounded less in religious conviction than in some more conventional right-wing ideology—not neoconservative zeal for remaking the world in an American image but a more conventional nationalism. Publicly, however, Cheney is as dogmatic, as impervious to evidence, as faith-based in this sense, as Bush is.[11]

Leaving aside the impenetrable niceties of the question of where Bush stops and Cheney begins, what is clear is that throughout the published reports that are the only sources of information about this secretive regime, there are many more instances of Bush gut-thinking his way to judgment and yanking his "advisers" in lock-step behind him than there are instances of rational debate. Bush held his truths to be self-evident. Indeed, the disillusion of Bush's first Treasury secretary, Paul O'Neill, flowed from his discovery that Bush was not interested in the expression of rival opinions from among his advisers in the first place. "O'Neill had been made to understand by various colleagues in the White House that the President should not be expected to read reports," wrote Suskind, O'Neill's amanuensis. "In his personal experience, the President didn't even appear to have read the short memos he sent over. That made it especially troubling that Bush did not ask any questions."

O'Neill, the former CEO of Alcoa, was a rational conservative. He had served under Presidents Nixon and Ford, each of whom (as O'Neill told his amanuensis, Suskind) expected to hear advisers hash out a range of alternatives so that he could set them against each other and choose from among them. O'Neill expected to encounter the same from Bush. He didn't. Bush was unfamiliar with—or allergic to—contrary opinions. Although war was his governing metaphor, he did not think about war as an actual planner of war does. He did not weigh alternatives. Bush was not, in other words, rational, or interested in becoming more so. Suskind concluded that President Bush "was caught in an echo chamber of his own making, cut off from everyone other than a circle around him that's tiny and getting smaller and in concert on everything." Bush's Environmental Protection Agency chief, Christine Todd Whitman, was reduced to making "blind stabs at deducing the mind of the President." He didn't "offer explanation, even to his most senior aides. . . . Mr. O'Neill knew that Whitman had never heard the President analyze a complex issue, parse opposing positions, and settle on a judicious path. In fact, no one—inside or outside the government, here or across the globe—had heard him do that to any significant degree."[12]

Confirmation about Bush's mental inflexibility when the chips were down comes from the man who was Osama bin Laden's prime nemesis in the White House from 1998 on, Richard Clarke. Clarke had worked in high-security positions for Ronald Reagan, George H. W. Bush, and Bill Clinton, who appointed him the first national coordinator for security, infrastructure protection, and counterterrorism—a position he retained in the younger Bush's White House, where he discovered that the Cold War mind-set of the new inner circle rendered its members altogether uninterested in bin Laden. Despite months of effort starting in January 2001, Clarke was unable to achieve a meeting with the inner circle (the "Principals") on the al-Qaeda threat until September 4, 2001.[13]

Clarke is not indiscriminately dismissive of Bush. It is worthwhile to slow down here and proceed slowly through his sentences on Bush's state of mind. He writes that "the critique of [Bush] as a dumb, lazy rich kid were [sic] somewhat off the mark." The national security civil servant strives to be precise, even generous. "When [Bush] focused," he goes on—Clarke seems to be suggesting that this was not an automatic event—"he asked the kind of questions that revealed a results-oriented mind, but he looked for the simple solution, the bumper sticker description of the problem." This speaks to a form of laziness that might better be called simple-mindedness. "Once he had that [the 'bumper-sticker description']," Clarke goes on, "he could put energy behind a drive to achieve his goal." In other words, he was lazy until his thoughts fit into a preestablished pattern—but once they fit, he was a fanatic. "The problem was that many of the important issues, like terrorism, like Iraq, were laced with important subtlety and nuance. These issues needed analysis and Bush and his inner circle had no real interest in complicated analyses; on the issues that they cared about, they already knew the answers."[14]

"Thinking with the gut" at the top, an airtight apparatus beneath—this was Bush's leadership principle, while a chorus of pundits, flunkies, and other admirers spent years admiring his ever-new wardrobe.[15] His willfulness he rationalized as faith.

This is not a trivial rationalization. The faith of the faithful moves onlookers even when it does not move mountains. Faith generates courage. With faith, men and women have defended the weak, withstood torture, resisted tyrants, and overcome all manner of frailties. But the faith that Bush practices cannot be understood as the faith of saints—the faith that withstands suffering and motivates sacrifice. Not even those who testify to Bush's faith mean the faith that walks through the valley of the shadow of death fearing no evil, the faith that emerges in fear and trembling and dissolves the torment of doubt.

The faith on which Bush bases his actions is, rather, a stupendous self-importance. It is the certitude of a man who takes his religion as an all-purpose certificate of approval. This faith is less adherence to any particular principle or ritual, let alone a coherent picture of the world, than it is the emotional set of a man who believes, most of all, in the imperative to act.[16] He is the decider; that is his measure as a man. He can justify his decisions because he has divine sanction from the Supreme Decider. David Frum, the conservative columnist who was a Bush White House speechwriter for a time, writes that the reason "why Bush was so confident" was "not because he was arrogant"—though Frum's case for Bush's humility is scanty—"but because he believed that the future was held in stronger hands than his own": in other words, that God was writing his destiny.[17] Shortly after September 11, 2001, Bush was reported "to have privately told friends that God has handed him this crisis."[18] Bush the son told Bob Woodward that his father, George H. W. Bush, "is the wrong father to appeal to in terms of strength. There is a higher father that I appeal to."[19] Bush's claim to be doing God's work extended to a claim to know God's purposes (and to know how God proposed to accomplish his purposes as well): "I base a lot of my foreign-policy decision on some things that I think are true," he said in 2006. "One, I believe there's an Almighty. And, secondly, I believe one of the great gifts of the Almighty is the desire in everybody's soul, regardless of what you look like or where you live, to be free."[20]

One of Bush's favorite adjectives is *strong*.[21] Individuals whom he admires—Pope John Paul II, Pope Benedict XVI, the German prime minister Angela Merkel—are "strong," the "higher father" has "strength," and most of all, Bush admires strength in himself. It would appear at first blush, from his relatively few unbuttoned interviews, that part of what he means by strength is consistency of principle. Look more closely and you see that consistency, as he construes it, embraces refusal to reconsider his judgments. Doubt is unmanly. Only certainty is righteous. Moral righteousness requires intellectual rightness, which in turn entails a refusal to rethink one's positions. Moral strength is wedded in turn to that cardinal American virtue, optimism, for optimism is proof of faith—the conviction that your decisions will be vindicated, if only in the fullness of time.

Optimism, in Bush's meaning, is more than a personality trait or a cognitive style. Optimism is the pulsing heart of religious faith. It is rock-bottom proof of strong character because it comes from "your very soul." Bush was "a natural raving optimist," wrote his former campaign aide Stuart Stevens, who meant it as a compliment.[22] In an Oval Office interview with a German tabloid reporter, on May 5, 2006, as his approval ratings were plummeting, Bush said:

> You cannot lead people unless you're optimistic about what you're doing. You've got to believe it in your very soul. . . .
> [I]f I'm going to be [wringing] my hands and if I'm all worried about the decisions I make are not going to lead to a better tomorrow, [people will] figure it out. And so when you talk to me today, I just want you to know I not only strongly believe in the decisions I make, I'm optimistic that they're going to work—very optimistic.[23]

God, strength, soul, optimism, will—the mind of George W. Bush is all of a piece. On what ground does Bush hold fast to his radiant optimism? God's ground. By virtue of his special relationship with God, Bush is anointed for a singular role in history. Once he was weak, but God made him strong, and forevermore what will keep him strong is the strength of the Almighty. He cannot be guilty of hubris because, like the devout ballplayer who points heavenward after sinking a basket or hitting the ball out of the park, his prowess is only on loan. He is God's proxy.

In the official story, Bush was forty years old when he bound his will to God's. On the nature of his moment of salvation from alcoholic desperation, no outsider can comment with much assurance. Yet it should not escape notice that it is decidedly useful to be born again and "accept Jesus Christ as your personal savior." From the moment he directly experienced the power of God—Christ having "changed [his] heart"—Bush became God's instrument. In other words, his own decisions became unimpeachable.

Now, a reflective believer in God might reasonably wonder whether Almighty God writes his or her personal destiny—at least consistently so. After all, billions believe in God, but not all who believe are always content with the destinies that come their way. Otherwise there would be no long history of "the dark night of the soul." If God writes all the destinies of all the mortals who believe in Him and who believe, further, that He writes their destinies, then the multiplicity of the results—after all, men as different as Jimmy Carter and George W. Bush profess to have been born again—is either proof that they are mistaken about what God intended for them or proof that the divergent manners in which the same God writes their varying destinies somehow fit together in a fashion strikingly, even disturbingly, unfathomable to ordinary thought— in which case the knowledge that your destiny is written by God may not amount to the utter assurance you are bargaining for.

But then what does this belief amount to? Might it be no more than a comfort for the humble—an after-the-fact compensation, a runner-up prize, as if to say, *I am small, but God has something special in mind for even the smallest of mortals*? Yet everything in the experience of the president of the United States of America already conspires to convince him that he is *not* small. After spending his first forty years in casual underachievement, he found God, quit drinking, and devoted himself to the bruising struggles of politics, to the point of transforming himself into the most powerful human being in the world.

Now the decider is entitled to decide because he does the work of the Decider in Chief. By the standards of worldly action he is not small or ordinary at all. He gives orders, people snap to attention, and individuals he has never met live or die. Millions pray for him. A supporter, a self-professed lifelong Republican, rose at a 2004 campaign rally, to say, "This is the very first time that I have felt that God was in the White House." Bush thanked him. At another, private meeting with a group of Amish in central Pennsylvania, Bush is reported to have said, "I trust God speaks through me." (The White House denied it.)[24]

Are such comments signals that Bush deliberately flashes to his true believers? What's clear is that in George W. Bush, first as candidate, then as president, the Christian right found a man it took as a literal godsend. Early in his political career, in 1988, when Bush served as his father's emissary to the religious right, he learned from his father's adviser, the Assemblies of God minister and motivational speaker Doug Wead, how important it was to "signal early and signal often"—that is, to pepper his speeches with biblical references that would serve as political winks and nods and thus arouse the party's religious base to fix upon him as its man.[25] All presidents signal to their constituencies; more maladroit than most, Bush may simply be less subtle about the signals he sends. "In 1998, 1999, 2000," Wead once said, "within five minutes of any meetings with evangelicals, within minutes, they instantly knew he's a born-again Christian."[26]

Wead added about the 1988 campaign, "When we'd talk about the numbers and where they were, he'd just about salivate: 'Wow, I could win the governorship of Texas with just the evangelical vote.'" To the question of whether Bush's religiosity is genuine, Wead, more subtle than some of his critics, told an interviewer, "There's no question that the president's faith is real, that it's authentic, that it's genuine, and there's no question that it's calculated. I know that sounds like a contradiction. But that will always be the case for a public figure, regardless of their faith, whether they're Islamic, or Jewish, or Christian." Wead continued,

"I would say that I don't know when he's sincere and when he's calculated. . . . George Bush doesn't know when he's operating out of a genuine sense of his own faith, or when it's calculated, and there must be gray areas in between. I think he operates instinctively."[27]

Relations between Bush and his religious base have been, by many accounts, warm and reciprocal. To reward the faithful and alert them that they were never far from his mind, Bush stirred a certain minimum of concrete actions into a regular diet of rhetorical affirmations. Accordingly, on his first day in the White House, he reinstated the Reagan-era ban on funding foreign contraception programs run by agencies that also conduct abortions.[28] Bush in office found many occasions to remind the Christian right that he was in tune with its members—directly in tune, short-circuiting the "filters" of national media.[29] In "faith-based programs," the word became flesh. Bush's Christian legions saw him as doing the Lord's work in a sinful world. If he fell short, they pressed him to live up to his reputation for righteousness.

Then the Satanic bolts from the blue on September 11, 2001, intensified Bush's conviction that he was an instrument of Divine Providence. Now he more openly expressed—possibly more sharply felt—his religious calling. His longtime friend, the 2000 campaign finance chief and first-term secretary of commerce Don Evans, told a reporter that Bush "believes he was called by God to lead the nation at this time."[30]

What exactly should be made of Bush's God talk? Bush's chief speechwriter for seven years, the theologically trained Michael Gerson, argued that Bush's speeches express a normal fealty to American civic religion. He denied that allusions to specific hymns and scriptural passages in Bush's speeches qualified as "code words; they're literary references understood by millions of Americans. They're not code words; they're our culture."[31] Gerson has a bit of a point: such references may well be understood by more Americans than would today recognize an allusion to Emerson, Whitman, or Hemingway. But it is disingenuous to deny that Bush's references to the Bible, Providence, and the like signal—sincerely, let us grant—that the speaker is conversant with Christian fundamentals.

Doug Wead is plausible. The signals that Bush sends to his followers are probably also sincere, or close to it. He flatters himself worthy of their true belief. In other words, the belief that God is writing his destiny, though superficially at odds with an inflated idea of his own importance (the "arrogance" that David Frum discounts), dissolves on inspection into a belief that he is supremely important—not only worthy of God's attention but distinctly needful of God's help, for he is not only saluted, courted, and loved but hated by multitudes. Narcissism glossed as godliness is narcissism to a higher power.

If it is Bush's self-glorification to believe that he has been chosen specially for his mission in life, his conviction is repeatedly confirmed and reinforced by his followers. Even the powerful and accomplished individuals who surround him and—as the saying goes—serve at his pleasure, the ones who do not wear their beliefs on their sleeves, tiptoe around him. Insiders who do not share his religious fervor, such as Dick Cheney and Karl Rove (and Donald Rumsfeld, for six years), evidently possess an abiding faith in him— never mind that evidence and logic have gone missing.

In his deservedly much-cited article of October 2004, Ron Suskind wrote that a senior adviser to Bush—one surmises it was Karl Rove—told him that

> guys like me were "in what we call the reality-based community," which he [the adviser] defined as people who "believe that solutions emerge from your judicious study of discernible reality." I nodded and murmured something about enlightenment principles and empiricism. He cut me off. "That's not the way the world really works anymore," he continued. "We're an empire now, and when we act, we create our own reality. And while you're studying that reality—judiciously, as you will—we'll act again, creating other new realities, which you can study too, and that's how things will sort out. We're history's actors . . . and you, all of you, will be left to just study what we do."[32]

The polarization between doing and knowing is stark. (The senior adviser might chortle to know that Marx put the point this way in his famous eleventh thesis on Feuerbach: "Philosophers have only studied the world, the point is to change it.") Ruling the world are *We*, anointed angels soaring upward and onward, "creating our own reality." Reduced to merely studying the world on which We act are the likes of *You*—listless, earthbound blue-state types dragging your bellies through the mud while the glorious godlike work— the creative work, the work of Creation—is performed by *Us*. As Goethe put it, in a line admired by Marx, *Im Anfang war die Tat*—in the beginning was the deed. The principle could also be called the "fixing of the facts and intelligence around the policy."[33]

In short, what makes Bush and his inner circle dangerous is not their ignorance alone, and not what some critics call "stupidity" in the sense of plain feeblemindedness, but their will to override logic and evidence. They act as though might makes not only right but truth. Their infallibility leaves evidence in the dust. Their own inflexibility they admire under the headings of "strength," "resoluteness," "focus," and "determination." It was an earlier phase of "resoluteness" that led them to ignore ample warnings of forthcoming terror attacks in 2001, including a warning by the CIA's George Tenet and James L. Pavitt, about a week before Bush's inauguration, to Bush, Cheney, and Condoleezza Rice that "bin Laden and his network were a 'tremendous threat' which was 'immediate,' " in Bob Woodward's words.[34] These warnings culminated in the CIA's famous "Bin Ladin [*sic*] Determined to Strike in US" presidential daily brief of August 6, 2001, the one dismissed by Condoleezza Rice at her confirmation hearing for secretary of state as merely "historical"[35]—because through September 10, 2001, Bush and his inner circle were convinced that the greatest dangers the country faced came from what Rice had called "rogue states and hostile powers."[36] This was their conviction, and they did not deviate from conviction.

But their willingness, or eagerness, to depart from evidence if it does not fit their mental framework goes beyond rigidity. It reveals a penchant for the fantastical—a penchant that goes beyond simple mendacity, too, because much of the time it seems to reflect either sincere (though hallucinatory) belief or the perverse, illogical, but somehow compelling fusion of fervent belief (in a delusional system) and utter cynicism (about whether one is describing or even approximating reality). This is the hodgepodge that George Orwell memorably designated as "doublethink."

Thus North Korea, Iraq, and Iran solidified into an "axis of evil"; "the war on terror" entailed war in Iraq; torture dwindled into "abuse"; General Musharraf's Pakistan held "free" elections; "privatization" morphed into "personal accounts." Bush is at home in the realm of Newspeak Lite, where euphemism joins hands with evasion and self-contradiction. Artful evasion, innuendo, and repetition exert pressure by default, so that in time a majority of Americans came to believe that al-Qaeda and Saddam Hussein were allies and that there were weapons of mass destruction in Iraq. (Significant numbers of people persisted for years in believing that these weapons *were* found.) *1984*'s "We have always been at war with Eurasia" found a parallel in the assumption that the United States had always been antagonistic to Saddam Hussein. "He has used chemical weapons against his own people," recited by the president and his inner circle with a never-ending air of shocked indignation, consistently obscured the fact that the United States had been colluding with Saddam in 1988 when he gassed the Kurds at Halabja.

Orwell's language of Newspeak clogged the public mind because it exercised a monopoly. Newspeak Lite circulated differently, resounding from White House press conferences and briefings, swept along by a right-wing amplification system on radio and cable TV, only half-heartedly contested by credulous ("liberal") mainstream media. It was one rivulet among rivulets, spilling through the world amid a torrent of sensations, stories, and trivia, that whole gushing, incessant stream of popular culture—TV, radio, music in every room and eardrum, on billboards and in computer pop-up ads, in elevators, malls, waiting rooms, and planes, a nonstop welter of attractions, interruptions, and interferences that amount to everyone's secondhand accompaniment or semireality.[37]

And here was the awesome power of Newspeak Lite: when logic and proportion made no impact on policy, truth became a weightless irrelevancy, a matter of mere opinion—he said, she said. After the White House declared a hundred times that Social Security was "in crisis," the debate started with a presumption that this must be so. Repeating their pet phrases as if objections were proof of deafness and slogans the mothers of reality, top officials rolled over pesky questions and occasional dissents. Professionals admired them for staying "on message."

To prevail, Newspeak Lite need not persuade. It suffices to cow the opposition, to smother doubt, to inoculate an inattentive and uninformed public against corrosive skepticism. As the example of Social Security shows, the White House does not necessarily prevail, but it does shift the question under discussion. (In this case, it primes the pump for the next privatization attempt.) When Bush declared about the grinding war in Iraq, on June 28, 2005, that "there is only one course of action against [terrorists]: to defeat them abroad before they attack us at home,"[38] and then again, on July 6, on arriving in Scotland for the G-8 meeting, that the war in Iraq was "laying the foundation for peace,"[39] he could not be faulted for failing to anticipate that a few hours later Islamist terrorists would commit mass murder in London, though it is certainly worthy of note that he was uttering cant, for terrorists did not cease attacking American allies after the United States went to war in Iraq—most lethally in Madrid on March 11, 2004. But when he repeated his phrase almost exactly, *two days after the London attacks* ("We will stay on the offense, fighting the terrorists abroad so we do not have to face them at home," he said on his weekly radio broadcast), what could he possibly have meant? Presumably, since he was reading from a radio script, this was no accident, no slip of the tongue.

Parsing such statements requires the finesse of a philosophical brain surgeon. (In honor of William Empson, a book on Bush's language might be called *Seven Varieties of Deception*.) When Bush repeated his falsehoods about Iraq, was he lying, half-lying, deluding himself, or displaying—or letting slip—his indifference to the truth? In 2005, did the president of the United States mean that London, like Madrid, was not "us"? Possibly so—a recursion to fortress America thinking, the luxury of the parochial, though, to put it mildly, in the week of G-8 this would fly smack in the face of solidarity with allies, the sort of expression we celebrated (briefly) when *Le Monde* trumpeted, "We are all Americans!" on September 12, 2001.

More likely, Bush was using language in an incantatory way. Phrases such as "before they attack us at home" and "laying the foundation for peace" do not speak—and may not even be intended to speak—a truth that invites confirmation or refutation by events. These are not statements about reality, though they employ language that seems to be either true or false. Bush might have said, "We will stay on the offense, and though terrorists may attack our people and our allies' people, because they have no respect for human life, we shall prevail," or words to that effect. Such an affirmation might have been as close to the Churchillian mold as Bush gets and would have committed no falsehood. But no. On June 28, Bush chose instead an affirmation that had already been falsified (in Madrid) and was almost immediately falsified again; and then he repeated it, denying evident fact. What shall we make of such statements? I can only think that they are meant both to obscure reality and to evoke the sort of sympathetic grunt that affirms, "You know what he means," when what he means is to depart from meaning altogether.

Bush's readiness to strip language of literal or even figurative meaning and indulge in the fantastical can be prettied up—as by David Frum—as "the Bush preference for imagination over memory."[40] Imagination is a wondrous thing, but not when it is mistaken for knowledge. When it is so mistaken, it is magical thinking. "Words often failed him," Frum wrote in tribute to Bush's underrated intelligence, "his memory sometimes betrayed him, but his vision was large and clear."[41] The word *vision* here slides from foresight—as in "visionary"—to hallucination; from the desirable to the actual. If a vision is "large and clear" enough, does this mean it need not be checked for accuracy? Does it no longer require evidence? Is it allowed to overrule contrary evidence with aplomb? If it is "large and clear" enough, a vision of Saddam Hussein's Iraq infested with weapons of mass destruction overrides knowledgeable doubts—thus the "fixing" of intelligence "around the policy." If it is "large and clear" enough, a vision of postwar Iraq falling into place because the United States will be "greeted as liberators" overpowers the doubts of the military and the State Department. The luminous vision of Iraq without Saddam overcomes any serious recognition of the forces and strategies requisite to a viable postwar society. When vision in this sense rides high, doubt is not just a nuisance; it is a virtual sin—a morale-blaster, a bummer, an act of sabotage.

When, on May 31, 2005, Dick Cheney proclaimed that the Iraqi insurgency was in its "last throes," it defies common sense to accept his subsequent explanation that he was hewing to the dictionary definition of "throes."[42] Nor does it seem likely that Condoleezza Rice was merely laying down a tactical gauntlet when she spoke of the Israel-Lebanon war of 2006 as among "the birth pangs of a new Middle East." Such bizarre metaphors are in-house go-aheads and signals to the base.

Now, so much is routine in the age of mass politics. To politicians, words are stratagems, for in politics language is both a communication and a commitment to action. Language is policy. The failure to justify policy is also policy. Under Bush, it reflects the Republican base's conviction that its faith is determining, that it does not require "elitist" logic and evidence. It is beyond such trifles.

All politicians trim, deflect, bull, and spin their way through public life. Language is a large part of image, and in America, image is the supreme bond between politician and public, the cement of legitimacy, the place where the follower and the leader meet. In the American political style, image skyrockets in significance because the voter looks directly to the leader, not to the party. The voter not only consents to the leader but feels an identity with him, feels at least respected and at best ennobled by him—and believes that to be worthy of the voter's choice, the leader must make him feel that their hearts beat together. In choosing the leader, the voter chooses a presence in his or her life. Do I want to let this person into my home ("comfort zone") for the next four years? Proverbially speaking, is this somebody I want to have a beer with? Successful leadership consists, up to a point, of mastering the projective game, flattering the follower that the leader is actually following *him.*

In this version, or parody, of democratic leadership, victory goes to the superior incarnation of popular ideals. Bush is decisive—or at least such is the image that he projects, as against the flaccid Al Gore and the "flip-flopping" John Kerry. In 2000, Bush won white voters without four-year college degrees by 17 percentage points. In 2004, he won them by 23 points.[43] During the 2004 campaign, a white New York City policeman of my acquaintance maintained, "You may not agree with Bush, but you know where he stands." Forcefulness makes Bush a man's man—damn the nuances. The tough mind in the hard body declares to the world, "Bring 'em on." The same decisiveness that clears brush and rides mountain bikes when it is not moving mountains brings freedom and democracy to a reluctant world. (In 2006, a reporter accompanied Bush as he "set a brutal pace" on his mountain bike in hundred-degree heat on his Texas property. " 'Air assault!' [Bush] yelled as he started one of two major climbs."[44]) It is freedom in action, the American verve that undertakes the errand into the wilderness, erects the shining city upon the hill, overthrows tyrants, rescues the vulnerable, conquers complacency, remembers the Alamo, and avenges Pearl Harbor. This is the will in all its muscular glory, the will of absolute certainty, setting the course, staying the course, not only against enemies in arms but against the mushy, flabby, indecisive, morally relative liberals who are their allies.

4

"The Un-Sixties"

In the minds of George Bush's followers—both those who remain loyal and those who backed away once backing away appeared popular—his iron will incorporates more than his steady manliness. It stands for perpetual revolt: the revolt of John Wayne against the herd of sheepish townspeople; of Midland, Texas, against suburban Connecticut; of Crawford, Texas, against Washington, D.C.; of Nazareth against Jerusalem; of outsiders against nameless Establishments, against the namby-pamby, cutting-and-running, stultifying pseudo-knowledge of doubters. Bush is properly tagged, by one of his yea-sayers, as the "rebel in chief," for he "operates in Washington like the head of a small occupying army of insurgents, an elected band of brothers (and quite a few sisters) on a mission. He's an alien in the realm of the governing class."[1]

The "governing class," in this view, consists of the gray and faceless half-men of "the bureaucracy"—as in, "I read the report put out by the bureaucracy," Bush's dismissive response to a 2002 Environmental Protection Agency statement arguing that human activities were responsible for massive climate change.[2] Not for the first time, Bush summoned a time-honored conservative theme with a vaguely Marxist class-struggle tinge—resentment by the forces of production of unproductive parasites who don't properly appreciate big business but resent it, regulate it, tax it, and lay it low.

There is a lineage to this impulse. The theme of a dangerous class of unshackled office-holders, rationalists running amok and taking over the world descends from Edmund Burke's *Reflections on the Revolution in France* (1790) and was later imported from Europe in James Burnham's quasi-Trotskyist *The Managerial Revolution* (1941). Burnham influenced William F. Buckley's *National Review* and wrote a column there. The same notion was applied specifically to the communist system in Milovan Djilas's *The New Class* (1957), then popularized for the United States in Irving Kristol's *Two Cheers for Capitalism* (1978). Bush in Washington, like an earlier fortunate son of wealth, John F. Kennedy,[3] fancied himself a guerrilla fighter against entrenched "elitists," to use today's insult of choice. (George Wallace, in truck drivers' language, used the more colorful term "pointy-headed bureaucrats.") Bush's enemies were the know-it-alls, those credentialed meritocrats too educated by half, who won prestige and credit that should more properly have accrued to their social betters—the likes of the Bushes. Where Richard Nixon was consumed by resentment of the wealthy and glamorous Kennedys because they possessed in abundance the savoir faire of which he could only dream, the objects of Bush's resentment were those undeserving arrivistes who, in the days of his youth just when he was coming into his heritage as a scion, smuggled themselves into the sanctum sanctorum and made off with the glory he felt entitled to.

Yale was where Bush first felt that his social standing was devalued. There, the young man of privilege found himself shorn of his rightful prerogatives. Yale, after all, was for Bushes. His grandfather and his father had been big men on campus—both star baseball players, both tapped for the secret society Skull and Bones. His father, a war hero who won the Distinguished Flying Cross, was elected president of his fraternity and graduated Phi Beta Kappa; his grandfather was destined to become a member of the Yale Corporation.[4] But the young Bush's experience at Yale was jarring, a comedown. He made the baseball team, all right, but not like first baseman Prescott Bush or first baseman and captain George H. W. Bush; rather, as a third-string pitcher.[5]

The younger Bush had the misfortune to arrive at Yale in 1964, as his forebears' Yale was crumbling. The young Bush's years in New Haven were the years of Kingman Brewster's presidency, when the institution was belatedly moving in the direction of meritocracy. Just two years before the matriculation of George W. Bush in 1968, Yale, under pressure, decided it was no longer going to be content to have the lowest Jewish enrollment in the Ivy League, at 12 percent. Whereas the class that entered in 1961 was 10 percent Jewish, the percentage rose to 16 percent the next year and to 30 percent the year after that.[6] (The class of 1966 was the first to be subject to Yale president A. Whitney Griswold's new policy of removing "economic social, religious or racial barriers to the fulfillment of . . . the democratic ideal of equal opportunity." Yale College first admitted women in 1969.) Under Brewster's hand-picked admissions director, the number of graduates from Andover and other similar prep schools plunged by 50 percent or more within a single year.[7] For the first time, Yale recruited at elite public schools such as Bronx Science and Stuyvesant. By 1967, George W. Bush's junior year, prep school graduates (who had been 56 percent of all entrants in 1960) were down to 39 percent of the freshmen.[8] "We were the last vestiges of the rich man's school," one of his fraternity brothers said later.[9]

During young Bush's college years, Yale's center of gravity drifted away from the WASP social establishment and toward intellectuals, upstarts, and interlopers—not only the brainy and the studious but, increasingly, the unkempt radicals and the marijuana-smoking counterculturalists. Compared to activist-friendly Harvard and Columbia, Yale was still on the straight side, but even at Yale young go-getters like John F. Kerry '66, an accomplished political debater (as well as an athlete), were the big men on campus. A blueblood heir would not automatically find himself graced by virtue of his lineage.

The young Bush worked out a different form of distinction: he had a gift for remembering names and a knack for promoting himself as the hail-fellow-well-met who assigned nicknames to everyone whose path he crossed. He thrived as a fraternity president, a glad-hander in his father's old haunts, "known as the jock-and-party fraternity," as his biographer Bill Minutaglio wrote, possessed of "maybe the biggest bar in Connecticut."[10] But the fraternities were no longer where it was at. When young Bush went out for his fraternity during his sophomore year, more than four hundred of his fellow students attended the organizational meeting; the following year, half that number showed up.[11] Fraternity values were old. The whole culture was telling him so—it was, after all, the sixties, and Bush was so fifties. There was, he felt, a pall of "heaviness" suffusing the campus.[12] "Yale had reinforced his feeling that if he were ever asked where he was from, he would say Texas instead of Connecticut," one of his cousins said. "It was very uncomfortable for him, as the son of his father, to be at Yale when there was so much antiwar and so much antiestablishment."[13]

The birthright of George W. Bush had been devalued by a social and moral upheaval that was not only offensive in principle but had the additional disadvantage of devaluing him. It was surely a sign of moral decay when the grandson of Prescott Bush and the son of George H. W. Bush had to settle for less than his due, when Yale's halls of ivy no longer served to shelter and exalt the Bushes of the world. Bush wanted wealth, but wealth was no longer an undisputed value among the campus elite.[14] Instead, Yale was full of intellectuals, arrogant, liberal, and guilty—a combination that weighed on Bush and drove him to a proud and defensive *anti*intellectualism.[15] Secret societies like Skull and Bones had become, said the *New York Times*, "hotly controversial on the campus."[16] The august *New York Times* sounded as though it had gone over to the enemy. To add insult to injury, one of the biggest men on campus, the chaplain William Sloane Coffin, a liberal of upper-class origins who had himself been inducted into Skull and Bones by George the Elder, had the gall to tell the young Bush to his face (or so the young Bush remembered) that George H. W. Bush, having lost the Texas Senate race to the liberal Ralph Yarborough, "was beaten by a better man."[17]

The barbarians were inside the gates, and young George Bush found himself on the front line. Rebellious against his father, though scarcely against the social class they shared, he now encountered a dark force that it was legitimate to rebel against—the interlopers and the attitudes they represented: moral decadence, intellectual arrogance, "the heaviness." By all signs, he kept his feelings under wraps, but he must have smoldered with resentment of the new culture of cultural radicalism with its combination of meritocracy and outré style. He was a cut-up. He drank.

But he remained a Bush, and therefore entitled—entitled to jump the line into the Air National Guard, entitled to take time off from the guard to work on a political campaign in another state just as he pleased, entitled to skip out on a physical examination just as he pleased, entitled to exit the National Guard early to enter Harvard Business School, and then, once possessed of his M.B.A., to call upon family funds when needed in order to keep his erratic oil career afloat.[18] His father pointed the way forward toward the winning combination: oil and Texas politics. The son would be a man of Midland, not Kennebunkport.

Bush spent much of his adult life ambling from pursuit to pursuit. If he stumbled repeatedly, at least he was familiar with the path on which he was stumbling. But as he entered his fifth decade, young George found a way to stamp his undistinguished business career with a distinct generational brand. He gave up the bottle for Jesus. Now he could unify his life. In 1992, Bush suffered through the losing cause of his father's reelection campaign and found himself confronting, again, his old nemesis—and this time more directly than before. "I got into politics initially because I wanted to help change a culture," he later told David Brooks, who noted that Bush was "referring to his campaign against the instant gratifications of the 1960's counterculture."[19] In 1992, the counterculture took on a distinctive name and face: the unrepentant, Hillary-marrying, adulterous, noninhaling, onetime draft dodger, and McGovernite Bill Clinton. But no matter how fervently the elder Bush's supporters insisted that Clinton represented moral decay in America, Clinton prevailed. When George H. W. Bush was brought low, his son reached into himself and found the mainspring of clear ambition.

Young George learned two political lessons from his father's failure. A Republican politician must keep faith with the conservative base over taxes. He must also excite evangelicals. This is best done when the candidate is himself one of their number, but it is sometimes done most effectively in disguise, framing the defense of moral restoration in the anodyne glow of "compassionate conservatism."

Rallying business with the promise of "tort reform," the promise of which would excite it to fill his coffers, Bush was now on the road to a surprise victory in the race for the Texas governorship two years later. Here, contemplating a run for the presidency, he came to appreciate the political clout of the moral conservatives. He was a deserving inheritor after all, but more: he could carve out a distinct place for himself in a great social movement—the great recoil against the destructive sixties zeitgeist of "if it feels good, do it." Politics would be the vessel of his defiance. By 2000, he would present himself as (in the words of a conservative writer who inspired him) "the anti-Clinton and the un-sixties."[20] Where robust conservatives had, with reason, accused George H. W. Bush of wimping out in the face of the enemy—caving in on taxes, failing to depose Saddam Hussein—Bush the younger would prove *he* was no pushover but rather a manly avenger, a staunch redeemer of fifties virtue, the true successor to Ronald Reagan.[21]

Bush would flout the moral degradation to which the interlopers had subjected the country, but he would do so without rough edges. He would side with "the culture of life," but in a kinder and gentler way, as "a committed family man devoted to traditional values and traditional beliefs, after his youthful fling with the culture of the sixties led him to reject it emphatically from firsthand knowledge of its destructiveness."[22] Born again, he would not only save himself but join in a great redemptive movement to save his country.

In the White House, Bush renewed his long-standing resentment, repeatedly taking down people who knew more than he did, people who tore down the country, *his* country. He was too earthy a figure to be bound by the pantywaist syntax of fussy elitists who did not, after all, rise to the level of genuine elites—Bushes. When reporters asked him to give reasons for his views or to reconcile today's reasons with yesterday's, he blithely declared that he did not have to explain himself. In a gray world where experts rode high, flaunting their methodical but godless science, he remained a golden boy, his resolve a bright bolt from the blue.

Contemporary politicians believe that they are hammers and phrases are nails: they drive home a point by repeating it. The public, after all, is inattentive, the whole ensemble of media has an infinite appetite, and off-message comments fly into an endless audiovisual afterlife online. But the spiky crudity of Bush's spoken style is more than self-discipline; it is a sign of his bond with his base. Bush's repetitive inarticulateness is in this sense, as his professional imitator Steve Bridges said, "endearing."[23] To his true believers, his claim of inerrancy certifies his genuineness. So does his negligence or insouciance in the face of self-contradiction or refutation by observable fact.

The evidence is voluminous and definitive. Self-deception, self-hypnosis, dissembling, and fabricating come so frequently to Bush, they must be said to be second nature. He goes far beyond the trimming, shading, bending, evading, double-talking—all in all, to use the knowing euphemism of the present day, the *spinning*—the whole kit-bag of dodges and deceptions that is standard equipment in politics. As Machiavelli well knew, impressions are components of power. Deception is a tool of state. And in a democratic society, there is a particular structure to lying. Leave aside the lies of state, little and large, meant to befuddle enemies and mollify friends. In the climb to power, there are lies and self-deceptions of flattery and lies and self-deceptions of audacity—such as the common claim that the politician knows how to solve the public's problems, or even what the public's problems are. Inevitably, once a politician rises to power, there will be issues on which supporters will be at loggerheads some of the time. Therefore, the art of assembling victorious coalitions is also the art of dissembling—speaking out of two or more sides of one's mouth. Given all the political cross-currents, what president of this complicated country has not found it convenient to shade the truth, at least on special occasions?

But there is a striking difference between Bush's lies and the lies of his predecessors. Lyndon Johnson, for example, lied tactically in order to accomplish political goals. Tapes of his presidential phone conversations reveal many occasions when this master of maneuver talks out of both sides of his mouth in order to assemble a fragile majority for, say, civil rights—a habit he had practiced brilliantly as senate majority leader.[24] About Vietnam, Johnson repeatedly deceived the public—first with respect to the 1964 Tonkin Gulf incidents that provided a pretext for the congressional war resolution, then about how the war was faring, lest the grim truth about lack of progress intensify pressure either to escalate the war or end it.[25] Bill Clinton lied to protect his political career from damage— Gennifer Flowers, Monica Lewinsky, overnight stays in the White House Lincoln Bedroom for champion donors.[26] Clinton also lied for vanity's sake, as, for example, about his weight.[27]

Bush lies and dodges self-protectively, too. He does so when he talks—or refuses to talk—about the holes in his Air National Guard record, his checkered financial history, his relationship with tainted cronies like the former Enron CEO Kenneth Lay, and other such matters.[28] He lies about his previous contradictions—or sends his press secretary out to lie for him—partly because he is too inarticulate to try finessing the conflicts. But in the sweep of his lies, Bush breaks new ground. Where Johnson was tactical, Bush is strategic. In this, he is more like Nixon. Bush lies about his political objectives. He lies about what he believes because he believes that he is on an exalted mission that justifies deep cover. In other words, his ideology dictates lying. His lies are in the service of ideals, even if phantasmagorical ones. He lied about when it was that he determined to go to war with Saddam Hussein, about the existence of Iraqi weapons of mass destruction, about the progress of United Nations weapons inspectors, about the clarity of the intelligence that said Saddam possessed weapons of mass destruction, and about Saddam's relations with al-Qaeda.[29]

But ideology aside, Bush adheres to a style of lying all his own. Sometimes Bush lies when he need not. Sometimes he is so specific in telling an untruth that the only reasonable conclusion is that he lies—that is, he knows that what he is saying contravenes the truth. Sometimes he lies about his personal history, as, for example, in his 1998 denial to a Texas reporter that he was ever arrested after his college prank of stealing a Christmas wreath. In fact, as reporters discovered late in the 2000 campaign, he was also arrested for drunk driving at age thirty.[30] He also lies about his positions. In his third debate with Al Gore, on October 17, 2000, for example, Bush declared that he supported a national patients' bill of rights and touted what he called "good law like we've got in Texas." Bush boasted, "We're one of the first states that said you can sue an HMO for denying you proper coverage. . . . If I'm the president . . . people will be able to take their HMO insurance company to court. That's what I've done in Texas and that's the kind of leadership style I'll bring to Washington."

But in fact, in 1995, during his first term as governor of Texas, Bush vetoed the Texas Patient Protection Act. In 1997, the state legislature passed it again by a veto-proof majority, and it became law without his signature.[31] (Sooner than expose the lie, journalists made mirth with Gore's inside-the-Beltway references.[32]) If Bush was not lying about what happened in Texas, one might think that in the heat of the debate, he was forgetting—forgetting not randomly but conveniently, forgetting in such a way as to leave a favorable false impression. But Bush had been making false claims about the part he played in the Texas patients' bill of rights all along—at least as far back as the previous winter.[33] Systematic forgetting in this manner is improbable to the vanishing point. Bush must have remembered the truth well enough to decide that he *had* to lie about it.

At other times, though, Bush may well be telling the truth about the untruths he believes. It is characteristic of ideological liars not to know, past a certain point, whether they are telling the truth or not, because they have lost track—if they ever *had* track—of what they really know. Knowing, anyway, is not the point, for Bush is in revolt against knowers—people who know. Thanks to faith, he is *in* the know, which makes him the master knower. An ideological liar's concept of truth is wholly tactical: truth is whatever works in the service of the higher belief. Anything can be said; it's only words.

Transcending Aristotelian logic with its irritating either/or's, yet refusing to "do nuance"—a sissy's recourse, not a real man's—Bush and his circle are willing to contradict themselves with aplomb and to overlook, or deny, the fact that they are doing so.[34] Contradiction is what lesser creatures commit. Those of "large and clear" vision enfold contradiction, painlessly, caricaturing Walt Whitman's "I am large, I contain multitudes." During the brief era of good feeling that followed the September 11 attacks, Bush declared to congressional leaders, on October 21, 2001, "Whether you're Republican or Democrat, we all want to win this war."[35] When his alter ego, Karl Rove, declared three and a half years later that the motive of liberals—including certain Democratic senators—was to "put our troops in greater danger," did Bush notice the contradiction even long enough to override it? It is hard to know, but the odds are that he didn't pause to think that he might be contradicting himself. Such pauses are for wimps.

This is where lying and secrecy intersect. It is damnably hard to distinguish between Bush's knowing lies and his sincere distortions in part because he and the entourage at the summit of his administration play their cards so closely. These are disciplined, close-mouthed people. Sharing a powerful sense of their mission, they share, too, an imposing zeal to clam up and protect themselves—and, in particular, their leader. They classify documents at unprecedented rates.[36] National security is, of course, the prime justification, but the administration's obsession with secrecy has mounted far beyond reasonable precautions, including, for example, such items as the names of the vice president's staff and his circle of energy policy advisers in 2001. Where national security does not serve, the mantra of executive privilege comes into play. The Bush circle will not leave behind the incriminating tapes that pinioned Richard Nixon and—in the verdicts of scholars, if not in the indictments of the criminal justice system—the garrulous, insecure, and manipulative Lyndon Johnson.

Bush signals again and again that he is a "real man." His bravado is not superficial, not just a matter of image, but an identity. A real man is never "sicklied o'er by the pale cast of thought." He decides from the gut, where resides his "native hue of resolution." His steadfastness runs deep. By contrast, those whom conscience makes cowards are the ditherers, the notorious "flip-floppers" and "girlie men," Hamlets who never get around to their "enterprises of great pith and moment" and so "lose the name of action." Bush is not displeased to be accused of bumptiousness, for the accusation only attests to the wimpiness of his accusers, who fail to appreciate that the can-do style is no idiosyncrasy at all but a sign of his manliness. His stiff power walk might or might not be the holding-it-together posture of a post-alcoholic, a so-called dry drunk who never learned much about his propensity for addiction because he didn't and doesn't go in for "navel-gazing," but he is proud of it—proud of his pride. As he said on accepting his second presidential nomination, "Some folks look at me and see a certain swagger, which in Texas is called 'walking.'"[37] Those hippie, prissy types who dispossessed him—they do not swagger. They don't know how.

The controlled manner in which he swings his hands outward as he speaks, one slight beat after the words come, suggests the earnestness of his striving to make himself understood but also the awkwardness that afflicts him as he is forced (as he sees it) to go to the trouble of striving to make himself understood. Why should he have to make himself understood at all? Why should he (a strange locution to which he frequently has recourse) "negotiate with himself"? Bush's relish for a power that need not trouble with reasons can be heard behind his fascinating remark to Bob Woodward: "I'm the commander—see, I don't need to explain—I do not need to explain why I say things. That's the interesting thing about being the president. Maybe somebody needs to explain to me why they say something, but I don't feel like I owe anybody an explanation."[38]

That this statement was not incidental is suggested by a similar version that crops up in Bush's response to a question at yet another unusually casual question-and-answer session, this one with five Texas reporters in August 2005:

> Asked about continued political challenges such as Iraq and Social Security, Bush said he doesn't care about the polls.
> Q. "But power is perception."
> THE PRESIDENT: "Power is being the President."[39]

Thus does Bush preach that power needs no reasons. Aware how flimsy are his powers of articulation, he revels in soaring over the mundane need for explanation upon which lesser men and women must rely. To justify himself would be to undermine his strong suit—his decisiveness. Explanations are what inferiors owe superiors, not the other way around.

Now, surely no one ascends to the presidency of the United States without possessing a certain taste for command. This essentially military style goes with the territory of political power. Yet Bush seems to take unusual pleasure in even the more trivial prerogatives of command. His longtime habit of assigning nicknames, often diminutives, to intimates is a dominator's quirk: he names you, you don't name him. Enron's Kenneth Lay was "Kenny Boy" until he fell from grace and had to be thrown overboard and demoted to who's-he status. Karl Rove is alternately "Boy Genius" and "Turd Blossom," the insult putting the brainier subordinate in his place.[40] Bush does the same with reporters and other acquaintances, for the same reason.

As if to underscore that the sixties lout Bill Clinton is no longer in charge, Bush enforced a dress code in the Oval Office. He toys with subordinates, deploying his powers just to prove that he can do it, as if turning an on-off switch. According to his former speechwriter David Frum:

> [T]he Bush staff rose to their feet with a snap that would have impressed a Prussian field marshal. When Bush was in a kidding mood, he would direct the staff like an orchestra conductor: He would press his hands palms down to direct them to sit and then, when they had taken their seats, raise his hands palms up to order them to rise again. Only then would they get the final palms-down. Even in the informality of Air Force One, the staff would leap up whenever Bush stepped into view.[41]

But the context of Bush's remark to Woodward about "not owing anybody an explanation" makes it even more interesting. Bush has just told Woodward that he likes "to be provocative"—to press his sometimes dilatory advisers, in order "to force decisions."[42] As even the effusive Frum acknowledged, Bush "is impatient and quick to anger"—these two come first on Frum's list of Bush's "many faults."[43] Bush's former religious adviser Doug Wead implies that he saw the same constellation of traits when he first contemplated the possibility that the younger Bush might someday run for president: "He's so decisive. He's so adamant, so dogmatic—makes a decision, never looks back. . . . I thought either he'd be terrific, or he'd be terrible. But he'd sure make news. There'd be sparks, because his personality today is the same as it was then [in 1988]."[44]

Marrying decisiveness to dogma, Bush's bulldozer spirit speaks to, and for, most of the Republican base—even as his popularity sinks. They admired it while it worked; some still do. His ferocious imagination or, even more generously, his idealism proves his ruggedness. His belief in the power of will is manifest in his commitment to "stay the course" in Iraq even as evidence mounted that the course headed deeper into a swamp. The purity of Bush's belief in the inerrancy of his will shines forth in his apparent inability, or refusal, to feel uncertainty. One remarkably well-informed source has said, "I've seen, even in this White House, I've seen people agonizing over decisions, but I've never seen him," that is, Bush. The speaker: Karl Rove.[45] Leslie Gelb, who directed the Pentagon Papers project in the Johnson administration, contrasted Bush's sublime confidence with Johnson's approach to Vietnam this way: "You can't listen to those tapes of Johnson without hearing a man in utter agony, knowing he's trapped. Bush doesn't think he's trapped. *Bush has reduced everything to will.* I've never seen any self-doubt or agonizing, or anyone who works with him suggest that."[46]

Faith without fear or trembling is a mighty weapon—until the day it ceases to work.

5

Men Riding out of the West on White Horses

When George W. Bush in a scripted but telling moment said that what some call swagger, "in Texas we call 'walking,'" he underscored a visceral truth: his go-for-broke West Texas manner. Another version comes from Mark Leaverton, who ran the Bible study group that Bush joined in Midland in the mid-1980s after the oil bust had picked up where the oil boom had left off. Leaverton said Bush's style belongs to the culture of his former occupation. He spoke of "the can-do attitude that people from Midland have. And that involves the oil business. You've gotta be a real optimist to be in the oil business. It's very risky. You can gain millions and lose millions on one well."[1]

More generally, Stuart Stevens, a Republican operative who worked on Bush's 2000 campaign, wrote admiringly:

> Bush did everything he could to assert not only his Texas roots but his *West Texas* identity. There's a classic photo of Bush at Harvard Business School sitting in a lecture wearing his Texas Air National Guard flight jacket, jeans, and cowboy boots. That said it all. He wore his Texas identity like a 1968 dashiki. *This is who I am. Don't expect me to change.*[2]

Stevens's simile was peculiar, for the dashiki was a garment adopted by young men in search of *new* identities, while Bush prides himself on the depth of his roots in Midland soil. But nevertheless, Stevens stumbled despite himself onto a parallel that is germane, for Bush appeared in politics bearing an identity as close to him as his own skin.

Conservatives have been fortunate in their heroes. Again and again in the course of recent decades they have been rescued by men of mythic style, Western frontiersmen of rugged appearance and a gift for no-nonsense plainness, wealthy, hard-driving, competitive men who could play the self-made part, muster the look of "hardiness and independence,"[3] men who, because they looked as though they ruled themselves, appeared entitled to rule others. In the words of the historian Patricia Nelson Limerick, "Westerners . . . should be able to choose a goal and pursue it, free of restriction and obstacle. They should not have other people telling them what to do."[4] These are men born into a myth—which is not to say a lie, for the myth has been an object of fervent belief for so long, it describes something central about how Americans imagine themselves and present themselves, how they live, and who they are. Square-jawed and erect, clean-shaven, with full hair, clear skin, and an outdoors appearance, they look the very image of sheriffs, Indian fighters, clearers of wilderness, hunters of game, ranchers, grazers of cattle, wildcatters, miners, extractors of natural bounty, riders of purple sage, men who regardless of where they were born had the good sense to "light out for the territory ahead of the rest"—at least, the Hollywood versions of the territory. If they are not the real thing, no matter—they look the part. And the part they look is the part of the action hero who preserves the bright core of the past and rekindles the old, banked fires of America's Manifest Destiny even in a citified and suburbanized nation. Through the instrument of his vigorous and straight-talking persona, the hero promises to reinvent the past and call it the future. Against the nay-saying counsel of fast-talking realists and other decadent types these men awaken dormant ideals and seize their moments.

During the long decades of New Deal—Fair Deal—New Frontier dominance, conservatives were a spent force in national politics.

Not until Barry Goldwater galloped out of the West with a Stetson, a jutting jaw, and a gift for leathery bluntness did they come to life. Appropriately, the jacket flap of Goldwater's 1960 book *The Conscience of a Conservative* starts by identifying the author as "the descendant of a pioneer Arizona family" (it does not mention that his father, on marrying, converted from Judaism) and in its second sentence goes on to speak of "the outspoken brand of conservatism and self-reliance stemming from his frontier background."[5] Goldwater was born in Arizona when it was not yet one of the United States. He was stamped with a rawhide spirit that predated the federal government's reach.

Goldwater was pulverized in the Johnson landslide of 1964, Johnson being a slicker kind of Westerner who had twice failed to win the Democratic nomination on his own but whom fate had now anointed the successor of the martyred John F. Kennedy. Resoundingly defeated, Goldwater's legions promptly reenlisted behind Ronald Reagan, Goldwater's most eloquent champion, who was spotted and promoted as gubernatorial material by a circle of wealthy Southern California Republicans. After winning the California governorship in 1966, Reagan started running for president and, after the self-demolition of the Nixon administration and a season of political exile, rode to the rescue. George W. Bush adroitly placed himself in this line, and at the moment of truth, during the long fall of 2000, he himself was rescued by the Supreme Court. Truly, a movement that can count on such rescues believes itself touched by angels. All these happy endings—were they not signs of a benign Providence, the power of positive thinking, or Destiny made Manifest once more?

Goldwater, Reagan, Bush II—this providential procession of Western leaders in ten-gallon hats, free men galloping over the ridge to save the embattled outposts of civilization, incarnate an American ideal.[6] Their differences—in particular, over religion— are not superficial. They are personal but also speak to changes in the American spirit evolving over the last half-century. Goldwater, descended from a converted Polish Jew, was not religious and eventually denounced the Christian domination of his beloved Republican Party. (His political descendant, Bush's rival for the

2000 nomination—though for various reasons not guaranteed an opportunity to succeed the Texan—Senator John McCain, shares with Goldwater an unhappiness about religious zealots' hold over the party.) Reagan was not much of a churchgoer, as it turned out, but could act religious feeling at will. Bush, famously, is himself evangelical in his own person.

The unifying streak remains, and it is regional. And the main line of leaders is notably joined by lieutenants who also hail from the West (Dick Cheney of Wyoming, Karl Rove of Utah), as well as the South (Lee Atwater of South Carolina, Rove's mentor). With a unanimity grounded in a spurious history of the American West, they share the myth that government intervention is dispensable, and convert it, peculiarly, to the notion that they are destined to lead. Cheney played on the mystique of frontier self-sufficiency when he debated Joseph Lieberman in 2000 and claimed that "the government had absolutely nothing to do with" the fortune he built as CEO of Halliburton, "out in the private sector." Just as the success of the railroads in the nineteenth century rested heavily on federal largesse, so did Cheney's oil-based fortune rest substantially on federal contracts, even if the deferential Lieberman failed to challenge Cheney's claim. Indeed, Lieberman's immediate response smacked of a certain envy: "I can see my wife and I think she's saying, 'I think he [Lieberman] should go out into the private sector.' "[7]

For the prospects of men like Bush and Cheney, the mythic advantage and the demographic both matter. The Sunbelt—not least Arizona, California, and Texas—is the American growth zone. Detroit is no longer one of the nation's ten largest cities, but Los Angeles, Houston, Phoenix, San Antonio, San Diego, Dallas, and San Jose are. The nation's population center—and its electoral heart—have been migrating southwesterly for the last fifty years. Politicians who speak for, and to, this shifting center of gravity hold an obvious advantage. If they can retain the old Confederacy and California, as Reagan did, they are well-nigh unstoppable. If they can hold the old Confederacy, the mountain West, and the Great Plains, that is almost as good.

But the myth these men stand for also speaks to a less provincial wish and attracts voters who live outside the South and the West.

They possess the stuff that the American dream is made on. Toughness rhymes with freedom in American ideals, and the combination is nowhere more vividly enshrined than in the sheriff who keeps the peace thanks to—what else?—the pistol known as the peacemaker. The men who voyaged from Europe simply continued their passage westward. Western freedom meant knowing that the land you crossed, you owned. So Jefferson felt when he consolidated the yeoman ideal by arranging for the Louisiana Purchase to extend the United States until the land ran out.

The movement from sea to shining sea was the movement toward independence—away from the confining order of Europe, away from the fancy ways of the well-born, away from the formalities of a settled way of life in decadent cities and stifling towns. In economic terms, it was the movement away from overpriced land to cheap land. In cultural terms, it was the movement away from the soft toward the hard; from the settled to the unsettled; from the over-civilized man toward the natural. It is where the call of the already-developed market yielded to the not-yet-developed. In that place where belief and reality intertwined (again, partly because reality was perennially remade in accordance with the belief, or "fixed around the idea"), entrepreneurship moved westward with the sun—along the rails that crossed the great mountain ranges; to the oil fields of Texas and Oklahoma; to the airplane factories of Kansas, Washington State, and California; to the nuclear laboratories of New Mexico and California; to Hollywood; to Silicon Valley. You could talk all you wanted about the closing of the American frontier—intellectuals have been talking about it for over a century—but the national spirit rebelled against such dour recognitions. As long as men on horseback, incarnations of freedom, keep riding out of the West—unbridled backwoodsmen, commanding men, horsemen (that is, commanders of animals)—the frontier was not really closed, all the grim historians be damned.

The essential source for understanding this mentality remains the classic 1893 paper by the historian Frederick Jackson Turner, "The Significance of the Frontier in American History." Turner today is no doubt more alluded to than read—as he certainly was until recently by this author, who, however, encountered him with a shock of recognition—and there are anachronisms, overstatements, and other flaws in his work. While there is more to American history than is dreamed of in Turner's philosophy—there is even more of the West, as his critics have pointed out[8]—this is of little moment. Turner succeeded brilliantly in describing the mystique that has triumphed in our time:

> Up to our own day, American history has been in a large degree the history of the colonization of the Great West. The existence of an area of free land, its continuous recession, and the advance of American settlement westward, explain American development. . . . American social development has been continually beginning over again on the frontier. This perennial rebirth, this fluidity of American life, this expansion westward with its new opportunities, its continuous touch with the simplicity of primitive society, furnish the forces dominating American character.

Turner thought that the rough-hewn frontier character, dressed in "hunting shirt and . . . moccasin," was democratic—and, moreover, responsible for driving America as a whole in a democratic direction—because the frontier was "productive of individualism. Complex society is precipitated by the wilderness into a kind of primitive organization based on the family. The tendency is antisocial. It produces antipathy to control, and particularly to any direct control. The tax-gatherer is viewed as a representative of oppression."[9]

Settling the frontier, in Turner's story, entailed cutting loose from Europe. "The separation of the Western man from the seaboard, and his environment," Turner wrote,

> made him in a large degree free from European precedents and forces. He looked at things independently and with small regard or appreciation for the best Old World experience. . . .
> The West was not conservative: buoyant self-confidence and self-assertion were distinguishing traits in its composition. It saw in its growth nothing less than a new order of society and state.

No wonder hidebound Easterners—conservative in the literal sense—were reciprocally suspicious.[10]

Turner made rather too much of the Western streak in the American character. In his search for a monocausal theory of American life, he downplayed other strands. He tended to assume that the frontier *mystique* described frontier *reality*. In his overreach toward an all-explaining "thesis" to get to the bottom of America once and for all, Turner could be, by turns, crude, simplistic, and vague.[11] He neglected other keys to American history: industrialization, the Civil War, economic depressions. He tended to collapse frontier life into a single archetype, obscuring its internal conflicts. He failed to note that—in the words of one of his most formidable critics, Patricia Nelson Limerick—"the American West was the arena in which an expanded role for the federal government first took hold"; that "in the Far West of 1890, one-half of the land remained federal property."[12] He probably exaggerated the degree to which free or cheap Western land served as a "safety valve" to keep Eastern wages high and protect the East from class conflict.

But if we think of him as identifying a common Western *mystique,* an ideal that spoke to something forceful and enduring in American character, Turner was right on the mark. His account of the frontier character—"strong in selfishness and individualism, intolerant of administrative experience and education, and pressing individual liberty beyond its proper bounds"—splendidly anticipates much of the nature, and most of the image and appeal, of George W. Bush of Midland, Texas.[13] Turner attributed the unboundedness and recklessness of the Western character to its freedom from government and from the civilizing qualities of densely settled society. These freedoms foreshadowed what would come to be known as the "American dream" of opportunity.[14] "It followed from the lack of organized political life," wrote Turner,

> from the atomic conditions of the backwoods society, that the individual was exalted and given free play. The West was another name for opportunity. Here were mines to be seized, fertile valleys to be preempted, all the natural resources open to the shrewdest and the boldest. The United States is unique in the extent to which the individual has been given an open field, unchecked by restraints of an old social order, or of scientific administration of government. The self-made man

was the Western man's ideal, was the kind of man that all men might become. Out of his wilderness experience, out of the freedom of his opportunities, he fashioned a formula for social regeneration.

In the cauldron of experience where ideologies are endlessly melted down and recast as if they were fresh, "self-made" alloys nicely with "born-again." And in the subterranean channels where the chords of popular feeling resonate with a leader, it doesn't matter that George W. Bush of Andover, Yale, Harvard, and Kennebunkport, as well as Midland, Texas, the grandson of Senator Prescott Bush, the son of President George H. W. Bush, fails to qualify as "self-made." The aura is everything, the facts next to nothing. Print the aura.

Turner insisted it was "a profound mistake to write of the West as though it were engrossed in mere material ends. It has been, and is, preeminently a region of ideals, mistaken or not." Specifically, "The Western man believed in the manifest destiny of his country."[15] Where there was so much opportunity, why shouldn't a Westerner be a man (in the mystique, *he* is almost always a *man*) of adventure and hope? For that matter, if progress is a consequence of the will, why shouldn't *any* American be an optimist? For Turner thought the West's culture flowed throughout the nation's veins. It included "that dominant individualism, working for good and for evil, and withal that buoyancy and exuberance which comes with freedom—these are traits of the frontier, *or traits called out elsewhere because of the existence of the frontier.*"[16]

In truth—though Turner did not go quite this far—these Western traits were "called out" *within* every American. You do not have to be a conservative to feel the force of the Western ideal, for the frontier runs through the minds, the hearts, and the souls of men and women regardless of region, class, or politics. You can hear the Western ideal in the words and intonation of Woody Guthrie, Bob Dylan, and Bruce Springsteen. (Did any folksinger ever affect an *Eastern* accent?) You can follow traces of the West in the work of Easterners from James Fenimore Cooper to Allen Ginsberg and Jack Kerouac, Midwesterners from Mark Twain to Ernest Hemingway, and, of course, the Western movies financed by Eastern European

Jews who passed through New York. Bret Harte ("The Luck of Roaring Camp") grew up in Albany, New York; Owen Wister (*The Virginian*) in Philadelphia. You could taste the West in the counterculture's East Village and North Beach, even if the new image of natural man was for a while displaced from the buckskin-wearing hunter to the buckskin-wearing Indian.

For most of American history, you did not have to set foot in the actual West to identify as a Westerner, at least in spirit. You could do it with style—with food, music, dress, and accent. If you were looking for a way to express hostility to Northeastern elites and their actual or imputed ways, the Western image was more tempting than the Southern—at least, outside the old Confederacy. The Confederate flag might be brandished to signify working-class toughness, but the South was tied up with slavery, white supremacy, and the war against the Union. Moreover, to the respectable Northern mind, it was coated with various unattractive cultural features: ignorance, slovenliness, the backward worlds of Tobacco Road, Al Capp, and Tennessee Williams. Emblems like the Stars and Bars of the Confederate battle flag might play well among unreconstructed white Southerners, but after the Ku Klux Klan receded from its Northern high water mark in the 1920s, they largely ceased to be attractive symbols of antielitism.

So Southerners, especially when making national careers in politics, often presented themselves as Westerners. Senator Estes Kefauver of Tennessee campaigned wearing a Davy Crockett–style coonskin cap. Lyndon B. Johnson, from the hill country west of Austin, played up his ranch—it was not a plantation. George W. Bush may sound to the outside ear like a Southerner, but he dresses like a Westerner, complete with his own ranch—if "ranch" is the right designation for a 1,583-acre property where the president grazes (according to his deputy press secretary) "four or five" cattle.[17] As Michael Lind has pointed out, Midland stands atop extractive Texas, not plantation Texas—the West Texas flatlands beneath which lies the largest expanse of oil in the continental United States. Bush's version of Texas matches Turner's description of the mystique of the little house on the prairie, not of East Texas cotton country.[18]

Class is always distinction—*our sort* are not *that other sort*—and the experience of class is always felt, in some measure, as a distinction of style.[19] In the New World, class differences were also felt as geographical ones. To be a man of the West was to be a man of the people, a man's man, an authentic, a man without pretense. The Westerner did not calculate. He was not shifty, a "flip-flopper." He might work in an office, but he felt at home in the great outdoors. He was a straight-shooter. He moved by instinct, by "gut." He did not put on airs. He had nothing to hide. He looked you in the eye. What kind of man (or woman) are you? Are you a "good man" or the other kind?[20] Anyone who failed to grasp this Western mystique would misunderstand Bush's otherwise weird statement after he first encountered the Russian president Vladimir Putin: "I looked the man in the eye. I was able to get a sense of his soul." If a man of Western demeanor ran against a candidate who sounded too smart, and thus "too big for his britches," he won—Eisenhower against Stevenson, Reagan against Carter, Bush against Gore. It made sense to wear string ties, cowboy boots, and Stetsons, as Bush did; to drink beer, not wine; not to be weighed down by book learnin' or expertise (though it might occasionally be useful to claim such recent reading as Camus's *The Stranger* and "three Shakespeares").[21]

The upstanding Westerner faced up to trouble. The Texas historian Walter Prescott Webb wrote of the image of the Texas Ranger as "'a man standing alone between a society and its enemies,'" an enforcer of the law who was also "a very quiet, deliberate, gentle person who could gaze calmly into the eye of a murderer, divine his thoughts, and anticipate his action, a man who could ride straight up to death."[22] This guardian of the public good was a man for whom bad deeds, as much as good ones, were personal.

It is squarely in this tradition that George W. Bush took the measure of buddies, enemies, and advisers alike by sizing them up for their personal qualities. Bush was not a man for committees, formalities, or "process." As Ron Suskind wrote, Bush "seeks a way to make sweeping, often complex matters intensely personal. Connects them to his gut, his instinct, for swift decision."[23] Decision-making committees were not for him. Formal procedures in which policies were debated and worked their way up a chain of command were not for him. Faced with a bewildering world populated by billions of people and thousands of leaders unlike himself, Bush "met America's foreign challenges with decisiveness born of a brand of preternatural, faith-based, self-generated certainty." His former deputy secretary of state, Richard Armitage, said (after leaving office), "There was never any policy process to break. . . . There was never one from the start. Bush didn't want one, for whatever reason. One was never started."[24]

Ignorance was bliss. Suskind went so far as to say that "the President made it clear to his most trusted lieutenants he did not *want to be informed*, especially when the information might undercut the confidence he has in certain sweeping convictions."[25] Bush also had a practical need not to know. What the president did not know, he could plausibly deny. He could not be held accountable. On the value of remaining in the dark, Cheney doubtless influenced Bush. As Gerald Ford's chief of staff, Cheney had implemented plausible deniability. He had learned from the late days of Nixon's presidency that the downfall came from the cover-up, not from the initial crimes.[26] So ignorance and mental slovenliness were not only congenial but culturally (and legally) useful. Ronald Reagan masked his ignorance of the world with anecdotes, actual, filmic, or imaginary. For decades, George W. Bush masked his ignorance of the world with his "gut" and his frat boy talent for joshing around—and an outstanding memory for names. The world was made to be mastered by masterful men, one face and name at a time. Once America had been the sort of place where real men were in charge. Under weaklings like Bill Clinton, spineless men of the sixties, the country had lost control. Now control could be won back. Bush fit as snugly inside his mythology as he did inside his jeans.

The frontiersman who ranged away from the Atlantic Seaboard was not encrusted by the *Old* World.[27] There is no sign that Bush was embarrassed at his lack of worldliness—if anything, he conveyed the impression that he was proud of it. If he forayed into the Old World, he did not make a point of it. It was easy for him to slide from not-European to anti-European—which became a GOP theme in his 2004 campaign, which cast John Kerry as "International

Man of Mystery" and "French." In 2003, Secretary of Defense Donald Rumsfeld brought disdain and contempt for Europe to a boil when he dismissed the antiwar climate of "Old Europe," meaning the French and German governments. He meant, perhaps, to distinguish that "Old Europe" from the "New Europe" into which NATO had expanded, what used to be Soviet-run Eastern and Central Europe. But many Americans understood that by "Old," Rumsfeld also meant bygone, loser, past: effete, not virile, not vigorous, unable even to defend itself. "Old Europe" was a museum.

Rumsfeld's disdain was a sentiment as old as the United States of America, an extension of Europe that in a certain sense conceived itself as the anti-Europe—democratic and neither royal nor aristocratic, vigorous and not effete, unbound by tradition, pragmatic. In one long strand of American opinion, Europe meant culture while America meant either nature or God or the combination— the wilderness as opposed to the city, the natural as opposed to the cosmopolitan, the raw as opposed to the cooked, the plowman as opposed to the pantywaist. But still, America for all of its history *needed* Europe—its ideas, its investment, its markets, its unwanted "huddled masses yearning to breathe free," at times its cachet. Beneath the disdain always sparkled the green-eyed monster. Envy, Tocqueville wrote, was the democratic sentiment par excellence.

The cultural side of American anti-Europeanism has a long, thick history—and not only among residents of the literal West and South. Throughout the nineteenth and twentieth centuries, American culture defined itself as the fundamental against the complex, the bold against the hesitant, the plain against the tricky; the redskin against the paleface; Walt Whitman and Herman Melville against the Victorians. Against the opera, America launched Buffalo Bill's Wild West show. Against the symphonic tradition, America offered jazz, blues, rock-and-roll, and country-western songs. Against Proust, Joyce, and American aspirants such as Henry James, Ezra Pound, and T. S. Eliot, America offered up Ernest Hemingway of Illinois, with his Old Testament cadences— never mind that he was, during much of his life, an expat, too. The European movie talked, the American movie *moved*. ("I saw a Rohmer movie once," says a character in Arthur Penn's *Night*

Moves. "It was like watching paint dry.") American cinema devolved into Steven Spielberg and George Lucas, whose "pure cinema" didn't need words, at least not many of them. Arnold Schwarzenegger could become an American icon not despite his limited facility with the American language, but partly because of it.

Today's anti-European clichés coexist with the Americanization of sorbet, Dijon mustard, Heineken, and merlot—and for that matter, TV reality shows, first devised abroad. But in the roughly half of the country that is comfortable with Republican rule, anti-Europeanism has been a triumphant accompaniment to messianism. The old Confederacy plus the mountain states and the prairie count roughly as half the national populace. Texas is the region's heartland. Oil is its definitive industry. The heartland of anti-Europe was Reagan's America and then, minus California, it became George W. Bush's. Majorities in the Sunbelt imagine themselves ruggedly self-sufficient. Only reluctantly does six-shooter country make concessions to the striped-pants State Department set. As long as Bush could get what he wanted by insisting that "you're either with us or you're with the terrorists"—an echo of Jesus' "He that is not with me is against me" (Matthew 12:30), by the way—the only diplomacy that mattered was follow the leader. (Of necessity, unable to get his way with Iran, North Korea, or Israel, Bush later retreated to a reality redoubt.) Watching UN-mandated inspections was like watching paint dry. "What if you'd missed?" John Wayne's Ethan Edwards is asked in *The Searchers.* "Never occurred to me," Wayne drawls.

What changed politically in the twentieth century was that Europe needed America. The interrupted Thirty-One Year War of 1914–1945 shattered European illusions. In the eyes of America's Atlanticists, Yankee indispensability in World War II extended into the Cold War. The proof of America's leadership of the "Free World" would lie in its ability to bring Europe along. Men like Dean Acheson, Clark Clifford, C. Douglas Dillon, and McGeorge Bundy—the "Wise Men" of the Truman, Kennedy, and Johnson administrations—thought that a rejuvenated America should take up the burden of reviving a decadent and dependent Europe. The problem was to make sure that Europe was up to its new role as willing but subordinate partner.

For more than thirty years, the Atlanticist elite was barely challenged. Today, it is a gaggle of ghosts. The cowboy counterelite that came to power with Ronald Reagan had neoconservative, ex-Democratic allies, but in the main it descended ideologically from Arizona's Senator Barry Goldwater, who suggested in 1961, "Sometimes I think this country would be better off if we could just saw off the Eastern Seaboard and let it float out to sea."[28] Donald Rumsfeld may hail from Illinois, but his plain-spoken disdain speaks for the whole cowboy elite. When Bush's America disdains Europe—pre-Sarkozy France in particular, objectionable not only for its foreign policy but as the most aristocratic of continental nations—it also sneers at the American Northeast. To Bush's America, "Washington, D.C." is an insult and "New York City" (meaning Manhattan) a sort of offshore entrepôt where Europe begins. (Westerners are not the only Americans to see New York that way. I once heard Susan Sontag refer to Manhattan as "an island anchored off the coast of America," and I confess I have used similar phrases myself.)

Frederick Jackson Turner took his inspiration from an administrative fact. The superintendent of the 1890 census had declared the frontier—a detectable, continuous line between the settled world and the wilderness—officially closed. More than a century later, the frontier lives on as a memory of a memory. But it is also a cultural foundation of tremendous reach and solidity, and Turner remains an indispensable historian of America because he understood how deep it goes. More than a century later, the frontier is still entrenched in the American mind. Voters who chose George W. Bush were not "conservatives" in the sense of conserving an actual way of life, as much as they were supporters of a legend of American possibility—a possibility they thought was once an actuality and could become one again. When they told pollsters they were comfortable with Bush, they meant that they were comfortable with themselves as the sort of people who could be comfortable with Bush—or rather, the image they held of him. Once again, as Faulkner understood, "The past is not dead—it is not even past."[29]

6

Pulpits of Bullies

The right-wing idealism of positive thinking should never be mistaken for dreaminess. It is faith militant. The Republicans' faith-based politics is, at least in significant part, a reflex of their religious zeal and its apocalyptic, Manichean scenarios. They are the Party of Virtue, and it is their mission to mobilize that virtue in the heart of a sinful world. The test of their virtue, in fact, is that they are willing to see it subjected to tribulation. Defeats are prologues to victories—the Bible is full of such sequences. Once the virtuous have plunged into the inferno of ordeals, their good works will be rewarded. The consequences of their virtuous struggle will be revealed, if not in this world, then in the world to come. This perhaps helps to explain the vigor with which the antigovernment party pursues government power. The test of true virtue is that it be visited upon the nest of vipers: Washington, D.C. They must carry the fight into the very lair of Satan. Embattlement in Babylon is the proof that they are, in fact, the Party of Virtue.

In the Calvinist root of the militant conservative mind, the world is flooded with sin, and goodness is always in jeopardy. In the born-again overlay, the flood of sin is God's test. Goodness is under siege—the godly stalked by the Antichrist—but will overcomes adversity. The two religious streaks come together where will meets opposition: in the struggle of power against a shape-shifting enemy. Modern conservatives ring various changes on these themes, but on and off during the last century the structure of their struggle has been the same. The Great Awakening is always at risk. Once, faith was called upon to march into combat against godless communism. Faith also had to combat modernity, a three-headed beast featuring political liberalism, corrosive secularism, and moral relativism. Now it confronts terrorists. These are all, in effect, phases of the same moon. They are the changing names of evil.

One need not believe in the Rapture or any other millennial tale to subscribe to this bipolar worldview. Here is what Karl Rove notoriously told a New York Conservative Party fund-raiser in Manhattan on June 22, 2005: "Conservatives saw the savagery of 9/11 in the attacks and prepared for war; *liberals saw the savagery of the 9/11 attacks and wanted to prepare indictments and offer therapy and understanding for our attackers.*" (My italics, but Rove's emphasis.) Rove added that liberals' motive remains to "put our troops in greater danger."[1] Over the days of commotion that followed, liberals mused about Rove's own motives. Was he desperately aiming to distract attention from the deepening morass in Iraq? Was he letting his mask slip and revealing the kind of character assassin that, in his core—if that is the right word—he really was?[2] In response to critics, the White House flacks Scott McClellan and Dan Bartlett remained unswervingly "on message," intoning their talking points—that Rove had been speaking only of liberals, not Democrats, and only of certain liberals (MoveOn.org, Michael Moore) and not others, although plainly Rove had failed to make any such nice distinctions. Rove neither apologized nor resigned. The leadership rallied round their take-it-or-leave-it principle, the code of all bullies: "If you're explaining, you're losing." (The line has been attributed variously to Rove, Lee Atwater, former congressman J. C. Watts, and time-honored political lore of indefinite provenance.) The road to political victory, Rove wrote in a 1985 strategy memo, is marked by a single sign: *Attack, Attack, Attack.*[3]

The endless repetition of talking points may well be largely tactical in its purposes, on the double theory that repetition is needed to punch through to an inattentive public, while wavering is the essence of liberalism, conveying an impression of woman-ishness or, worse, effeminacy, the limp-wristed "flip-flop" label hung on the decorated war hero John Kerry by the draft-dodgers George W. Bush, Dick Cheney, Karl Rove, and the rest. The Republican leadership is surely capable of such calculations. But a better explanation, a more economical hypothesis, is that this bulldozer approach to politics runs deeper than tactical calcula-tion. It is an article of faith. It expresses not just Bush's credo, not just what the Republicans like to call their "ideas," but the party's, and the conservative movement's, *way of life*.

Though tactical compromises may at times be called for, the per-cussive absolutism of a Tom DeLay (who took to the House floor during the impeachment debate of 1998–1999 to declare that what was at stake was "moral relativism versus absolute truth"), the pounding Bush refrain that what is within reach in Iraq is "victory," resounds through the career of Karl Rove. Rove's zeal in pursuit of victory, and the relish with which he conquers and pulverizes scruple, is the subject of the compelling book *Bush's Brain: How Karl Rove Made George W. Bush Presidential*, written by two longtime Texas reporters, Wayne Slater and James Moore. The book is replete with instances where, very likely, Rove or someone like Rove resorted to dirty tricks to win elections. (The book inspired an excellent 2004 film by the same name, directed by Joseph Mealey and Michael Shoob.) So is an article by Joshua Green in the *Atlantic*, itemizing a number of vicious episodes in Rove's career—including his surreptitiously dis-tributing flyers attacking his own candidate in an Alabama race to arouse a sympathy vote (1996) and orchestrating George W. Bush's whisper campaigns against Texas governor Ann Richards in Texas (1994) and primary rival John McCain in South Carolina (2000). Green concluded, "Anyone who takes an honest look at his history will come away awed by Rove's power, when challenged, to draw on an animal ferocity that far exceeds the chest-thumping bravado common to professional political operatives."[4] One witness to a moment's eruption of Rove's ferocity was Ron Suskind, who first encountered him through the (deliberately left?) open door to his White House office talking to an aide about someone Suskind called "a political operative who had displeased him." Rove was saying, "We will fuck him. Do you hear me? We will fuck him. We will ruin him. Like no one has ever fucked him!" "This went on without a break for a minute or two," Suskind wrote.[5]

The movie of the Republicans' collective bio-pic should come with a soundtrack of gangsta rap. Manichaean rhetoric is the theme music of their drive for power. Harshness, insult, and dark innuendo reverberate from the party high command down through its media to the base, and back up. For this purpose, wholly owned media are extremely useful—as Bush would put it, there are no "filters." The media amplify not only the right-wing command's notions but its style. The means of communication evolve over time, but what remains the same is Republican bluntness. The continuity is straightforwardly acknowledged in these sentences—in part (but only in part) self-promotional—by Richard A. Viguerie and David Franke: "Conservatives didn't build their alternative media empire overnight. It was the result of decades of hard work—mastering direct mail in the 1970s, talk radio in the late 1980s, and cable television and the Internet in the 1990s."[6]

Throughout these decades, right-wing propaganda, heavy on spleen and percussion, has cascaded endlessly through direct mail, talk radio (liberated from the constraints of the Fairness Doctrine in 1987), and cable television, and, in daily print, the *Wall Street Journal* editorial page, the Unification Church's *Washington Times*, and Rupert Murdoch's *New York Post*.[7] The right's media roll out a nonstop war game, specializing in sprees of demonization: the sneers and rants of Rush Limbaugh (whose weekly audience has been estimated at 13.5 to 20 million at various times), Michael Savage, Sean Hannity, James Dobson, Bill O'Reilly, Glenn Beck, Laura Ingraham, Ann Coulter, and hosts of other sonorous brawlers with listeners in the millions. These effusions of malice and mendacity do triple duty: they give many listeners an identity, a way to name and interpret their resentments; they reinforce that identity and mobilize the base to vote; and at the same time, they exercise a gravitational force on the so-called mainstream media.

Through such channels of bombast, speaking in the name of "regular people," Republican politicians keep in touch with the movement-conservative voice, and vice versa—the politicians never have any doubt of the subjects that are inflaming their base. "Well," the Christian Right's senator from Kansas, Sam Brownback, told a constituent complaining about "the liberal media," "they have the newspapers and TV, but we have radio."[8] There is no left-of-center equivalent to the evangelical broadcasters who, according to Mariah Blake, "openly pushed the Republican ticket in the run-up to the 2004 election," even "launching and promoting massive voter-registration drives with the apparent goal of helping Republicans clinch a victory. . . . James Dobson held pro-Bush rallies that packed stadiums and told his 7 million U.S. listeners that it was a sin not to vote."[9]

In talk radio, politics engenders commerce, which in turn engenders politics: there is a chicken-egg loop. Relentless pugilistics and demonization accord with a certain public taste for shrillness and melodrama, which then generates and regenerates the demand for a take-no-prisoners style, not only on Fox News but in heavily commercial endeavors like WABC (Limbaugh's home base) and Clear Channel, by far the largest owner of radio stations in the country. The common style runs from muscularity to resentment tinged with sarcasm—right-wing populism from A to C. The general style is bombastic, melodramatic, percussive—that is to say, compelling: punditry as extreme sport. One prototype template was installed on public television during the Reaganite eighties by John McLaughlin's up-tempo talkfest-as-food-fight. Another strand derived from apocalyptic, prophetic evangelical Christians, its lineage stretching from Father Charles Coughlin's thirties anti-Semitic-cum-populist demagoguery. In the nineties, Rush Limbaugh tinkered with the model and bellowed his way into millions of hearts and spleens, mixing a touch of mirth and post-sixties sarcasm into a radio preacher's urgency and ad hominem viciousness. Imitators cropped up around the radio dial. The formula was set: the successful pundit doesn't discuss, he brays.

Here was a model for the round-the-clock uproar of celebrity froth, crime news, terror fright, weather hysteria, liberal-baiting, and pictures within pictures that Rupert Murdoch and the long-time Republican political consultant Roger Ailes launched with Fox News in 1996. Murdoch's far-flung business interests—and acumen—support some loss-leader enterprises (like the *New York Post* and the *Weekly Standard*) that make him a political player in the key markets of New York and Washington. But mainly, Murdoch adroitly melds commercial formulas (a blonde squad, hyperkinetic sound effects, all crisis all the time) with brawling personalities and daylong propagandistic blasts in the guise of news. His financial breakthrough with Fox News rests on his having begun with successful over-the-air entertainment stations. Starting with those and able to dig into his very deep pockets, Murdoch could place his propaganda network on so many cable systems that by 2006 he had access to almost 90 percent of American households.[10]

As right-wing radio and television emerged, liberals barely paid attention at first or tried to wish the menace away. They lacked entrepreneurial zeal; perhaps, despite their populist rhetoric, they lacked confidence that they could connect to mass audiences. In the early eighties, magazines such as the *Nation,* liberal foundations, and philanthropists preferred to build up small-circulation ventures rather than risk pricier cable TV. They were satisfied to corner markets that already belonged to the left—in the range of a few hundred thousand readers. Liberal philanthropists funded documentary films but shied away from founding new media. The left's own talk radio candidates, such as the populist Jim Hightower of Texas, were not smash successes.

Most of the right-wing programs have small audiences—Fox News viewership rarely rises above 1 or 1.5 percent of all households (roughly 1 to 1.5 million).[11] But they are a force. To them, much power is attributed—and in politics, reputation is the prologue to fact, moving money, making things happen. Authoritarian to the bone, their audience includes many "dittoheads"—true believers so-called because their response to Limbaugh was "ditto, Rush, ditto." (The closest thing to an equivalent on the left are the Jon Stewart and Stephen Colbert Comedy Central shows, with audiences of the same order of magnitude, and passionate ones at that, but as satirists—liberals, moreover—they are not in the business of lining up dittoheads.) The knowledge that these channels are at work day and night, offering positive feedback for the White House line of the day, taking their agenda from Bush, Rove, and the RNC, not only heartens the right-wing base but hovers over the mainstream, pressing it to play defense. To compete with Fox News, CNN hires William Bennett and Glenn Beck. Shamed by right-wing bloggers for the shoddy features of a 60 *Minutes* report on Bush's National Guard evasions, CBS discards Dan Rather.

In June 2006, Francine Busby, a local school board member in northern San Diego County, was the Democratic candidate in a special election to fill the congressional seat left vacant after the longtime incumbent, Randy ("Duke") Cunningham, having been indicted for taking bribes from military contractors, pleaded guilty and resigned his seat. Five days before the election, Busby attended a campaign forum. Most of the people in attendance were Latinos. A man in the back of the noisy room, speaking Spanish, "mumbled"—Busby's word when she described the scene to me—a question of which she heard only two words: *ayudo* (help) and *papeles* (papers). She took him to be asking whether he could help her campaign if he wasn't registered to vote. But she blundered. Instead of asking him to repeat the question, she responded with the words: "You don't need papers for voting."[12] Immediately, she did follow this sentence with another: "You don't need to be a registered voter to help." But no matter. An anti-immigration Minuteman in the audience had her on tape, which he passed on to right-wing talk shows. The next day, the San Diego right-wing radio talker Roger Hedgecock was playing clips of this statement. The day after that, Sean Hannity and Rush Limbaugh picked it up.[13] The day before the election, the Republicans inundated the radio airwaves with ads saying, "That's right. Francine Busby says you don't need papers to vote."[14] In all, she said, the

Republicans spent $4.5 million to defeat her—in a heavily Republican district.

Before the "papers" incident and its reverberations, Cunningham's nationally notorious corruption had given Busby a reasonable chance of winning. Even her gaffe might not have been decisive in the absence of talk radio and Republican ads. But she was compelled to prove that she had not beaten her husband. In the end, she lost by 4,732 votes, less than 4 percent of the total.[15]

The net effect of the right's echo chamber has been to help normalize the right's view of the world, spraying years' worth of Teflon on Bush, heightening the sense that (on one side, at least) ignorant, scabrous, often scurrilous views are legitimate, reasonable, and worth hearing. With the center dragged rightward, conventional discourse bends toward false equivalences—as if the balance of American media were demonstrated by the fact that it runs a gamut from "right" (Rush Limbaugh, Fox News, the *Wall Street Journal* editorial page) to "left" (the *New York Times*, the *Washington Post*, the *Los Angeles Times*, ABC, CBS, and NBC).

But to posit these as equivalent sides is laughable. One can argue that the mainstream media skew tacitly liberal on social issues, but there exists nothing close to a left-of-center equivalent of Fox News, with its penetration of most cable markets, or the right-wing Sinclair Broadcast Group, which owns fifty-eight television channels that reach, in sum, 22 percent of American households and, during the 2004 campaign, planned to require its owned stations to broadcast an anti-Kerry documentary until an advertising boycott campaign convinced it to water down the film.[16] Public television has never offered a stew of bombast skewed liberal the way *The McLaughlin Group* and the *Journal Editorial Report*, staffed entirely by the editorial board of the *Wall Street Journal*, have skewed to the right. As for the *Journal's* editorial page, it is almost completely closed to liberals, whereas, by contrast, the *New York Times*'s op-ed page makes a point of commissioning and choosing commentaries that counterbalance the (generally liberal) editorials, and the *Los Angeles Times* also cultivates a balance in columnists. During a twelve-week period in the run-up to the Iraq war, the *Washington Post* ran thirty-nine hawkish op-ed pieces to twelve dovish ones, a ratio of more than three to one.[17]

The right's pulpit bullies enforce political uniformity in a way that the mainstream "liberal media" neither wishes to nor does. In the realm of editorials themselves, Michael Tomasky's 2003 study demonstrated that right-wing editorial pages were far more consistently "on-message" than were "liberal" ones. Comparing 510 editorials during the Clinton and Bush II administrations, in the *Wall Street Journal* and the *Washington Times*, on the one hand, and the *New York Times* and the *Washington Post*, on the other, Tomasky found a drastic difference in partisanship: the right-wing editorial pages were more intensely rhetorical and "far less willing to criticize a Republican administration than liberal pages are willing to take issue with a Democratic administration." Only one of forty *Journal* editorials during the Bush administration criticized Bush. Whereas the *New York Times* ran as many anti-Clinton as pro-Clinton editorials, the *Journal* supported Bush 75 percent of the time and opposed Clinton 83 percent of the time.[18]

Likewise, the right's think tanks—to use the term of art for the ideological havens more devoted to propagandizing for their positions than thinking through new ones—are cited more frequently than their less-heeled liberal equivalents are.[19] And likewise, too, the guest lists on the Sunday morning network shows are skewed. As Eric Boehlert reported, in 2004, *Meet the Press* had room around its round tables for thirteen times as many conservatives as liberals, though during the first ten months of 2005 the ratio slumped to a mere 3-to-1. Between 1997 and 2005, Sunday morning talk show guests on all three major networks leaned rightward. Even during Bill Clinton's second term, Republicans and conservatives outnumbered Democrats and liberals 52 percent to 48 percent, this margin widening to 58 percent against 42 percent during Bush's first term. Even during the sixteen months when the Democrats controlled the Senate in 2001–2002, the number of Democrats on the Sunday shows actually declined.[20]

In news coverage, too, even as Bush's Teflon wears thin, the proprietors of the mainstream often bend over backward to demonstrate that they are not those damnable "liberal media" of conservative song and story. Whatever journalists may privately think, the result is a public display of credulity. At worst, watchdogs with laryngitis lick the hands that feed them. At best, there are exposés of administration deceptions, but until the Democrats took charge of Congress in 2007, these were often consigned to the back pages. On the whole, then, where the largest questions of war and peace were concerned, especially after the trauma of September 11, 2001, it is not too much to say that most news organizations spent most of the Bush years rolling over for an alternately (and sometimes simultaneously) fanatical, inept, mendacious, and clueless administration. In the run-up to war, television in particular gave him the benefit of many undeserved doubts. When he claimed to accomplish his mission, they saluted. They buried their doubts and, when the time came for apologies, displayed remarkably little curiosity as to how they had acquired so many sins to apologize for.[21] In fairness, however, it was hard to address the reality of the Bush administration without conveying the impression that the press was precisely what it didn't want to be—an opposition press.

Mostly, the mainstream media take care to keep up a spurious impression of balance: *Some say that the emperor is naked, others say that his new clothes are easy on the eye.* A dramatic and almost certainly influential case is that of the Swift Boat charges leveled against John Kerry in 2004. Historians of the mad pageant in which Americans chose their president in 2004 will someday note with astonishment that the quote-unquote Swift Boat Veterans for Truth, many of its members inveterate liars more swift than truthful, succeeded in hijacking the presidential campaign for the better part of the month of August, nearly one-third of the total time left to John Kerry after his apparently triumphal convention. Journalists escorted them into the limelight with a bodyguard of publicity. It is true that candidate Kerry miscalculated the explosive power of their charges and thereby lost control of his campaign. It is also true that journalists performed as accomplices to liars and half-truth tellers, thereby buying them piles of publicity that money couldn't have bought. For a full two weeks, clips of the group's ads, with interview supplements, wallpapered cable news and talk radio. Their claims then percolated into the rest of the media. Whatever Kerry said about health care, Iraq, and jobs instantly became Topics B, C, and D; the Swift boats of the Vietnam War were Topic A. A low six-figure ad buy became the slander heard 'round the world.

Wayne Slater, the *Dallas Morning News*'s senior political writer and coauthor of *Bush's Brain*, told me:

> This is [Rove's] pattern. Go after an opponent's strength and leave no fingerprints. If basic media had largely not reported this when it was largely a phenomenon of the blog-Web-Limbaugh world, there would still have been this powerful clamor: "Why don't you guys go after this?" Now that we're yelled at so much by Fox News and Limbaugh, the error is to bend on the side of the charges. The Bush people win by sheer publicity.

Slater didn't know what else reporters could have done. "Our obligation is to report," he said. "There are two things to say: one is, an organization is saying something; second, evaluate whether these charges have any merit. I have a problem being used as a stooge to transmit information that may well be irresponsible. But if the gate's closed too much, I don't like that, either. I'm not positive that there was anything to be done that significantly changes this."

I reminded Slater that an earlier rumor purporting to link Kerry to a young girlfriend had been successfully confined to the right-wing Internet world of Matt Drudge and Co. when major networks and newspapers refused to touch the smear, at least long enough for the woman in question to come forward with a flat denial. That ended that. This time, the mainstream media could have held their stories about the anti-Kerry ads until reporters had had a chance to read *Unfit for Command*, the book by John O'Neill, who had played Inspector Javert to Kerry's Jean Valjean since 1971, and evaluate his charges.

"A good idea," Slater said. "But it denies the idea of writing about conflict."

O'Neill was interviewed everywhere and often uncontradicted; or even when contradicted, he rolled on, blowing smoke to be magnified in one mirror after the other.

The Republicans who purchased the anti-Kerry ads well understood that reporters would see "a story"—would be fascinated by the charges and such conflict as might develop about them, that they would be reluctant or unable either to ignore or to refute them. They aggressively exploited the media interest in balance—some think the earth is flat, others disagree. Story after story alluded indiscriminately to veterans contradicting one another—without clarifying that no documents supported O'Neill's slurs about Kerry's medals, and neither did any of Kerry's crewmates. What emerged was a messy picture of charges and countercharges piling up indiscriminately in a "vituperative," "hypernasty," "mean," "vicious" campaign of "slime." Reporters did not, in general, report that what seemed to be driving John O'Neill and his allies was not so much a casual interest in Kerry's medals as anger at Kerry's antiwar charges of 1971, the subject of their second ad. Rare were the correspondents such as ABC's Jake Tapper, who showed some of the anti-Kerry group contradicting themselves and said of them, "None of them served with Kerry on his boat. His actual crewmates reject their charges" and "none of the charges are supported by naval records."

The Kerry campaign reacted late—Kerry himself delayed more than two weeks before responding. Although the Swift-boat charges had dogged Kerry for decades, Kerry seemed to think it would be beneath him to respond. One network reporter told me that the whole affair was "half Kerry's fault, half the press'." Another said, "We've been trying to get stuff from Kerry's side that they won't release. There's a big suspicion that this campaign hasn't vetted their own candidate." *Newsweek*'s Trent Gegax, who covered the Kerry campaign, called O'Neill's accusations "a ridiculous story. It was ridiculous to carry on for weeks when the ads were built on claims that weren't backed up by any documentation. There were misstatements and out-and-out lies that kept this going." He thought that "Kerry himself was afraid that [if he rebutted the first ad directly] it would hit the national news that night. The Kerry people dug themselves into a hole—relying on the media to do their job. They kept trying to defend something they shouldn't have to defend. Why didn't they say, 'Let's talk about where Kerry was and compare it to where George Bush was'? They didn't fight back hard. Ultimately, it's not the media's responsibility to do that work for them."

This recent history, of course, ill-comports with the conventional narrative of journalism in our time. From roughly 1955 through 1965, didn't journalism play a heroic part in spreading news about the civil rights movement and exposing racist violence?[22] Over the following decade, didn't the press bring down two mendacious and overreaching governments, Johnson's and Nixon's? Didn't David Halberstam, Seymour Hersh, and others expose the U.S. government's lies in Vietnam? What of journalism's crowning achievement, as Bob Woodward and Carl Bernstein unraveled the Watergate crimes?

All this happened. But, in fact, journalistic defiance in those years was not exactly usual. In ordinary times, big media are uncomfortable with opposition to power. The glory years of Vietnam and Watergate, however noble for Hollywood purposes and J-school lore, unnerved the journalistic mainstream. Especially when media conglomerates depend on the national government for largesse, the institutions of journalism are vulnerable to assault by Fox, Rush Limbaugh, and the dittoheads barking over their right shoulders. The media bend over backward to prove, even to themselves, that they're not left wing. If journalists regularly called falsehoods falsehoods, they think they would undermine the standard of fairness that secures their professional status. Thus they trap themselves in the self-parodying notion of objectivity immortalized by *The Daily Show*'s Rob Corddry: "My job is to spend half the time repeating what one side says, and half the time repeating the other."[23]

The journalistic surrender to power, manifest in the executive ingratiation of the Bob Woodward of 2002–2005, and the *New York Times*'s credulous neoconservative Judith Miller, is more representative.[24] But even a milder version of the legend does not sit comfortably with the media proprietors, especially given two additional factors: (1) broadcast corporations rely on administration favors and (2) government prosecutors inspect journalists with baleful eyes. The real, imagined, or anticipated threat to deprive them of access cows journalists, although access, in fact, affords more inhibition than revelation.[25] The mainstream quivers at the accusation "liberal." To live down an inflated reputation for speaking truth to power, they are more acutely attuned to noises right than left. Thus the hypersensitivity at many media outlets as to whether they are doing right by conservatives. Early in 2005 I was present at a meeting summoned by *New York Times* editors, reporters, and business staff where one reporter asked, "Should we have affirmative action for conservatives?" Political editors expressed relief when the Democratic congressman William Jefferson was found with $90,000 cash in his freezer and charged with criminal conduct in 2006—they could then balance the systemic corruption of Republican members of Congress connected to the lobbyist-bagman Jack Abramoff against a Democrat's isolated malfeasance.[26]

In May 2001, the *Washington Post* political reporter (later editor) John Harris, in an unusually reflective dot-connecting piece, wrote:

> The truth is, this new president has done things with relative impunity that would have been huge uproars if they had occurred under Clinton. . . . Above all . . . there is one big reason for Bush's easy ride: There is no well-coordinated corps of aggrieved and methodical people who start each day looking for ways to expose and undermine a new president.
>
> There was just such a gang ready for Clinton in 1993. Conservative interest groups, commentators and congressional investigators waged a remorseless campaign that they hoped would make life miserable for Clinton and vault themselves to power. They succeeded in many ways. . . . It is

Bush's good fortune that the liberal equivalent of this conservative coterie does not exist."[27]

The mainstream media's generosity toward government claims
about al-Qaeda–Saddam connections and Iraqi weapons of mass
destruction has been amply documented, even, belatedly, in the
New York Times and the *Washington Post* themselves. But on other
fronts as well, these papers and the rest of the mainstream cut Bush
plenty of slack. It was business as usual to scant the substance of
candidates' and presidents' views in favor of their tactics and
strategies. But when the president is a serial obfuscator and fab-
ricator—not to say flip-flopper—this inside-dopester coverage
works to his advantage.

So many small exposés take place, but the dots, once unearthed,
are usually reinterred unconnected. Patterns go unrecognized. "If
there's anything missing," the *New York Times*'s former Washington bureau chief and executive editor Max Frankel told me, "it's the
single voice pulling it all together."[28] Especially in television's once-
over-lightly collages, the deep patterns that make comprehension
possible and actionable remain obscured. Few suggestions are
heard that Bush systematically arrived at decisions in an uninformed, irrational manner. Diehard Democrats may already know
that the Republican Party doesn't incidentally or occasionally stoop
to please big corporations, it does so systematically; but many
independents and Republicans do not. Infrequent reports on fox-
henhouse cohabitation in the coal industry, say, did not refer to
examples from drug, hospital, utility, oil and gas, and other
sectors.[29]

Every Washington journalist I have spoken with in recent years
agrees that the Bush administration is more clammed-up and
robotically on message than any other in history. How to cover
the White House (in anything other than gauze) therefore poses a
professional problem, and it troubles the Washington bureaus.
Several serious reporters told me they fled the White House beat
after tiring of closed doors and puffery—the equivalent of the desert
travelogues that were the best that most reporters embedded in Iraq
could muster during the march-on-Baghdad phase of 2003. One

former White House reporter for a major newspaper told me, "This White House is extremely difficult, if not impossible, to cover. The editors need to realize their journalists are like in straitjackets. When it came to [Monica] Lewinsky and [Bill] Clinton's campaign finances, White House reporters had help from investigative reporters. Where are they now?"

But the investigations that would go to demonstrate the day-in-day-out corruption, malfeasance, ignorance, and partisanship of the Bush years are costly—even more so under Bush than during the Clinton years. Reporters are scarcer than they used to be, and extensive investigations require that reporters be dislodged from daily beats for months of work that may, in the end, prove fruitless. With dead-tree circulations in apparently irreversible decline, newspapers are in a cost panic. Meanwhile, predatory investors hold large stakes in chains like Knight Ridder, which was forced to sell off in March 2006 because its profits were in the low 20 percent range—far higher than the average firm's, but no matter. The profits of 15 percent or so that Wall Street considered desirable if not obligatory in the nineties are, in the early twenty-first century, considered deficient, probably because investors are pursuing what newspaper consultants call a "harvest strategy" predicated on the assumption that metropolitan newspapers are "mature" businesses facing dwindling growth, so that the best way to realize their value is to maximize profits and run. (Previously, in fact, publishers considered single-digit margins acceptable.)[30] Only the family stockholders of the *New York Times*, the *Washington Post*, and the *Wall Street Journal*, who occupy an exclusive tier of stock ownership, can sometimes fend off raiders and insulate their firms from fierce market pressures.

But this media elite, too, has other reasons to mute its criticism or narrow it. When reporting on social issues, these three newspapers do tend to tilt toward the liberal side,[31] but on other matters, their institutional mind thinks that to respect the nation, one must respect the government. Washington journalism in particular is as enamored of conventional wisdom as it is desperate for access. Professionalism, as conventionally understood, demands a show—at least—of balance. Reporters have had a symbiotic relationship with officials since time immemorial.[32] On the Washington fashion beat, there is always an authority standing by to comment on the emperor's bright new garb. Once establishment institutions go looking for reasons to be establishment institutions, they can always find them. This was true before George W. Bush took office and it will be true after he departs.

But this is not to say that the variously bland, euphemistic, lazy, smug, shallow, supine, and otherwise de facto conservative news organizations are by themselves responsible for America's long conservative ascendancy. To assume as much is to grant them too much power and, implicitly, to urge them on to a mission that they will never accept. They operate as one set of forces in a larger field of forces. Too true, the overall media imbalance is an impediment for liberals. Also too true, the mainstream media do a good deal to promote certain agendas and images above others, to certify that certain controversies are legitimate and others not.[33] They are *the media*—the means by which issues are named, forces identified, curses delivered, and positions declared to be in and out of bounds.

But they are *only* the media, relaying in mysterious ways the consensus reached by elites outside the newsrooms. And in fact, their legitimacy is eroding. Challenges to their authority emerge not only on right-wing talk radio and cable TV but in the liberal blogosphere. Although the times when the media as a whole act as a force unto themselves can be decisive—see under Swift Boats—those are rare. More often, their power lies in their ability to limit the terms of debate—a significant force, at least in the absence of intense public mobilizations, but still only one force in the larger political field.

Still, in the end, there is not only a journalistic but a political consensus that journalists are not obliged to be a political opposition. They can further opposition or dampen it, and in a run-up to war, to take one huge example, they can be mighty pulpits for bullies. But when political life at large falls afoul of public neglect and ignorance, and the party system is tilted toward know-nothing politics, and a single party stands astride government, and the president of the United States brooks no serious opposition, it would be astounding if large commercial organizations converted themselves into battalions of resistance. For that, there is politics.

So we turn to the opposition that, throughout recent decades, strives to make up for lost time and structural weakness, sometimes shoulders its burdens and sometimes shrugs them off, strains its muscles, falls short, quarrels over its failures, strains some more, and in fits and tries to remake itself on its long slog uphill.

PART TWO

Wilderness: Fits and Starts

If I said, "'A microphone is on the table' is the message," ten Republicans around the table would say, "A microphone is on the table," "A microphone is on the table," "A microphone is on the table." Ten Democrats around the table would say, "A microphone is on the table," "It's next to a glass," "There's all these people sitting around," "It's in a room with a chandelier," "There are windows in the room."

—Nancy Pelosi

7

Parties and Movements: A Brief Excursus on Democratic Dilemmas

In heaven, possibly, ideals speak for themselves—from their lips directly into the hearts of lesser beings. But on Earth ideals require translation, namely, action. If the world were logically ordered, politics would begin with ends—so Plato and Aristotle would insist. But a little experience demonstrates that the ends crash and burn without means. So, over time, human beings have learned that their ideals need means, vessels, and escorts—and that's where the trouble begins. The need for means is the requirement exacted by an unforgiving world, and in this requirement, and the possibility it creates of a fatal mismatch between ends and means, lies the taproot of political tragedy. Ideals are the necessary motives of practical action, but ideals without wherewithal are pipe dreams, and even worse, ideals yoked to the wrong means are likely as not to turn into nightmares.

In democracies, the people who either bear the ideals or bury them, or both, are politicians. And organizations of politicians, called parties, are the indispensable means of political power. But parties are, to say the least, impure vessels. They consist, by definition, of politicians, namely, people who aspire to political power, along with staffs who are also possessed of personal ambition. They win public support by making promises, but they head for the compromised land. They may have started out with passions, may insist that their sojourns in the compromised land are only short-term, but during those sojourns they are insiders, and insiders have interests—their own prerogatives and advantages. Officeholders like to retain their offices, toward which end parties are helpful—for cultivating, choosing, and selecting candidates, and funding and organizing their campaigns.

But most Americans are less than attached to parties, even the ones they vote for. With good reason, they think that parties bear the stink of corruption; that even at best, parties are the property of professionals while they, the citizens, are only rank amateurs—and they like it that way, for they have private pursuits, a pleasing luxury of liberal societies. And for the most part, except during fund-raising spurts or in those places where machine remnants deliver the equivalent of Thanksgiving turkeys, the parties return the favor: day by day, they offer citizens next to nothing. In the United States, national parties scarcely exist. Walk the streets of any city in the United States and you will be hard-pressed to find a party office, let alone a meeting. (Consider, by contrast, the West European cities, even midsized towns, that feature such offices emblazoned with their party logos.)

In 1965, the economist Mancur Olson wrote in his classic study of the dynamics of political groups: "The average American . . . will not be willing to make a significant sacrifice for the party he favors, since a victory for his party provides [only] a collective good. He will not contribute to the party coffers or attend precinct meetings. There are on the other hand many people with personal political ambitions, and for them the party will provide . . . benefits in the form of public office." Olson, following Tocqueville, went on to mention America's seven hundred thousand elected officials—more than forty years ago—as well as the businessmen who contribute to the party for the purpose of access.[1] And Olson was writing at a moment when party loyalty was still relatively high and political independence hadn't developed the prestige it later came to enjoy.

So much is elementary, perhaps. But it is crucial to understand that by the time Olson set pen to paper, the conservative movement was already jarring the conventional wisdom. That movement set out to take over the Republican Party, warts and all, to convert it into a conservative party, and over the next decades succeeded. For the most part, the party welcomed right-wing activists. They were energetic, assured, reliable cadres. They were well organized, used to getting together ritually: Sunday mornings at church, weekly kaffeeklatsch meetings. They turned out to canvass and they turned loyalists out to vote. Despite continuing tensions, the Republican Party became, and continues to be, a splendid conduit for idealists of their stripe. Theirs was a very long march, proceeding in fits and starts—a grand success in 1964, with the nomination of Barry Goldwater, followed by his apparently calamitous but actually fruitful defeat; the regrouping in California under Ronald Reagan from 1966 on; Reagan's narrow failure to wrest the presidential nomination from Gerald Ford in 1976; his triumphal comeback in 1980—and crucially, the Christian right's commitment to turn the Republican Party to its use, to reap a host of resentments, repeal liberal values, and recoup the ground it had lost in the barbarian sixties.[2]

Movement disgruntlement never ceases; neither does party high-handedness. Therefore, the relation between movement and party is a more or less tense collaboration. This is not a matter of personalities: tension is inherent in the structure of the movement-party relationship. In no small part because of the inordinate cost of television advertising, American politics is absurdly expensive. (In 2006, the winning candidates alone in House and Senate races spent more than $750 million, up from $420 million in 1998. In 2004, those winners spent $666 million; Bush and Kerry raised an additional $963 million between them.[3]) In the absence of public financing, the party is beholden to big money, while the movement wants purity. The party belongs to professionals, while the movement consists largely of amateurs.

So at various times the movement yelps that the party leadership is imprisoned by the get-along-go-along attitude of a Washington establishment or is directly for sale. Examples are legion. Reagan negotiated with the Evil Empire and actually seemed on the brink of tossing away nuclear weapons. Bush I betrayed his promise and, however his lips read, raised taxes. As for Bush II, in the eyes of some conservatives, his "Global War on Terror" masked the "nation-building" that he campaigned against in 2000; for others, it masked reckless empire building and the disastrous war in Iraq. He bulked up the federal government with new entitlements, budget deficits, and debt as steep as the eye can see. To purists, his tax cuts, however huge, were not huge enough; his antiabortion actions were sketchy; his advocacy of constitutional amendments was merely symbolic. Far from abolishing the Department of Education—a longtime conservative hope—Bush stuffed it with new functions, not least the national tests mandated by "No Child Left Behind." He proved, in short, to be an apostle of "big-government conservatism."

Hard-line conservatives of several stripes accordingly assumed a posture, at least, of revolt. "Warning to the Republican Party: Conservatives are unhappy again," Richard A. Viguerie and David Franke ended their 2004 book, *America's Right Turn*.[4] In May 2006, Viguerie wrote in the *Washington Post*:

> The current record of Washington Republicans is so bad that, without a drastic change in direction, millions of conservatives will again stay home this November. . . . Conservatives must stop funding the Republican National Committee and other party groups. (Let Big Business take care of that!). . . . I've never seen conservatives so downright fed up as they are today.[5]

Just before the midterm election of 2006, the free-market fundamentalist and former House majority leader Dick Armey also took to the *Washington Post* with "Where We Went Wrong," declaring that "Republican lawmakers forgot the party's principles, became enamored with power and position, and began putting politics over policy."[6] Such formulations were echoed by the Christian fundamentalist Ken Connor, the former head of the Family Research Council (and a Florida Republican lawyer during the Terri Schiavo affair), who wrote after the 2006 election that "Republican leaders seemed to think of social conservatives as easy dupes," and that many "prominent Christian organization and leaders . . . have been seduced by the Washington, D.C., political culture. They have identified themselves so closely with persons and parties that they have lost sight of principle. . . . Christian conservatives became enablers of corrupt Republicans."[7]

Still, movement conservatives have nowhere to go—except out of politics altogether. Periodically, figures on the religious right advocate retreat from the fleshpots of Washington and the rest of a tainted political world. This threat to abstain may not seem entirely empty. After all, evangelical Christians largely absented themselves from politics for decades until the Warren Court's decisions on school prayer and mandatory Bible reading in 1962–1963 convinced them that they needed to throw themselves into the fray. In 1999, Paul Weyrich, the longtime right-wing leader who in the late seventies had offered the term *moral majority* to Jerry Falwell, was so revolted by the Senate's failure to convict Bill Clinton of high crimes and misdemeanors as to issue an open letter declaring, "I no longer believe that there is a moral majority." The United States, Weyrich wrote, "is very close to becoming a state totally dominated by an alien ideology, an ideology bitterly hostile to Western culture. . . . [P]olitics itself has failed." It followed, then, that conservatives should "secede," he maintained, to a refuge, "some sort of quarantine . . . where we can live godly, righteous, and sober lives," for example, by home-schooling.[8] In the event, few prominent conservatives sided with Weyrich, and soon Weyrich was back at work endorsing Republican candidates. The secessionist impulse is likely to devolve into a gesture when conservative leaders have a sizable stake in Washington power, prestige, and money.

Still, given such intense feelings, it is unsurprising that the right's long movement-party collaboration had to be made—it was not born. From Reagan to Bush the Younger, the party's leadership finesse was always essential. A politician less adroit than Ronald Reagan might not have succeeded in brokering a deal between social and economic conservatives that both sides could live with in their common drive toward power. (Reagan was blunt, if somewhat experimental, about his objective. "The time has come," he told the American Conservative Union on February 6,

1977, "to see if it is possible to present a program of action based on political principle that can attract those interested in the so-called 'social' issues and those interested in 'economic' issues."[9]) Under George W. Bush, economic conservatives—ostensibly rational— had to swallow their own objections to swollen federal government in the interest of satisfying a venal base with "earmarks" and other material privileges. Meanwhile, movement conservatives of a religious bent had to be willing to accept a long-term strategy for limiting abortion (via legislation banning "partial-birth abortion," and certain statewide bans), rather than go for broke with a probably doomed constitutional amendment.

But whatever conservatives' grumbles about the intractable corruption and sluggishness of Washington, D.C., despite defections and bitter protests that the party has betrayed conservative values— declarations that must be considered disingenuous in the light of movement conservatives' passion for George W. Bush as long as his approval ratings ran high—the conservative movement is safely locked into the world of Republican power. The party is conservatives' institutional haven, their world of networks and money, their revolving door, employment agency, and mobility ladder, the Elysian field of their pleasures and sweet corruptions. It is also, decisively, the home of their highly practical hearts. They threaten, but they do not bolt. They harbor no Ralph Nader. (The most they could muster for a breakaway in 2000 was an enfeebled Pat Buchanan, who, however, did end up helping Bush by winning the inadvertent votes of Florida Jews.) After Goldwater's defeat in 1964, when purist conservatives spoke of bolting from the Republicans, one of their chief funders, Walter Knott of Orange County, of California's Knott's Berry Farm, gave them a wise old uncle's talking-to: "I think that you have to work through a [mainstream] party. . . . [I]f you don't, you would be pretty ineffective."[10] Pretty ineffective was what the conservative movement was not willing to be. Since the sixties, the movement knew that its fate was inseparable from the party—*its* party.

Liberal idealists, on the other hand, do not control the Democratic Party. In the main, they have gone their own ways, fighting their own issue campaigns through their distinct organizations, for decades. "The left establishment," in the words of the peerless political reporter Thomas B. Edsall, "has placed a far higher priority on specific, narrow legislative and policy goals, on grass roots demonstration projects, on ad hoc victories, and on culturally inflammatory initiatives that expend moral capital, than on building political power through Democratic Party victories."[11] This is not the mentality of an army, but of an assortment of eight sometimes overlapping, sometimes quarrelsome interest groups—labor, the helping professions, the antiwar residents of university-area neighborhoods, environmentalists, African Americans, Hispanics, feminists, and gays.

Liberals had to stare long and hard at the calamity of George W. Bush's reign to start coming to terms with the party's impurities—impurities that they might strive to minimize but that would surely not disappear. The Democratic Party, for its part, spent the better part of forty years in considerable comfort with its ineffectuality. As a national party, the Democrats got used to feebleness on the ground. Power gravitated to the candidates and their personal, temporary machines. FDR may have wanted to nationalize the party and downgrade the Dixiecrats, but his commitment to administrative power left his party in a subordinate position.[12]

"Parties played a limited role in the 1960's," wrote Joel H. Silbey, a leading historian of American parties. "They had, by then, lost much of their force as coordinators and shapers of political activity, and as the main conduits for articulating and organizing popular demands."[13] The Democratic Party awkwardly basted together three quite different organizational bases—machines, unions, and liberal activist groups.[14] While the Goldwater cadres led a Republican revitalization movement, the Democrats proceeded to crumble, in no small part because of strains over civil rights and Vietnam. As president, Lyndon Johnson "slashed the budget of the national committee and concentrated its resources in the White House," wrote Eugene McCarthy's biographer Dominic Sandbrook.[15] Johnson, in the words of the political scientist Sidney M. Milkis, "deemphasized party politics in favor of a presidential coalition—and an alliance with social movements. . . . LBJ and his aides viewed state and local governments, and the party organizations that influenced them, as obstacles to good government, to the 'enlightened' management of social policy."[16] In 1968, according to Sandbrook, "no more than a fifth of the population lived in areas with a dominant Democratic Party organization."

The seventies were hard on the Democrats, who practiced personal politics, their improvised organizations cropping up to run what the political scientist David R. Mayhew called "capital-intensive campaigns" as the machines, the unions, and the activist groups withered. As the Republicans were strengthening their party apparatus, the Democrats entered the eighties as little more "than an arena for competing candidate organizations."[17] Neither Jimmy Carter nor, later, Bill Clinton did much to build the party. Clinton, in particular, was inclined to strive for bipartisan consensus, even when the Republicans repelled his health-care initiative and triumphed in the midterm elections of 1994. By contrast, Ronald Reagan, in office, knew how much he owed the Republican Party—movement he had escorted to power. He raised money for Republican candidates at all levels. He gave back. All the more so did George W. Bush, who, spurred by his narrow escape at the hands of the Supreme Court in 2000, once in office "made unprecedented efforts to recruit Republican candidates, engage in partisan campaigning, and utilize the administrative presidency to achieve partisan objectives." One measure of his commitment was that in early October 2002, a month be-fore the midterm elections, the Republican National Committee had *six times as much* available cash as its Democratic counterpart—six times as much to campaign for a vote of confidence in Bush while the Democrats tried to ignore the party's harsh assaults and the impending Iraq war.[18] Republican presidents viewed the party as an instrument to accomplish their goals. Democratic presidents, by contrast, agreed, in a sense, with the liberal issue groups: the party was not exactly *theirs*.

In many states, as a result, the Democratic apparatus has been threadbare and impoverished. On the ground, the national party was a ghost—at least until 2004, when years of bad results finally upgraded party-building on its agenda. In 2005, Howard Dean won the chairmanship of the Democratic National Committee on a platform of putting national operatives to work in all fifty states in an effort to make the party nationally competitive. (Dean's pitch as party builder was so popular among Democrats that his rivals for the position all followed suit in swearing allegiance to the same goal.) This was an innovation precisely because, astonishingly, many states, including swinging Ohio, up to that moment lacked *a single one*. And although at this writing Dean has succeeded in implanting at least two organizers in every state, the party's entities (the Democratic Senatorial Campaign Committee and the Democratic Congressional Campaign Committee) prefer to raise money for candidates—in select districts at that.[19] Not until 2006 did these committees exercise clout (whether wisely or foolishly is disputed) to promote desirable candidates. The Democratic Party is largely, in other words, a bank—and at that, one that is open only during occasional hours.

With this half-apparatus, half-phantasm, many professional liberals cannot be said to have even a love-hate relationship. It is more like tolerate-hate.

In June 2005, in a Washington Hilton ballroom, at what is probably the largest gathering of liberal activists in the country, the Take Back America conference, I heard Kim Gandy, the president of the National Organization for Women, declare that "the Democratic Party can't seem to decide whether it wants to be Republican Lite." She called out her betes noires of the day: John Kerry, who had said the Democrats needed to elect more antiabortionists; the left evangelical Reverend Jim Wallis, the previous speaker, who supports "faith-based" initiatives; and Bono, who "crossed the line" to seek collaboration on Africa with pro-lifers. "If this is what it means to be a big tent," Gandy declared, "then I say let's keep the skunk out of the tent."

The Reverend Jesse Jackson Sr. declared, in one of the more maladroit statements in contemporary politics, that progressives are "the third rail of American politics." The two rails, he explained, are the two parties. The third is "a strong independent force"—such as abolitionism at a time when the two parties disagreed on how nice to be to the slaves. The reverend was uncharacteristically maladroit—or revealing—in his metaphorical choice. If he were acquainted with the electrical systems of subways, he would know that the third rail is lethal.

Gandy and Jackson both drew standing ovations.

Like movement conservatives of an earlier stripe, liberal activists would often rather be right than be president. They have their reasons, even if they don't have much clout. Perhaps if they speak up loudly, forcefully, repeatedly enough, they will eventually transform the debate and get the president and the Congress of their dreams. In a more populist vein, they may think that by standing four-square on principle, they bring to the surface popular ideals that were only latent before; they speak in the people's true voice. (Bush is even more radical: on such questions as Iraq, Social Security, global warming, and stem-cells, he prides himself on *leading* public opinion. John McCain has some of the same fervor, as on Iraq. So did Barry Goldwater.) It is precisely because idealists believe that they can discern the public good that they must be ever on guard against trimmers.

Yet to get what they want, the activists will probably have to cultivate irony, to sense the inescapable truth that the realization of their hopes depends on politicians who are sometimes defiantly not idealists, who are subject to cross-pressures (many of them financial), and who tend to strike activists as phony, smarmy panderers, connoisseurs of euphemism, self-promoters who will run over you if you stand between them and a TV camera, and, moreover, as having other fish to fry, namely, narrow interests.

Passion tends to melt away irony, and idealists accuse insiders of heartlessness. Moral certitude also plugs the ears, so activists incline to think that only the venal or the ignorant could fail to see things their way. All in all, they tend not to be interested in inches, only in miles. When the party fails to oblige, they clamor, in full prophetic voice, against self-seeking insiders who have brought the hacks, the flacks, the dopes, and, worst of all, the money changers into the temple. To which the party, composed of no-nonsense professionals, replies that the outsiders are naifs, ignoramuses, hicks, strangers to "this town," grandstanders, or, worse, uncompromising wreckers who haven't the faintest idea *how things work*. So offense inspires defensiveness, which in turn generates more offense.

Neither outsiders nor insiders have all the arguments. Politicians may be only modestly principled, but they can claim legitimacy while begging indulgence for their realism—they are tested, after all, in the exacting laboratory of popular politics. They can claim to be down in the trenches while idealists are building air castles. Proudly or wearily, aggressively or with pathos, they point out that parties are the engines that turn the wheels that move the government that, in turn, moves things in the real world. Far be it from them to claim that the party is a splendid institution brimming with saints, a fun place for bright-eyed idealists to spend time, or a fully fair or fully equal prefiguration of justice incarnate. They know the party is more humdrum than that—the sort of imperfect human contrivance built to obtain the cooperation that a complex society needs to get its work done. People have interests, and parties collect disparate elements with disparate interests, and the disagreements have to be brokered. That's what parties do. They assemble human beings who maneuver, combine, conflict, recombine, and compromise. Politics is their livelihood. You may dislike this fact of political life, as you may reject the law of gravity, but there it is. You get political results with the party you have, not with the party you wish you had.

The principle that democracies need parties and that political power does not develop without them applies to partial, withered, corrupted democracies, as well as to the most fully developed democracies that have ever existed. Parties may be corrupt, fatally riven, degenerate, or stupid, or more than one of the above, and if they are badly enough so, they die. (A case in point: the American Whigs before the Civil War, torn apart by the single unignorable issue of their time, slavery.) In those cases, other parties arise—and they are not perfect, either. There are parties for sale, parties that amount to nothing but personal vehicles for bosses and celebrities, parties that devolve into hereditary machines. Many are the possible distortions of good democratic practice. But even a bad party does not depart the scene unless a critical mass of its partisans feel strongly enough that the old party has failed, and break away in favor of a different vehicle, a new or transformed vehicle for political power—another party, that is.

There is a realistic case for idealism, too. It starts with the recognition that there is much more to politics than parties. Today, in a time of rampant disillusion with politics—moreover, a time when tens of millions of Americans cannot even rouse themselves to a state of illusion in the first place—parties are incapable of replenishing themselves. If they are lucky, they include self-perpetuating machines that thrive because they offer material rewards—urban machines are the prototype, but the inside-the-Beltway apparatus of staffers, campaign consultants, managers, fund-raisers, and so on are other enduring components. But this is not enough. Parties that rest on nothing but blind ambition are doomed—in democracies as in one-party states.

For parties do not move themselves. They need fuel. Their fuel consists of popular energies, which, when they become more or less substantial, we call movements, and when they are not, should more properly be called currents, moods, or fads. But in democracies of the Western type, and particularly in the United States of the last half-century or so, movements are the carriers of ideals. When people in large numbers feel a political passion, they form a movement. Movements agitate, organize, mobilize. Movements flow. They are liquid. They may evaporate. They may solidify into establishments of their own—may become parties or parts of parties. In any event, they aim to change the political weather, if not the climate. They exert pressure on institutions—churches, businesses, universities, professions, what have you. When all else fails, they may overturn these institutions. Movements are, as the German New Left said of itself in the sixties, extraparliamentary.

Movements may aspire to policy changes or transformations in political climate and culture, even in whole ways of life. There are movements that make noble gestures and accomplish nothing more than to exist: think of the "White Rose" movement of 1942–1943 against Nazism, consisting of a handful of students in Munich who passed out leaflets denouncing Hitler and paid with their lives. There are movements that affect indifference to consequences, that aspire to nothing more than "speaking truth to power," expressing, even in theatrical fashion, "the power of the powerless." (And it is no accident, as they say, that this phrase comes from a dramatist, Vaclav Havel.) But in more-or-less democratic societies, parties must aspire to one thing above all: victory. If a party is not a machine to win and organize power, it is nothing at all.

Not surprisingly, we owe to a general, Douglas MacArthur—a man who spoke in his farewell address, amid purple evocations of the warrior's sacrifice, of "the horror" of war—the brutal truth that "in war there is no substitute for victory."[20] Only superficially is this a banal judgment. If we couple MacArthur's observation with Clausewitz's dictum that war is an extension of politics by other means, we may deduce that in politics, too, there is no substitute for victory. This statement is so profoundly true as to be tautological. The fiercest advocate of out-on-a-limb politics claims the status of a not-yet-recognized prophet; claims that today's defeats—in behalf of Barry Goldwater, say, "a choice not an echo"—are only the necessary prologues to a victory that will surely arrive, if not tomorrow, then the day after tomorrow. But to say that in politics, as in war, there is no substitute for victory is not to say that one victory is everything or even that a series of victories constitute triumph. After years out of power, Democrats may claim that there's nothing wrong with their party that victory can't cure. But such a claim is radically belied by the curious presidency of Bill Clinton.

8

Movements versus Party: 1964–1980

Bill Clinton, the most talented Democratic politician since Lyndon Johnson, and partly for this reason the most suspect and the most despised, was so masterful as to baste together the disparate segments of his party—provisionally, at least—and convince each of them that he was actually *their* man. He picked his way through the ruins of the party of Jimmy Carter, Walter Mondale, and Michael Dukakis, the party of three successive versions of post-sixties Democratic hope and three successive crushing defeats, and somehow (not least, with the help of Ross Perot and his self-funded crusade for fiscal conservatism) turned this party of steady defeat into an instrument of presidential victory.

Clinton was the consummate barker for the big tent. By contrast, each of the Democratic candidates who preceded him represented only a segment of the party's past: Carter, the Jeffersonian citizen-farmer in the post–civil rights South, Mondale the New Deal's career politician, and Dukakis a college graduate's idea of a competent manager. All these attempts to model a post-sixties Democratic presidency fell afoul of an ardent Republican right rejuvenated by Ronald Reagan, in large part because it was able to corner the states of the old Confederacy and win the votes of the white working class. Reagan won 66 percent of white voters without college degrees in his two presidential runs.[1]

Clinton, once ensconced in the White House, sometimes seemed the Democrats' very redeemer—a man of the sixties who in his demeanor and accent defied the stereotype of a liberal yuppie, who could win back Reagan Democrats, especially white men, because he didn't have to stoop to prove that he was in the cultural mainstream, who didn't have to show off his taste for pork rinds, who wolfed down fast food with evident relish, who wasn't just an avatar for the alumni of sixties movements, who knew how to trim down the rough edges of radicalism in such a way as to connect to popular forces. He was still, however, precisely the sort of sixties embodiment that young George Bush despised. More than twenty years after his own stupendous defeat, George McGovern said of Clinton, "He seemed to take away the lesson of not being caught too far out on the left on defense, welfare, crime. From then on he would take steps to make sure those were marketed in a way to appeal to conservatives and moderates." According to Clinton's biographer David Maraniss, "in Clinton's heart of hearts, McGovern believed then and later, he would always remain 'closer to where we were in '72 than the public thinks.'"[2]

The neat trick of profligate sincerity ("waffling," to those who despised it) was evidently in Clinton's nature. In some sense he actually *did* feel everyone's pain. He had an extravagant need to enfold his suitors in an appreciation that passed for love, so by temperament he seemed born for impossible missions. Before he became the master triangulator between Democrats and Republicans, he was the master triangulator between the dominant factions of the Democratic Party—the ensemble of interest groups who were the chief inheritors of the sixties, plus the Democratic Leadership Council's center. It was Clinton's rare, perhaps ill-starred art to step up to irreconcilables and embrace them.

Part of his skill lay in manner—his much-noticed capacity to read political personalities in order to grasp their singularity (he had "a novelistic sensibility about people," said one of his Yale friends).[3] Having read their desires, he could mediate between them, woo them, manage them.[4] But much of Clinton's skill also lay in matter. As a crafter of policies, he could attempt the impossible because he knew how to operate as a one-man party of reason. "He often found his organizing principles by dissecting contrary advice," wrote his chief speechwriter, Michael Waldman,[5] adding this observation about Clinton's dialectical nature: "[H]e was at his most creative and fertile as a policy-maker when he set up his advisers a la Roosevelt so there were conflicting factions, rather than approaching questions in a linear way."[6] When he presided at "town meetings," with experts or ordinary citizens, he practiced not only indiscriminate sincerity but a down-home version of the rationality that the presidential scholar Fred Greenstein found in Dwight D. Eisenhower and Paul O'Neill saw in Nixon and Ford, in stark contrast to George W. Bush.

In Clinton's talent for following everyone's arguments to their logical endpoints, his detractors saw nothing but opportunism and dithering: an absence of principle compounded by a self-indulgent taste for endless wonkery. But Clinton was confident that he could bring disputants around to supporting his eventual decisions by giving everyone the impression that he was taking their views into account even as he was talking them into acquiescence. Hence his supporters saw in Clinton the embodiment of a kind of principle—the will to strive for the sort of synthesis in which one rejects the old dichotomies (after first entertaining them) in favor of new departures. Clinton was not afraid to practice negative capability, that quality of suppleness named by the redoubtable John Keats: "When man is capable of being in uncertainties, Mysteries, doubts without any irritable reaching after fact & reason."[7] Or rather, in Michael Waldman's account, Clinton began with negative capability and used it to "reach after fact & reason."

In fashioning this ideal, Keats was not thinking of politics, but rather (*especially* was the word he used) of literature. Great literature, Keats thought, was the product of luminous uncertainty stretched to the highest expressive power. Hamlet versus Claudius and himself, Macbeth versus Duncan, his wife, and himself— Shakespeare, Keats's own example of "a Man of Achievement," animated the Mysteries, transformed collision into dialogue and the stuff of uncertainty into suspense. It would have been exceedingly strange if Keats had recommended this same love of suspenseful dialogue for *political* power, a human condition that entails, among other things, a willingness to create the impression of reducing "uncertainties, Mysteries, doubts" to rubble.[8] Power is action, after all, and action leaves the defeated behind and terminates the path not taken. Yet Clinton was a man who practiced a literary aesthetic in an uncongenial world—the world of action. He relished the clashes and dissonances of politics. "Clinton's love for the human comedy of politics undercut any puritanical drive to reform it," Waldman wrote.[9]

Clinton's art of the possible was easily scorned, but it was no minor artistry after a full quarter of a century when the Democratic Party seemed both impossible and artless. Democratic haplessness from the late sixties onward was all the more jaw-dropping because not so long before, the Democrats gave the impression of being America's default governing party—not only the majority party but the party of government, in fact, the pragmatic party, the party that *delivered the goods*. If for no other reason than that their programs delivered the goods, they made loyalists out of beneficiaries: union members, the helping professions, the unemployed, veterans, government job-holders, and recipients of Social Security, educational grants, and welfare, not to mention their families.

So the Democratic coalition steered by Franklin D. Roosevelt and his heirs ruled almost without interruption from 1933 through 1968. They were more than the weather; they were the climate. However awkwardly, through crescendos and diminuendos, they commanded majorities unified by a commitment to federal power in behalf of a general increase of liberty and equality and, not least, lubricated by economic growth distributed in a fashion that appeared fair, or fair enough. If the Democrats were often not so solid as they appeared, resting as they did on a corrupt bargain of convenience by throwing the ethnics and the liberals of the North together with the white supremacists of the South, they could take credit for delivering enough material progress to enough different factions to satisfy enough expectations.

For more than a full generation, then, the Democrats were not only the party of solidarity, the party of the common patriotic endeavor, but the party of reason. Their elites were commanding, knowledgeable, full of verve, men and women of stature blessed with the affections of common people, annealed by one crisis after another—coming to power in the wake of the Great Depression, confronting fascism and war, then communism. In peacetime and wartime the Democrats summoned up a succession of energetic, confident, sometimes eloquent men as national leaders who rose to their occasions—Roosevelt, of course, in 1932, then Harry S. Truman in 1945, then the impassioned civil rights standard-bearer Hubert Humphrey in 1948, John Kennedy in 1960, and Lyndon Johnson in 1963. And even during six of the eight years when Eisenhower wrested away control of the White House, the Democrats managed Congress so masterfully as to become partners in rule.

From the travail of the Great Depression through the opening years of the travail of Vietnam, the Democrats were the party that coupled brain to brawn. The right stood against evil, but the liberals stood for progress—the preservation of some time-honored tools toward that end, the devising of new tools where necessary. Democrats stood for faith in national action, a romance of popular government on a foundation of material progress. The romance made sense because—in no small measure thanks to the Democrats—government was the ascending institution in American life, the leading instrument for getting it done, the indispensable manager of warfare, welfare, mobility, prosperity, and security. What more did Americans want? Government became the prime instrument for social achievement, the locus of reason in the service of common ideals. Government not only supplied grand results, it delivered more pleasure than pain, made more people feel bigger than smaller—a lot more. Even as they sung their ballads as self-sufficient yeomen, Jeffersonian traditionalists, especially in the South, appreciated the farm supports, other subsidies, and military-industrial bases that Democratic presidents deposited throughout the onetime Confederacy.

For decades, then, while Republicans worshiped at their traditional altars, cherishing business and small-town establishments, fulminating against taxes, resenting and resisting federal power, the Democrats summoned initiative, intelligence, and, hard as it may be to believe from our present-day vantage point, a romantic mystique in behalf of a government that could solve social problems in the interest of justice: sharing prosperity at home, spreading good works, and containing communism abroad. As the party of muscular popular government, liberals appeared to solve the conundrum of how to advance at once the two not-always-compatible goals of liberty and equality. The trick was to make government more useful to more people than it irritated. As long as the Democrats looked like plausible guardians of the nation, then faith in government thrived, and the party could withstand a good deal of disgruntlement—as in 1948, when simultaneous left- and right-wing revolts spawned not only a third party insurgency (Strom Thurmond's racist Dixiecrats) but also a fourth (Henry Wallace's fellow-traveling Progressives), yet the Democrats were able to triumph nevertheless, because under Truman, as under Roosevelt, they stood convincingly for get-it-done government and get-it-done government, at home and abroad, was what the majority wanted.

So the Democrats recovered for another twenty years of liberal and quasi-liberal reform—even during the Eisenhower interregnum—until, under pressure of events, the double disgruntlement of 1948 exploded in the convulsions of 1968. The Southern civil rights movement, moving north, cost the party much white support. As big business's covenant with big labor hollowed out, the cities were left to decay, crime ballooned, whites fled, and moral entrepreneurs of a neoconservative bent identified crime with "black power." The white working and middle classes were shoved out of their place in the sun. Where was their government? Fighting in Vietnam, and quagmired at that. What good were the experts, the McNamaras and the Bundys, the men whom David Halberstam was to dub "the best and the brightest"? At what were they really expert?

After 1932, the New Deal–New Frontier power constellation ruled America for more than thirty-five years, virtually two generations. It was, as W. H. Auden wrote about Freud, "a whole climate of opinion"—and like many such climates, it felt like nature itself: inevitable. But it would be a distortion of history to claim that the Democratic climate dissipated from natural decay. Movements brought it down.

To simplify a complicated history, the New Left of the sixties was a movement uprising that took off from a party foundation—presupposed it, took it for granted, defied it, revolted against it in style and substance, and finally, willy-nilly, in the grip of a historical irony it did not anticipate, helped to explode it. The movement took for granted a full-bodied Democratic Party in power, administering a half-achieved welfare state, buttressed by trade unions and urban machines, established, operational, and compromised, but in principle and in practice flexible enough to accommodate radicals.

To the eager young organizers of the New Left, of whom I was one, the liberal-labor establishment felt like a fait accompli, a fixture of American life—worthy of respect and appreciation, up to a point, but fossilized, stuck, arrogant, cowardly, badly in need of renewal, perhaps even supersession. From inside, however, the liberal-labor establishment didn't feel like an establishment; it felt divided and embattled. True, the liberals' largest single population, organized labor, continued to grow. Between 1955 and 1965, the AFL-CIO added 297,000 members, to reach 12,919,000.[10] But most of labor wasn't so liberal, and labor's liberals, led by Walter Reuther's United Automobile Workers, were as mindful of their failures as much as their wins. Liberal members of Congress often felt outnumbered and outmaneuvered by the Dixiecrat-Republican alliance.

Little of the liberal-labor reform program was taken seriously by the Democratic leadership in Congress or by John F. Kennedy's White House. Certain fighting labor liberals such as Walter Reuther had been on the outs with the middle-class darling Adlai Stevenson, and despite their fervent support for Kennedy in the 1960 campaign, they were decidedly frustrated junior partners during the New Frontier. They well knew that the young—even young workers—lacked the passion and élan of the old-timers.[11] (Fearing that they would become marooned in history, the aging leadership of the UAW helped to finance the young activists of Students for a Democratic Society [SDS].)[12] Embattled on many fronts, labor's liberal warhorses saw themselves as combatants stymied by status-quo interest-group accommodationists, such as AFL-CIO boss George Meany, and hard-pressed to win even meager victories from reactionaries in business and government.

At the New Left's beginning, for all its pride in distinguishing itself from the liberal establishment, movement-party cooperation was not so unusual. Civil rights movement figures, including Martin Luther King Jr., maintained cordial—if strained—relations with Democratic officials up to and including the president. The civil rights movement was justifiably enraged at the Dixiecrats who ruled the South, but as late as 1963 the major groups, including the radical Student Nonviolent Coordinating Committee (SNCC), cooperated, if tensely, with liberals in and near the Kennedy administration who were channeling antiracist energies into voter registration, which would ultimately benefit the Democrats. SDS in its early years declared itself an alliance of "liberals and radicals." The New York City wing of early SDS grew out of reform Democratic clubs that were committed to the project of "realigning" the Democrats into a liberal party, while Republicans and Dixiecrats would fuse into a conservative party (ultimately, this would turn out to be a case of the curse of getting what you wish for), and for all the utopianism of SDS's Port Huron Statement, the document also endorsed realignment. During August of the years 1961, 1962, and 1963, SDS amicably collaborated with the campus branch of Americans for Democratic Action, the liberal lobby founded as an alternative to fellow-traveling "progressives" in 1947, in a "Liberal Study Project" encamped at the annual meeting of the National Student Association to lobby student government representatives in behalf of civil rights and a left-liberal foreign policy.

But SDS followed SNCC into a more radical disaffection. As the movement mushroomed, New Left energies disrupted the party's accommodations with the status quo. At the 1964 party convention in Atlantic City, the SNCC-organized Mississippi Freedom Democrats claimed to be the legitimate Democrats. When party liberals worked out a compromise that postponed absolute triumph for four years while granting a symbolic victory in the here and now, radicals thought the postponement an insult and the symbolic victory mere tokenism. Relations between the New Left's transformative spirit and the party's managerial liberalism degenerated from mutual suspicion, an intimacy of a sort, into radical rupture.[13] The movement and the party separated, then divorced. Watts rioted. SNCC expelled whites and launched a "Black Power" campaign. These events contributed to the rupture, but nothing contributed so much—and so irreversibly—as Lyndon Johnson's fateful escalation of the Vietnam War from 1965 onward. In the heart of the New Left, coalition with liberals came to look (in Staughton Lynd's words) like "coalition with the Marines."[14] In action as well as in words, radicals posed a pointed question: "If the Democratic Party can wage genocidal war in Vietnam, what difference [does] it make" whether Democrats or Republicans were in charge?[15]

Johnson's 1964 landslide victory over Barry Goldwater seemed to confirm the radicals' notion that American conservatives were no more than a spent force. Establishment liberals felt more like a hindrance than a precondition for radical success. During the mid-sixties, the years of its radicalization, the New Left rarely paused to realize that it depended on Democratic power and that this power might be shaky. New Leftists would have bridled at the thought that they *were* dependent on precisely the precondition that they were rebelling against. Over the next years, with Johnson ever more devoted to the evidently illiberal Vietnam war, rebellion was more compelling than indebtedness. Why *shouldn't* the New Left feel increasingly cavalier about the rickety condition of the machine? What would be so terrible if it fell apart?

In 1964 and 1965, young radicals were being terrorized, even murdered, in their nonviolent fight against white supremacy in Mississippi and throughout the Deep—and *Democratic*—South.

In 1966, the civil rights movement was marching against segregation in the North—which meant confronting such urban Democratic machines as Mayor Daley's in Chicago. The movement already distrusted the corrupt and racist machine Democrats. Now Daley's white working-class base mobilized against Martin Luther King, who was leading demonstrations for open housing. SDS community organizers in Chicago were battered, harassed, raided, and arrested on phony charges by Daley's police, then convicted in his courts.[16] Soon the police were cracking down on peaceful antiwar demonstrations. Polarization deepened—to the breaking point. And now, tensions in style heightened tensions in politics. Long hair, psychedelic drugs, and let-it-all-hang-out manners collided with short hair, alcohol, and the well-scrubbed look. For both sides, everything seemed to be at stake at once— ideals, styles, strategies, even identities. In this hallucinatory setting, culture looked like class, class looked like culture. The machine mobilized against the movement, the movement mobilized against the machine, and the middle ground dissolved.

The Democratic Party came unstuck. It couldn't straddle. The new civil rights laws, liberalism's huge achievement, cost the party its Dixiecrats. Johnson, to his everlasting credit, came around to promoting a wholehearted expansion of civil rights in the knowledge that the South would be lost for a generation—while his Vietnam War appalled the left. In politics as in the rest of life, timing counts, but during 1965, 1966, and 1967, when Johnson was escalating the war, Democrats turning against the war couldn't turn against it fast enough to keep pace with the estrangement of the burgeoning antiwar movement. By 1968, even Mayor Daley opposed the Vietnam War, but that was only in camera, in whispers to the enfeebled President Johnson. It didn't become public knowledge for years.

Here was one of those junctures when individuals can change history if everything goes well. In 1968, Robert F. Kennedy just might have had the mystique to hold together a bare party majority—a cross-class, black-white-Hispanic, liberal-radical fusion that once in power and out of Vietnam might have cemented a new vital center. That is a long chain of "might's," and the counterfactual is unknowable. In the event, with Kennedy cut down in mid-campaign, the party was hopeless at amalgamating old and new politics—cut to footage of Mayor Daley's gleeful cops smashing away at long-haired demonstrators in the streets of Chicago in August 1968. In November of that year, with the last-resort standard-bearer Hubert Humphrey wriggling frantically, unable to break definitively from the Vietnam War, much of the party left sat out the election and much of the party right deserted for George Wallace or Richard Nixon, leaving the Democrats to be crushed by the law-and-order alliance of old Republicans and resentful white supremacists.

In short, as the Democratic alliance cracked up, its rebellious energies spun wildly away in centrifugal motion, each break-away side seized by moral indignation and therefore not so easily placated as merely aggrieved interests would be—the left-and-countercultural wing of the party, personified by Eugene McCarthy, seceding mainly in horror at the Vietnam War, and the right-and-traditionalist wing, personified by George Wallace, seceding mainly in horror at civil rights. What remained in the feeble crusade of Hubert Humphrey and, four years later, Edmund Muskie was the party's aging, labor-based core built on a shrinking base, its confidence eroding, its whites evacuating, its leaders discredited.[17]

The party's decomposition had many causes, but central to the process was a resounding loss of faith in the national government. For thirty years and more, Democrats had looked to Washington, D.C., and seen there the indispensable resource for the common good—Social Security, military might, economic growth, whatever the moment required. The government not only *meant* well, but it *did* well, thanks to its ability to mobilize experts. The participants in the upheavals of the sixties were, in fact, shatterers of that faith. They thought that where it counted, the national government had become grotesque, inept, somehow *alien*, and *needed* shattering. The experts, in their eyes, might even be sinister—heavy-handed when they promoted high-rise slabs of "projects" as urban renewal, callous when they imposed Kafkaesque rules on welfare recipients, even murderous when they went to war. When New Politics

Democrats looked at the federal government, they saw crackpot anticommunists who knew no better approach to an unruly world than napalm pouring down from the bomb bays. When Wallace Democrats looked at the federal government, they saw uppity black people egged on by "pointy-headed bureaucrats" into forced integration. When the anti-Washington rhetoric grabbed them, they were no longer impressed by the impressive material benefits, the rural electrification, government dams, and cheap water that had rained down on their congressional districts. Now there was no center to hold. In the 1968 election, not only did the Democrats lose all but one state from the old Confederacy (five went to Wallace, the rest to Nixon), but even while winning the labor stronghold of Michigan, they lost half the voters in Michigan counties where the United Auto Workers, the quintessence of working-class liberalism, had long prevailed.[18]

Two successive conquests by Richard Nixon, the second a forty-nine-state landslide, no less, signaled that the New Deal faith had withered into nostalgia. The Republicans were in the process of annexing the Wallace Democrats—in fact, the entire region where they were based. The Democrats' cross-class, cross-race, cross-regional, cross-generational unity was smashed. The party was in chaos. In the wake of Humphrey's defeat, the custodians of the old party were dethroned by the angry, aroused late-sixties movements—blacks, feminists, anti-imperialist radicals—or, if not by the movements as a whole, many of which were slow to relinquish revolutionary illusions, then by the reform edges of those movements, activists who had decided that there was some payoff in becoming insiders.

Cut loose from a party that had by now, in effect, lost its disciplinary force, the New Left had itself imploded. Many of its veterans retreated from politics altogether in favor of religious pursuits, professional training, the communal life, and whatnot. The militant fringes hastened after various revolutionary fantasies. Without any anchorage, they were left standing in air, that is, nowhere at all. Most of the rest broke into distinct identity blocs—women, African American, Hispanic, and others. The identity blocs deployed their own range of strategies, some motivated by an enthusiasm for radical reconstruction, others by practical politics. To describe their own comparable polarity, the German Greens usefully distinguished between *fundis*, or fundamentalists—purists, in other words—and *realos*, or realists. Some American realos entered into local and state politics, won elections, and tried to build machines of their own. Sometimes they succeeded.

The Democrats reformed themselves. Primaries proliferated, bosses were deposed, smoke-filled rooms emptied out. Indeed, the movements could move into the party because the old party was a shell of its former self. The Vietnam debacle had tipped the Democrats into the hands of George McGovern, who succeeded in changing the party far more than he succeeded in impressing the electorate. The party reforms over which McGovern presided toppled the largely Catholic white ethnics, labor, elected officials, and urban machines that had dominated the northern wing of the Democrats for some forty years, smashing their lock on nominating power, empowering activists with added primaries, and granting delegate seats to women and minorities.[19] Down with Mayor Daley, up with the Reverend Jesse Jackson! The symbolism was stark. The sixties revolt of movements against the establishment raged on, this time directly inside the party itself. Post-sixties activists reemerged as "progressives."

As the dust settled, the activist-reformists found themselves not in the Age of Aquarius but in the Age of Nixon and Agnew. What were they to do? One reasonably practical course presented itself: as the Democrats crawled out from under the colossus (and the equally colossal errors) of Lyndon Johnson, the insurgents found room to move and shake in the party—racial minorities, feminists, environmentalists, gays, all of them eager to make the case that they were the true reincarnations, the postmodern-day extensions of their parents' liberalism. So, disciplined by events, political amateurs turned pro and outsiders reinvented themselves as insiders. They were tamed now, shrewder, and more reformist, and proud of it.

Under the leadership of these children of Betty Friedan, Gene McCarthy, Bobby Kennedy, and Ralph Nader, the sixties movements evolved in the course of the seventies (devolved, in the eyes of the old party establishment) into insurgent groups, each with its own issue turf, its own legend and lineage, its round table of knights, its friends in high places, its bone to pick with the lackluster Jimmy Carter. They were a modest counterestablishment of interest-and-identity groups. With every passing year they were less infused with the militant temper of a moment that was already rapidly receding into an irrecoverable past, a moment when it had felt to millions of not self-evidently self-delusional radicals that some sort of revolution to roll back centuries or millennia of error and wickedness was not only desirable but actually under way.

Even white male veterans of the New Left, ill at ease in the new organizational dispensation, found places for themselves in the new, or no-longer-exactly-old, Democratic Party. In local and state-wide campaigns, some electoral, some more like lobbies, working with women, they would be the craftsmen of broad political coalitions. They thought they could cross class lines in behalf of populist reforms, and at times they succeeded. They flourished in strongholds such as California, Massachusetts, Connecticut, and New York and in college towns like Berkeley, Madison, and Ithaca. Some of their projects lasted into the eighties and the nineties: Citizen Action (later, USAction) in many states; Tom Hayden and Jane Fonda's Campaign for Economic Democracy in California; Massachusetts Fair Share; and Connecticut's Legislative Electoral Action Program, among others, building little machines of their own, sometimes with union support, hoping to create cross-race, economics-minded, election-contesting alliances. Outside the party, ACORN, the Industrial Areas Foundation, and other such groups worked to organize the poor, with benefits that would eventually accrue to the Democrats even if the organizers themselves were formally nonpartisan. A loose national association for state and local legislators focused movement energies on practical policies.

The party had no choice but to make a place for these insurgencies. They were rambunctious, increasingly well organized, and convinced that they were the future. Without them, the party would have hollowed itself out, for labor, the remaining core of New Deal politics, was shriveling. While AFL-CIO membership continued to rise until the mid-seventies (to 14,070,000 in 1975), the additions came from the ranks of government workers, whose numbers would soon crest, and the aggregate soon began to sink—to 13,109,000 in 1985.[20] As a percentage of the workforce, union "density" was on its long way down.

The new party groups had loyalists to mobilize, passion in abundance, money to spend, even an impulse to federate. During the Carter years, these post-sixties groups tried to form a more or less coherent bloc, a Progressive Alliance against the "misuse of corporate power" that in the words of the historian Kevin Boyle embraced "over one hundred labor, civil rights, feminist, environmental, and other progressive organizations that by then enjoyed powerful positions in the Democratic Party's decision-making process."[21] In truth, while they were clear about their shared enemy, big business, the ideals they affirmed—industrial policy, national health insurance—had only diffuse public support, if that.

And if their alliance was so diffuse as to be incoherent, the same could be said of Jimmy Carter's administration itself. The U.S. government had been defeated in war, its criminal president deposed, American uplift was wearing thin, and the country quivered with a rising unease.[22] The Democrats' old bedrock principles—containment, growth, an expanding welfare state—felt slack, and new principles were slow in emerging. In the precincts of left and center alike, Democrats looked like quilters of scraps, not weavers of principle. Carter's speechwriter, James Fallows, wrote tellingly about Carter as a "passionless president," a well-meaning, small-town man whose ambition at a propitious moment carried him to the big city but then found himself at a loss for a big idea: "Carter thinks in lists, not arguments; as long as items are there, their order does not matter, nor does the hierarchy among them."[23] Michael Waldman, later Bill Clinton's chief speechwriter, called Carter "an anti-president."[24]

Carter struggled to stave off his enemies as they arose, but they multiplied and took the initiative, and he was repeatedly blindsided. As a candidate, he promoted his character as his credential, but in office he seemed a creature of accidents, at a loss for a grand design or even a label to encompass a national goal for an off-balance country that after assassinations, riots, war, and impeachment craved normalcy but was denied it. Perhaps most disconcerting of all to the public, Carter was beset by rampant and unprecedented stagflation—a neologism had to be coined to describe the mysterious outbreak of inflation and unemployment simultaneously, something that the going economic theory (and the going economic theorists) said should not be happening. *Stagflation*: this ugly term seemed to demonstrate that Democrats, supposedly the party of reason, no longer knew how to manage what they were supposed to be good at managing—the economy.

In 1980, the progressives rallied behind a challenge to Jimmy Carter from the liberal hero Ted Kennedy, but it proved toothless. It was a better time to crusade against government than for it. As Ronald Reagan gained strength with his restorationist alliance of pro-business and religious conservatives, the Democrats could not stanch the white, male flow. As Republicans thundered rightward and the Democrats floundered, making laundry lists of issues rather than stating clear values or issuing general calls for renewal, an independent candidacy developed in 1980 for the liberal Republican John Anderson, and the left formed a Citizens Party to run the environmentalist Barry Commoner, but both lacked popular bases and failed to arrest the Democrats' decline.

In new circumstances, intellect did not help. During the seventies, the progressives' claim that government knew how to fuse mind with power to make life better lost its hold. Nationalist fervor and tax revolt looked like sure bets. Washington bureaucrats were too smart for their own good and dreamed up the Vietnam War: a disaster. Local bureaucrats were too smart for their own good and dreamed up busing: another disaster. Government was at least supposed to know how to run the economy and the larger world, but then came the oil embargo and stagflation: more disasters. In a majority of American minds, things didn't look right in the federal government. While Jimmy Carter was president, the percentage of Americans who said they could trust the government in Washington "just about always" or "most of the time" fell from 41 to 25 percent.[25] (In the far-gone mid-sixties, before the Vietnam escalation and everything that went with it, almost three-quarters had thought Washington trustworthy.[26]) The zeitgeist wasn't on the side of experts in general or their stock-in-trade, expertise. Instead, it was time for a politics of resentment mingled with reassurance, of piety mingled with cowpoke myth, delivered flawlessly in a husky voice by a man who had been warning for years that government was a jackbooted army stomping on freedom.

In sum, the reeling Democrats in the seventies had fallen out of love with power, while liberal-left movements, suspicious of power in the first place, interpreted the New Left ideal of participatory democracy as a trumpet call to go local and launch community organizations. While right-wing foundations were endowing think tanks, promoting books, and founding campus newspapers, aiming to conquer the nation by channeling ideas from the top down, liberal foundations poured money into grassroots groups, aiming to defend the powerless, piecemeal, against overwhelming odds. Despite the Democrats' ability to win the national election in 1976 in the wake of Watergate, the battle was ill-matched.

Some veterans of the New Left got the message: build infra-structure and evolve into a political machine. Community activists felt largely indifferent to Jimmy Carter, but Reagan's victory in 1980 concentrated their minds about the value of political power, convincing them that if they remained outsiders they would be consigned to the margins, and that from here on out they had better take electoral politics seriously—which meant, like it or not, the Democratic Party. The Connecticut Citizen Action Group (CCAG), for example, "spent years worth of angst-ridden discus-sions about whether we should get involved in electoral politics," the group's former director, Miles Rapoport, and a veteran of Harvard SDS, told me, "the two arguments being one, that if we don't, we're fighting with one hand tied behind our back, or two, it is inherently a compromising playing field, we will lose the edge and start to become indistinguishable from the Democratic Party." Rapoport was among those who thought "we need to be serious about power," which entailed electoral politics. In the early eighties,

> We . . . formed an organization called LEAP, which was the Legislative Electoral Action Program . . . a coalition of CCAG and some environmental groups and some women's groups and some of the progressive unions in the state, deciding to run people for office, run our own for office wherever possible, that was sort of our theory, take activists from organizations and encourage them to run.

Rapoport himself served five terms in the Connecticut legislature and one as secretary of state.

Such activists were Democrats of convenience, at first. Running for local and statewide office, their hearts did not belong to the party. They were people of causes, issue people. In Connecticut, for example, they fought budget cuts. They were pro-choice. They campaigned for an income tax. (After a fifteen-year campaign, thanks also to a severe fiscal crisis and a plucky independent governor, Lowell Weicker, they succeeded in passing a progressive income tax, and withstood a backlash at the ballot box.)[27] "Part of our theory was that the Democratic Party was firmly ensconced in conservative hack hands . . . a pretty tightly knit group [that] needed to be fought," Rapoport said. Although Connecticut was known for having a "strong party structure," it was essentially "an aggregation of individual politicians' fiefdoms," Rapoport said. "It was certainly not a source of ideology, not a source of creative thinking about bills. It was an administrative apparatus and a fund-raising apparatus." Between campaigns, there was not much of a party at all—only local committees composed mainly of "apparatchiks" whose jobs came through patronage. Within a few years, the progressive caucus numbered close to a majority of the Connecticut House Democrats.[28]

Such victories were tantalizing—largely in states that tilted Democratic. But overall, the Democrats' chaos did not diminish.

They lurched from one crisis to another. Over the quarter century starting with Ronald Reagan's run against Jimmy Carter, the fragments wobbled, scattered, contended, regrouped, and degrouped in a fruitless search for a new coalescence—a theme for the pudding. Democrats intuited that they needed to rule from a revitalized center but had no idea where to position it. Unreconstructed New Dealers and chastened New Leftists, Populists, Atari Democrats, and assorted other bearers of New Ideas came and went. None of them, it is fair to say, set out a stirring, comprehensive idea of what the national government was for. They liked the *idea* of a center to rule from but couldn't find it.

Meanwhile, Reagan's Republicans had an answer to the questions that had been growing more urgent during the long years of social and economic crisis: What was the government *for*? What did it know how to do? Reagan could declare confidently that government was not the solution, it was the problem, but liberals were queasy about any equivalent declaration in favor of government. Which parts of government? Performing which tasks? Liberals no longer had the momentum, no longer carried conviction when they declared themselves in favor of tried, tested government—an apparently *permanent* government made up of faceless bureaucrats stacked up in huge, faceless Washington buildings; *old* government. They sounded old, even though Walter Mondale was seventeen years Reagan's junior.

Liberals were mindful that government, the noble vessel of reform that they rode throughout the twentieth century as Progressives, New Dealers, and Great Society partisans, was losing its nobility where it counted—in public. Trust in government "to do the right thing," which had plummeted with Vietnam and Watergate, bounced around under Carter only to sink again under Reagan, with the portion of the public saying that they "just about always" or "most of the time" trusted Washington sinking from 50 percent in June 1983 into the low 40s in 1986–1987 and continuing to slump during George H. W. Bush's term, down to a low of 20 percent in March 1992.[29] In April 1986, a *Time* poll asked the trust-government question of thirty- to forty-year-olds this way: "Compared to your views in the 1960s and early 1970s, do you feel you are more likely now to trust government to do what is right or are you less likely to trust government?" Thirty-eight percent answered "more likely" and 53 percent "less likely." (Five percent volunteered "the same.")[30] No matter that programs like Social Security and Medicare remained popular. Government as a whole had the reputation of a steam locomotive in an age of jet planes.

Democrats presuming to govern in these circumstances would have to affirm that they could make government safe—that they were the center.

9

An Unlikely Steward: Bill Clinton and Liberalism in the Nineties

Enter Bill Clinton, confounder of stereotypes, crosser of lines—a very intelligent man who was not haughty, an accomplished politician who was not without passion but (or therefore) delivered results, a Southerner who won Northern hearts, a man of Northern education who won Southern hearts, a ladies' man who could hang with the guys, a believer in government who knew why people mistrusted government and took it as his mission to restore their trust, a man for all constituencies. To make a political career in Arkansas and then go national, in fact, he had to be exactly that, because the Democratic Party was well along in the process of transmutation into a fundamentally divided party, a party deeply cleft by an economic and cultural wedge that first showed up in the sixties. Close to 40 percent of Democratic voters were drawn from the professions, with the remaining 60 percent drawn from among the less solvent, the blue collar, and the darker-skinned.[1] To speak to (let alone for) this 40–60 mélange of a party, Clinton talked about a new politics. You might laud or revile him for his flexibility; exalt him as a master of new politics and an overcomer of stale polarities, or despise him as a master trickster, an illusionist and a waffler. On this score, journalistic fashion itself waffled. But whether you admired or suspected Clinton's amalgam, or hedge, or whatever it was, you had some trouble grasping it, naming it, stating it ringingly.

Simply to win nomination in the first place, Clinton had to be dexterous and original—a man for all wings of his party. Even his enemies had to admit that he had *the knack*—that was the "slickness" his enemies loathed and his friends, with a wink and a nod, relished. To make a Democratic career in Arkansas politics at a time when the Republicans' Southern strategy was kicking in and whites were deserting the party in droves, Clinton had to escape the confines of antiwar politics and the 1972 McGovern campaign. Married to a powerhouse of a woman who insisted on keeping her maiden name, he had to prove he was still a good old boy. He did so, riling corporate timber and trucking interests during his first two-year term as governor, but he also offended his base with an unpopular auto license tax that he stumbled into in an inept attempt at compromise with irate truckers.[2] The young governor in a hurry, he had tried to do everything at once, at the cost of political finesse.[3] At thirty-four, in 1980, he was defeated.

Defeat concentrated his mind on relocating closer to the political center. From then on, he would pick his policy priorities in such a way as to impress political majorities. As he ran again in 1982, his wife would for the first time call herself Hillary Rodham Clinton, or Mrs. Bill Clinton.[4] "If I hadn't been defeated," he wrote in his memoir, "I probably never would have become President. It was a near-death experience, but an invaluable one, forcing me to be more sensitive to the political problems inherent in progressive politics: the system can absorb only so much change at once; no one can beat all the entrenched interests at the same time; and if people think you've stopped listening, you're sunk."[5] *The political problems inherent in progressive politics*: to radical idealists, them's fighting words.

Accordingly, as Clinton made his move into national politics, liberals sniffed—and Clinton seemed not to mind. In the great game of the pursuit of political power, what did they bring to the table anyway? While liberals were awaiting rescue out of some reincarnation of their golden past, the other side of the party, in some mixture of confidence and desperation, was getting itself together. In 1990, Clinton was successfully courted to become chairman of the largely Southern-based Democratic Leadership Council (DLC), "undoubtedly," in the words of its semiofficial historian, for what it "could do for his national aspirations."[6] There was everything practical and nothing airy about the help the DLC apparatus could offer an ambitious, talented young politician: the DLC put at Clinton's disposal "an ongoing Washington operation, staff backup, funding for travel, substantive support on issues development . . . and unlimited opportunities to get national press attention."[7] When Clinton formally announced his candidacy for the White House, he availed himself of one of the DLC leaders to help him write the words "the change we must make isn't liberal or conservative. It's both and it's different." Borrowing phrases from the DLC, he spoke the words *middle class* thirteen times, *responsibility* twelve times, and *opportunity* ten times.[8]

The change we must make isn't liberal or conservative. It's both and it's different. No wonder Clinton was not the first choice of movement liberals—the silver-tongued Mario Cuomo was, or Jesse Jackson, the voice of post-sixties interest-group liberalism. Neither of these liberal worthies would have taken time off from campaigning in January to rush back to Arkansas to see that the life of a brain-damaged murderer on death row was extinguished. (On coming to the end of his last meal, this man, Ricky Ray Rector, who had shot himself in the head after murdering two people in a convenience store, asked that his pie be put aside until later.) Liberals were never easily reconciled to the reality that Clinton, who believed deeply that there was no substitute for victory, held some views that were repugnant to them—or, as he would have preferred to put it, that he was his own man and not their wholly owned subsidiary. But Cuomo and Jackson declined to run against George H. W. Bush, leaving unreconstructed liberals with no alternatives but the unpromising populist Tom Harkin of Iowa and Jerry Brown, the human kaleidoscope. Labor doubted Clinton: was he not the governor of a right-to-work state where union representation was near bottom among American states? Did he not support NAFTA, which they viewed as draining away American jobs? Was he not dependent on DLC-based Wall Street money and committed to free trade and fiscal discipline?[9] Congressional liberals saw him as a DLC man, indifferent to their core constituencies, and indeed, the DLC was where his early congressional backers came from—though the organization's leadership not infrequently doubted whether he was reliably theirs.[10] But for his part, while availing himself of many talented people in the DLC orbit, Clinton discouraged the DLC from launching all-out war on party liberals. Clinton's liberal supporters—like the journalist Sidney Blumenthal—admired his "ideological deftness" and took him at his word when he said, "I got all sorts of grief about my involvement in the DLC. But I never would have gotten involved if it was going to push the country to the right."[11] Clinton himself worked to square the circle, declaring at one New Hampshire campaign event that he was "trying to be . . . a middle-class moderate offering radical change."[12]

"Reaganism was about the end of policy," Blumenthal wrote early in the 1992 campaign. "The intent was to immobilize government, leaving the action to the private sector. Clinton is about the renaissance of policy"—reinventing government, in a phrase he borrowed from an adviser.[13] Playing to both sides of the Democrats' 40–60 split, Clinton convinced educated voters that he was serious about training the mind and retraining the worker—education for competitiveness. He convinced the victims of globalization that he "put people first." Government would be leaner, meaner, cleaner—more effective—because he would move beyond "the brain-dead policies of both parties."[14]

Such squaring of the circle was Clinton's gambit for success, first in the Democratic primaries and then in the general election, where thanks to Ross Perot's quixotic candidacy Clinton won all of 43 percent of the national vote. In the meantime, the Democrats lost nine seats in the House while standing pat in the Senate. These raw facts probably suffice to explain why Clinton's was an uphill presidency, a flawed and thwarted attempt at progressive achievements during an inauspicious time—inauspicious because the right controlled the national agenda, because Clinton's hold on the Democrats in Congress was tenuous and brief, because his promises (of a middle-class tax cut, above all) fell afoul of the pile-up of Reagan-Bush I budget deficits, and because the ballot results were profoundly ambiguous.[15] Each segment of a fractious party could legitimately claim some credit for Clinton's victory. Each over-claimed, and none was in a compromising mood. Each demanded payoff for its contribution. Half rewarded, half spurned, each faction felt the spurning more acutely.

Clinton did enjoy a few heady moments in the esteem of his party's left wing. There was a surge of liberal rapture when Bill Clinton won the election—and who, at first, wanted to dwell on his 43 percent of the vote? Wishfulness ballooned. I remember a party of left-liberal journalists in New York, early on election night of 1992, almost all of us wildly overestimating the number of Senate seats that the Democrats would pick up—after twelve years of Republicans in the White House, surely it was *our* turn for a landslide. In San Francisco, a street party of thousands erupted on Castro Street, America's gay capital, blocking off traffic as (in the words of a reporter)

> the crowd moved to pounding disco and house music blaring from eight giant speakers on a flatbed truck. . . . The crowd roared when Clinton mentioned AIDS first in his victory speech, saying it was among the most pressing problems facing the country. San Francisco Supervisor [and leading lesbian activist] Roberta Achtenberg, speaking to the crowd by telephone from Clinton's national headquarters in Little Rock, said: "I know that he knows what we've done for him in San Francisco." Achtenberg told the crowd that the new president will "pay back" the overwhelming support he received in San Francisco.[16]

Activists who had been exiled from power for a decade or more quickly made plans to attend the inauguration balls, where the anthems ranged from Fleetwood Mac's bubblegum "Don't Stop (Thinking about Tomorrow)" to Leonard Cohen's luminous and grave "Democracy Is Coming to the U.S.A."

But it was as if Clinton were being stalked on his honeymoon. He began his first term saddled with a sixties reputation, and for his legions of enemies, this was enough to justify an assault on his character. Already in May 1993 I came across a calendar called "365 Reasons to Hate Bill Clinton," on sale in right-wing book-shops. Clinton had moved into the White House a bare four months earlier. Stumbling through his early White House months, he had proposed few laws and signed fewer. At that moment, Monica Lewinsky was a nineteen-year-old college student in Oregon, Kenneth W. Starr a corporate lawyer dabbling in conservative political campaigns. Vince Foster, the White House deputy counsel and Hillary Clinton's former Little Rock law partner, was still alive, though depressed, having been flayed by the *Wall Street Journal* for unspecified corruption, so there could not yet be any question of blaming the Clintons for driving him to suicide or actually sub-orning his murder, ostensibly because Foster knew where some documents or—who knows?—bodies were buried. Yet someone had already divined 365 reasons to *hate* the man already known (in the words of a bumper sticker) as CLINTON—COWARD, LIAR, SOCIALIST.

The claim that the scandals caused the hatred runs afoul of the inconvenient fact that the hatred preceded most of the scandals. True, the Whitewater affair, a barely penetrable story of a bad real estate partnership involving the governor, the governor's wife, and a fast-talking investor, had cropped up, though no criminal charges ever materialized. "Travelgate," "Filegate"—right-wing labels for accusations of petty White House malfeasance—were barely known and unknown, respectively.

No matter. Other minuscule charges followed, and so did con-gressional hearings keeping them in the news. A far-right smear machine was hard at work, insisting that Bill Clinton was, if not the literal Antichrist, a close approximation: perjurious, adulterous Slick Willie, admitted draft dodger and reputedly serial womanizer who had taken part in anti-Vietnam war demos in England, traveled to Moscow, and married a card-carrying feminist who was the first professional woman to take up First Ladyship in the White House. Clinton was, in their eyes, the sixties incarnate. Worse, he also knew how to play politics—he reveled in schmooz-ing but also in policy details—and he had the knack of bouncing back. It wasn't bad enough that he was personable, or that he promised to baste together the left and the center of the Democratic Party—he won elections (five out of seven in Arkansas, including his last four in a row). The hard right viewed such successes as infringements upon their God-given prerogatives.

Back home in Arkansas, unreconstructed racists had long been retailing horror stories about Clinton, who got on with black people, but nationally the demonizing frenzy began while he was barely into his 1992 campaign against the senior George Bush, and it never let up.[17] Scandal sheets munificently funded by Clinton-hating fat cats scared up every imaginable charge (and some unimaginable ones) to the effect that Clinton was not only the longtime lover of the lounge singer Gennifer Flowers but a drug-smuggler, a serial adulterer, a rapist, the father of a black baby, and so on. These were not drive-by insults spattered at random. "The attacks on Clinton," observed the *New York Daily News*'s Lars-Erik Nelson early in the 1992 campaign, "have been peddled first and foremost by the *Star* tabloid, the *Boston Herald*, the *New York Post*, the TV show 'A Current Affair,' and the Fox television network," which "have in common [that] they are all either owned or formerly owned—and all are currently staffed by long-time associates of—Rupert Murdoch, the one-time Australian who delights in his ability to destroy political candidates on three continents."[18]

One month later, the *New York Times* jumped in with a front-page story implying a sleazy relationship between the governor and a man whose savings and loan association, founded years later (a fact that the *Times* headline obscured), was subject to state regulation. Whitewater allegations, implications, and offshoots cascaded through the respectable news for years, promoted by Clinton-hating Republicans. Congressional investigations ensued. Special prosecutors vetted by Republican judges proceeded to prosecute anyone they thought to prosecute, remote as he or she might be from any particular knowledge of Ozark real estate. Jim McDougal, the Clintons' business partner, was a half-demented alcoholic who kept changing his story, and it didn't seem to matter. When the relevant federal agency cleared the Clintons in 1995, major news organizations (including the *New York Times*) could barely be troubled to notice. After years of grand juries and headlines, no one was ever convicted of any charge related to the Clintons' failed investment in Ozark real estate—unless we count Jim McDougal's hapless ex-wife Susan McDougal, who, reasonably suspecting a perjury trap, refused to answer a Starr grand jury's Whitewater questions and was jailed for contempt of court for eighteen months. As Clinton's later special assistant Sidney Blumenthal wrote without exaggeration, "never before had a sitting president been so assiduously investigated about a matter that had occurred before his election."[19]

In this inauspicious climate, through a combination of Arkansas naïveté (or ineptitude), fierce attacks from the right, and a mainstream press ready to pounce, it is not surprising that Clinton quickly lost the initiative—during his first week in office, in fact, with the Zoë Baird nanny scandal, gays in the military, and the barest possible congressional victory for his budget. Unruly events and minuscule scandals mastered him. On gays, on health care, on welfare, on NAFTA, Clinton was damned when he did and damned when he didn't. Under unrelenting pressure and lacking a clear mandate, smacked around in the headlines, Clinton sometimes doubted whether there was a point to all his tacking—whether he was tacking toward any political pole at all. Fewer than three months into his first term, according to his assistant, George Stephanopoulos, Clinton felt adrift, telling his staff one day, "[W]e are making incremental, day-to-day decisions because we don't have a core vision."[20]

A generous case for Clinton as practical liberal can still be made—indeed, it seems to be the case Clinton sometimes made for himself, or at least implied when speaking to a liberal aide. On the subject of campaign finance reform, for example, during the run-up to the 1996 election, Michael Waldman recalls Clinton sounding off against "these reformers" who "think that if you wave the wand you'll get reform. Look what happened with health care."[21] Clinton may well have thought that if he won the gratitude of business groups by giving them NAFTA, he would secure their support for a universal health-care plan that would please labor (among other party constituencies) and override party differences. Big business would join him (all but the insurance industry, which had a huge stake in the existing private-run patchwork) because it was alert to the increasing portion of its costs that was going for health care—not only for present employees but for retirees as well. This gambit of Clinton's, if it worked, would have a double payoff. It would deliver progressive reform for present-day Americans— and, if successful, would be a gift to the Democratic Party that would go on giving. It would solidify middle-class loyalty to the Democrats for a generation or more.

Health care was Clinton's big gamble, his make-or-break maneuver to recover the reputation of government, and thus of the Democratic Party. His attempt to build an automatic constituency for a massive government program stretching into the future was precisely what astute Republicans feared. Under George W. Bush, they would engender their own trademark program (the sort you would call "an entitlement program" if you didn't like it) in the hope that it would operate in exactly that fashion—the so-called faith-based initiative, which would work its way throughout domestic and foreign policy like a tapeworm.[22]

In 1993, Republicans were understandably leery of a grand-scale disbursement that the Democrats could use (making friends, influencing people, winning votes) as they had once used such programs as the National Youth Administration, the Civilian Conservation Corps, and Aid to Dependent Children. Precisely for this reason, William Kristol circulated a memo urging Republicans in Congress to oppose *any* health care reform.[23] The Republican Policy Committee's Eric Ueland said in 1994 that Democrats had "created a theology around health care that insists that St. Bill and St. Hillary will deliver to the middle class an entitlement from which the middle class will never be able to unwrap itself. And as a consequence, Democrats will be the governing majority in this country for generations to come."[24] The redoubtable power broker Grover Norquist and other conservatives were mindful of how popular the Clinton plan looked at the start. Norquist told a journalist, "Our fear was that if they got health care they would turn the United

States into a social democracy where a majority of people viewed the state as central to their lives the way they do in Europe. It would make more people dependent on government and the more people are dependent on government the more likely they are to be Democrats."[25]

As it turned out, Clinton had only two years to produce results with a Democratic Congress. His record did not win fanfares. His party, however Democratic, was not so friendly. The health insurance industry savaged his health-care proposal, and other business interests did not rise to its defense. The bitter truth—a truth so bitter, in fact, that not all liberals would cotton to it—was that well into the next decade, the deficits that Ronald Reagan had piled up, largely because of military expenditures that he was unwilling to pay for with a boost in income taxes, would severely hinder any substantial growth in domestic programs. Reagan's budget director, David Stockman, had acknowledged just this happy by-product of Reagan's tax cuts. As his amanuensis, William Greider, wrote, "[I]t put a tightening noose around the size of the government."[26] Reagan's revenge would weigh on a Democratic president as long as the deficits lasted—well into Clinton's second term.

Reagan's revenge worked. He would casually increase the government payroll without paying any price in conservative esteem. He could do it unexceptionally, by procuring missiles and fighter planes, and he could do it symbolically—firing the striking air traffic controllers was a good start—and perhaps most of all he could do it rhetorically by talking down government as he turned it to his uses. Reagan's terms were less colorful than the metaphor with which Norquist would later regale journalists on demand—"I don't want to abolish government. I simply want to reduce it to the size where I can drag it into the bathroom and drown it in the bathtub"[27]—but it came to the same thing.

So it was not altogether ironic when, early in his own first term, having found out that congressionally mandated spending caps would drastically truncate any new spending initiatives, Clinton was reduced to bellowing sarcastically to his staff: "We're all Eisenhower Republicans . . . and we are fighting the Reagan Republicans. We stand for lower deficits and free trade and the bond market. Isn't that great?"[28] A booby-trap had been left on his doorstep by Ronald Reagan.

Meanwhile, as liberals were in the process of trying to make up their minds just how happy or unhappy to be with Bill Clinton (and possibly Clinton himself was trying to make up his mind along with them), he was in the process of being defined to a larger public by those who had no doubt: they loathed him. On talk radio and in the bought-and-paid-for right-wing press—a right wing to which there was no symmetrical left—the Clintons were Enemies Number One and Two. Mainstream pundits relayed these charges with glee while dignifying them as "the character issue." Slash-and-burn criminalization and accusations of personal folly substituted for political argument. Mainstream media were quickly squinting at Clinton through jaundiced eyes.[29]

Quickly, much of the Democrats' left wing abandoned him, too. In the eyes of many liberals (and more radicals who were not yet ready to call themselves liberals, though it was hard for them to say just what they did want to call themselves), Clinton's reputation ran quickly downhill from the inauguration revels. Cries of sellout blared forth. The left railed against his failure to abolish discrimination against gays in the military. It railed against his successful campaign for NAFTA, his abandonment of the controversial Lani Guinier, and the ignominious failure of a health-care program that many thought barely adequate in the first place (for while conservative Democrats abandoned the principle of universality altogether, many liberals held firm for single-payer and gave Clinton no points for trying to tailor a universal program palatable to Congress). Once again, the left gave a Democrat no points for effort, no credit for decent intentions: power was proof of corruption.

I contributed a minor huzzah, writing a column chiding Clinton for the puniness of his "stimulus package," which I called "Stim-U-Pac." It was out of the ordinary, to say the least, when the left economist Richard Rothstein itemized Clinton's progressive achievements in the pages of the *American Prospect*, noting the stimulative value, as well as the justice, of Clinton's Earned Income Tax Credit,[30] and the left historians Maurice Isserman and Michael Kazin published an article called "As Bill Goes, So Do We" in the *Nation* (May 30, 1994). Isserman and Kazin noted that FDR would not have become the left's half-hero in the depths of the Great Depression if he had had to operate without a robust union movement pushing him to the left—and to contend with a hostile Congress to boot. They chided movement purists in these terms: "The literature and folklore of the left are full of warnings of the peril of cozying up to power. . . . But we're less alert to the equally insidious seduction of being permanent outsiders."[31] Many a *Nation* reader was scandalized.[32]

Then came the 1994 midterm elections. Gingrich's congressional revolution roared into Washington, stripping Clinton of any chance that he could foster any major liberal-thrilling reform. In shock at the magnitude of the Democrats' losses (fifty-four seats in the House, eight in the Senate, with the Democrats losing the House for the first time since the sixties and the Senate for the first time in eight years), Clinton made a beeline for the big picture. The Republicans' midterm upsurge must have amounted to more than a rejection of one administration plan in particular. Clinton saw the Republican sweep as a rebuke to activist government in general. He concluded—in the words of his chief speechwriter, Michael Waldman—that "he had underestimated the public's distrust of government." "By the end of 1994," Waldman wrote, "confidence in government had fallen in the Gallup poll to 15 percent, its lowest level in history." Clinton followed such polls—he inhaled every scrap of data he could. He had gambled that he could complete the New Deal with a universal health-care program that brought competition to managed care and would skirt the charge of Big Government, but his clumsy program, developed in secrecy and mocked as "Hillarycare," won no friends right or left, fell afoul of the health insurance industry's campaign to demonize national government anyway, and went down in flames. "The problem with the Clinton plan," Waldman concluded later, "was not that it was single-payer but that the public thought it was."[33]

There were, in fact, other reasons for the midterm debacle besides Clinton's overreaching on health care. An assault weapons ban cost the Democrats votes; so did tax increases; so did "don't ask, don't tell." Democrats were afflicted by an abundance of retirements, and by race-minded redistricting—a collaboration of right-wing Republicans and black Democrats—that concentrated Southern black voters in "majority-minority" districts and left white Democrats outnumbered by the GOP. Perhaps Clinton's 1992 victory only stalled the gathering Republican onslaught for a couple of years. Clinton himself seemed to think so. Licking his wounds after the midterm election, Clinton concluded ruefully (again according to Waldman), "It has been an anomaly in our country's history . . . that the public wanted a strong, semi-permanent governing class—a desire bred by the history of the Depression, world war, and Cold War." In ordinary times, he decided, Americans were too restive, too proud, to unwilling to be trod on, to submit to Washington know-it-alls. His effort to circumvent Big Government looked too much like Big Government. Trust in government, he decided, "would have to be rebuilt, slowly and consciously, before the public was ready to embrace a progressive agenda again."[34] "After a while," Waldman told me, "he remembered that he was a liberal president in a conservative country. He was reminded."[35]

Gingrich's rocketing revolution demonstrated with the subtlety of a kick in the gut that the impulse to smash Washington was a live force, not a spent one. Gingrich was the half-educated autodidact as failed college professor, suburbanized and updated heir of George Wallace's antigovernment, antibureaucrat theme of 1968, that rough-spoken revolt in a truck driver's voice having been modulated by Richard Nixon into middle class *ressentiment*, though Nixon in the main confined his populism to rhetorical flourishes, not a governing principle. But in the seventies, as the tax revolt mounted, the anti-Washington mood converged with rising evangelicalism, which in turn overlapped with a growing general suspicion of experts verging, indeed, on a suspicion of reason. After the Carter interregnum, Reagan remolded the conservative-populist revolt against the welfare state and spun it into a governing principle disguised as "supply-side economics."[36]

Clinton co-opted Reagan's balanced-budget movement, making more headway with it, in fact, than Reagan or the senior Bush did. In the eyes of fiscal conservatives, this might have counted for something, just as it subtracted from Clinton's standing with old-fashioned liberals. Moreover, it might have impressed serious conservatives that Clinton was a whiz kid who didn't put on airs—Georgetown, Yale, Oxford. If anyone could have reestablished the value of intellect in government, he ought to have been the one. Instead, his very successes, such as they were, offended and outraged movement conservatives for all the old reasons.

Meanwhile, the left had scarcely warmed to Clinton after the debacle of the midterm elections. Many were enraged that he signed a Republican welfare reform bill in 1996, even if the version he signed was somewhat less punitive than a bill he had vetoed previously. With a stroke of his pen, Clinton thought, he would signal "his determination to change the Democratic Party and drain away the public's anger at government."[37] But to liberals, this looked like rank opportunism. They were already suspicious of him for distinguishing between Americans who "worked hard and played by the rules" and Americans who presumably didn't. Why did he have to truckle to the right on this question of principle, they wanted to know, when he was running ahead in the polls against Bob Dole? What did he have to be afraid of? Three liberals who held high positions in the Department of Health and Human Services resigned in protest, including Peter Edelman, the husband of his (and his wife's) longtime friend Marion Wright Edelman, who, like Lani Guinier earlier, instantly was lionized as a liberal martyr. Overall, liberals were unimpressed by Clinton's microscopic feel-good programs and continuing "triangulations," his attempts to scramble back into the public's good graces by confining himself to "small successes."[38] Liberals were inclined to think that he was not one of them, that he was in thrall to corporate contributions, and Clinton at times fed their fears, as when he apologized publicly for having raised taxes on the wealthy.[39] But liberals were also loath to acknowledge that only an extraordinarily dexterous politician could have come to power in the first place, let alone compiled a record of any practical accomplishment whatsoever.

In his flowing ambiguities, Clinton was the perfect personification of the Democratic Party as a whole—flexibility raised to the level of principle. While the Republican mantra was *Attack, attack,*

attack, Clinton's was *Understand, explain, assuage*. Yet while many liberals were convinced that Clinton was digging liberalism's grave, he was convinced that he was digging the foundation for restoration. In Michael Waldman's words, Clinton's second electoral victory was proof that "he had taken the steam out of the intense anti-government animus that had driven the modern Republican Party for decades."[40] Soon, he would say out loud that "most people are conservative most of the time. They turn to the progressive party in a time of crisis. Then, that party becomes less progressive, or people turn to the other party. . . . JFK was a conservative liberal, the only way a liberal can be elected in America."[41]

In fact, whether his signing the welfare bill was politically necessary or not, Clinton succeeded in his objective of restoring trust in government—at least as much as polls can register. The sum of those who said they trusted the national government "just about always" or "most of the time," which was mired at 15 percent in April 1994, rose to 25 percent in November 1995 and October 1996, then to 31 percent in January 1998, to 34 percent in January 1999 (in the midst of the impeachment campaign!), to 42 percent in July 2000—back into Reagan's range.[42]

It was strangely as the liberals' uneasy, imperfect champion that Clinton departed in 2001—when it no longer mattered. He was appreciated more by contrast with his successor than by dint of his achievements in office. True, eliminating the deficit helped to unleash an investment boom. At the low end, Clinton enlarged the Earned Income Tax Credit and boosted the minimum wage. The proportion of Americans living in poverty fell by one-quarter during his tenure in office. But liberals tended to take for granted the economic improvements that took place during Clinton's presidency. If they came to appreciate him at all, it was late, and reluctantly—as the victim of a right-wing crusade.

And victim he was—first of Newt Gingrich, then of Ken Starr. Eventually the assault on him was so venomous and effective as to galvanize liberals into defending him. No sooner did Clinton fight Gingrich to a standstill than he waded into the Lewinsky imbroglio and the not-so-tender mercies of Starr and a Republican Party bent on impeachment. Even after welfare reform, his demonization revealed to any liberal who had missed it earlier that Clinton was their bulwark against a right wing of unlimited virulence. The Clinton they viewed as a sell-out was, as far as Gingrich was concerned, a "counterculture McGovernik," "an enemy of normal Americans." Rush Limbaugh, with a listening audience of some twenty million, fabricated obsessively about him. Jerry Falwell sold a video maintaining that he was a "murderer." To any number of crackpots, Clinton was "every bit as advanced a witch as was Adolf Hitler."[43] As liberals at last discovered how thoroughly Clinton was loathed by the right, they decided that he must be worthy of their affection. He was no longer a waffle at home on every plate, a man for all reasons, but the moving target of their targets, the enemy of their enemies.

It seemed that, policy aside, what liberals wanted from power was martyrs. During the year of Clinton's near-death and trans-figuration, it dawned on many veterans of sixties movements, including practitioners of identity politics, that Clinton was, for better or worse, their president. In fact, he embodied the sixties (he had "inhaled" them, as Tom Hayden put it to me)—and this was half the reason that he was hated. (The other half: he was a winner.) He was the antiwar, draft-dodging, noninhaling, Hillary-marrying, gay-friendly graduate of elite universities—a Martha's Vineyard vacationer who had somehow, for a while, carpetbagged his way into the South's good graces only to be revealed, in the end, as a roué of the sexual revolution and no friend of the bubbas. Against the will of the DLC, he had appointed a cabinet that "looked like America."[44] No less an eminence than Toni Morrison declared that Clinton was "the first black president."[45] If Bill Clinton could not be loved as a leader, he could be supported, admired, even cherished as a martyr.

But once Clinton left the White House, and Al Gore was denied his succession, the intraparty truces expired and the Democrats' inter-necine war resumed—or perhaps it is more accurate to say that, under Clinton, the clash never ceased but was only muffled. Party liberals, and what remained of the movement left, thought it laughable to suggest that Clinton was saving liberalism: to say so was like saying that you had to destroy a village in order to save it. Once the Republican assault on Clinton was turned back, congressional liberals got back in touch with their profound resentment. During one week in 2004, I happened to hear two liberal congressmen, Neil Abercrombie (D-HI) and Major Owens (D-NY), give vent to harsh attacks on their party's most successful leader in a generation. What struck me was not the substance of their criticisms but the intensity of their acrimony. These men were holders of safe House seats, firm institutional bases for liberal-cum-progressive politics—this could explain their indifference to the national political balance of forces, yes. But there was more.

Reduced to minority status, the party's office-holders had entered into a sullen, helpless state. They were strong enough to keep their seats—a rather easy matter, given the way both parties used computers to arrange statewide redistricting to nullify competition—but were an emasculated minority when it came to actual influence. They had even lost some of the perks of minority status. In 1995, Gingrich, operating under cover of the "Contract with America," had gutted Congress of staff positions that had served progressive interests. Such committees of Congress as the Arms Control and Foreign Policy Caucus, the Office of Technology Assessment, and the Democratic Study Group, with their rapid-response capacities, received what the longtime progressive staffer Lorelei Kelly called "a mid-level lobotomy."[46] So Democrats were enfeebled, feeling a diffuse sense of deprivation, without a clear target. But even then, why all the venom against Clinton?

Principled anger and helplessness, to be sure. At one time or another, Clinton had offended all the institutional pillars of the Democratic base—labor, minority groups, feminists, gays, environmentalists. The logic of their disaffection led some into Ralph Nader's crusade, fueled by imperious resentment at having been shut out from influence. Nader sometimes maintained that he was equally contemptuous of "Tweedledee" Democrats and "Tweedledum" Republicans, but his actions put the lie to this claim. His overriding concern was to punish the Democrats, as he did by deciding to campaign in close states such as Florida, rather than in sure-shot Democratic states where he could easily have picked up a large number of votes. This latter course of action might have helped him to reach the magic figure of 5 percent of the vote, which would have sent federal election funds to the Green Party in 2004. Nader was so patently vindictive toward the Democrats as to rejoice in public—the morning after the election—that he had put the Democrats in their place.

It was only a left-wing fringe (though, as it turned out, hardly an insignificant one) that would go so far as to break off and support Nader over Gore in 2000. But Clinton's failure to impress the left—and Gore's, too, to his chagrin—was also a failure of rhetoric. What was the fuel in the clunky party machine? Who were the enemies against whom Clinton invited all good Democrats to unify? What would the banner say? In accordance with the modesty of Clinton's achievement, he did not declare a new public philosophy. "The era of big government is over," the shock line of his 1996 State of the Union message, was not exactly an announcement of what the next era ought to be. It was a placeholder, not a principle. Clinton registered many practical achievements in the project of "reinventing government"—he actually did make governing more efficient, getting more done with fewer public employees. But publicity for Clinton's achievements was scanty. When Clinton and Gore held a South Lawn ceremony to announce their cost-cutting results, media mentions were rare, and the *New York Times* mentioned them not at all. Clinton's attempts to emblazon this work failed to interest journalists—or liberals. "Lean and mean government" didn't cut it. Even worse, there was no comprehensible name for his governing idea; no Newer Deal or Newer Freedom, no Twenty-First-Century Bridge. (Neither "New Covenant," of the 1992 campaign,[47] nor the "Third Way" of 1998, seized many imaginations.) This was not just a failure of sloganeering or, to use the trendier term, branding. His rhetorical shortfall was the price Clinton paid for his finesse, a by-product of his ability to "hold two opposing ideas" in his mind—and also of his overestimation of his "ability to function" under paralyzing circumstances.

Still, without question, Clinton was a political master—the uniquely gifted politician of his generation. The combination of his acumen and his persona won him two electoral victories in a row—the first Democratic presidential streak since FDR (or Kennedy-Johnson, if you like). Under the deeply unfavorable circumstances, it was unlikely in the extreme that Clinton could have accomplished more than he did. From a liberal point of view, he was more thwarted than triumphant.

But however you evaluate Clinton's successes and failures, when the glow faded and the dust cleared, the Democrats were still straggling. Disgraced, reviled, impeached, besieged by a merciless opposition and a hostile press, Clinton left office with a booming economy, a budget surplus, and approval ratings of two-thirds,[48] but his political heir, Al Gore, effectively renounced him in the course of a hapless campaign (while trying to repackage Clinton's political style as "practical idealism"). Had the right wing of the Supreme Court not shut Gore out of the White House, Michael Waldman suggested, we might have seen Clinton's presidency as an undisputed political success "for having realigned public attitudes toward progressive government."[49] As it happened, we were deprived of the chance to know what a third term of a sort of Clintonian politics would have looked like—and in any event, the September 11 attacks would have derailed any easy evolution. What *is* clear is that Clinton, like Jimmy Carter—indeed, like Lyndon Johnson—did not found an enduring movement or a party either cogent or comfortable in his image. No trademark program is hitched to his name. Clintonism, it seemed, was little more than the personal aura of Bill Clinton.

Or was there, in fact, an unlikely heir? A fiscally conservative, socially liberal, draft-evading, label-refusing, well-educated, policy-literate, professional-woman-marrying, multiterm Democratic governor from a low-population state who inspired warmth and hatred in equal measure? Myriad are the differences in temperament, style, and policy between Bill Clinton and Howard Dean. Vis-à-vis Republicans, Dean in 2004 was pugnacious, not so much bridge-builder as bridge-burner. Dean was an NRA member, Clinton a gun-controller. There was no equivalent during Clinton's ascendancy of Dean's signature issue, Iraq—to name only one difference between the political environments of 1992 and 2004. But it is surely worth noting that Dean, like Clinton, adroitly squared his circles, spliced his appeals, mixed and matched his positions in order to establish himself as a sort of New Democrat. The main reason the party left was taken with Dean was that, on Iraq, Bush was so obdurate—for Dean, contrary to reputation, was not hell-bent against war in Iraq under any and all circumstances, only war in the unilateralist manner on which Bush insisted. And while the force of Dean's style was not so compelling as to carry him to a single primary win, he did succeed in rising to the top of the Democratic National Committee, pledging to build the party organization for the long haul. Could it be that Clintonism survives as the realist note that will thrum in the Democrats' background whoever their candidates may be?

Those with a taste for half-filled glasses will draw some comfort by carefully picking their facts to warm up the glow around the post-Clinton Democrats. They will note that Al Gore did win the popular vote in 2000 and was chased out of the presidency only by extraordinary muscle—by an electoral apparatus appointed by George W. Bush's governor brother and the intervention of a court majority appointed by his party. They will go on to note that even Bush's ability to win a shade less than half the popular vote was predicated on a fundamentally dishonest campaign in which Bush presented himself as a "compassionate conservative" and a "reformer with results" at home and an opponent of "nation building" abroad, rather than the inegalitarian tax-cutter and hard-right unilateralist he revealed himself to be once in office. They will further observe that Bush's popularity started to sink almost immediately after he entered the White House; that he made the most of the political gift of the September 11 attacks, but even then, his popularity started to sink just afterward, with a bump up for the onset of the Iraq war and another bump up for the capture of Saddam Hussein. Still, even those with the American gift for keeping on the sunny side of the street will be hard pressed to deny the obvious: neither a strong Democratic Party nor a vital liberal movement survived the end of Bill Clinton's terms. It does not detract from Clinton's achievements to acknowledge that both the party and the movement floundered after he left the White House.

Which is why the mobilization of 2004 was so interesting—and promising.

PART THREE

Emergence: The Tent and the Principles

Emergence. 3. *Evolution*, the appearance
of new properties or species in the course
of development or evolution.
Dictionary.com Unabridged (v 1.1)

10

The Party as Movement, 2004 and After: The Deaniacs, the Purple States, and the Netroots

The hilly swaths of highway around Scranton, Pennsylvania, run thick with Wal-Mart trucks as bulky as whole towns. Cars are festooned with magnetized ribbons, yellow and red-white-and-blue, most of them manufactured in China, the inexpensive way to signify support for American troops in Iraq. Down the tired residential streets of Scranton, the state's fifth largest city, American flags are more common than weeds or the little statues of the Virgin Mary that adorn the front lawns of weathered wood and brick houses. One hotel features a black POW-MIA flag. There's a lot of past here, a lot of patriotism, a lot of true memory and some false.

Around the Lackawanna County courthouse, a handsome pile of gray stone that dominates the central square downtown, stands a forest of memorials, among them monuments to George Washington, to William McKinley of next-door Ohio, to four local soldiers who won the Congressional Medal of Honor (two in the Civil War, two in World War II), and to John Mitchell, "Champion of Labor, Defender of Human Rights" and president of the National Mine Workers Union during the great coal strike of 1902, which won the eight-hour day and the minimum wage for the miners. There is also a three-sided column dedicated to "Faith, Hope, and Charity." Across the street, a sign in a billiard parlor window reads "Restoring pride in Scranton." Many a downtown storefront stands empty.

A century of convulsive change leaves huge demographic gouge marks. In 1900, Scranton was not only a steel center but the hard coal capital of the world and the thirty-eighth largest city in the United States, with a population of more than 100,000. During the 1930s, Scranton's population reached 150,000. But the county started hemorrhaging jobs long before "outsourcing" became a cliché. The handsome old train station, built in 1908 with a classical facade, an ornate clock sandwiched between two bronzed eagles, and gold leaf trim,[1] is now a Radisson Hotel. Scranton, 93.5 percent white, is full of retirement homes. It's a city that's lost half its population in the last seventy years and one-sixth in the last quarter-century.[2]

But during the fall of 2004, Scranton was also a center of political rejuvenation. Here, as in scores of other American battlegrounds, in a country that was said to have shrugged itself away from public life for good, remnants of working-class Democratic machine politics encountered the spirit of do-good activist volunteerism and each found the other (more or less) friendly and indispensable. Thanks to the magnetic attraction of swing states, modest Scranton, like dozens of other cities, towns, and suburbs in Pennsylvania, Ohio, Florida, Nevada, New Mexico, and elsewhere, was propelled into the thick of the broadest, most formidable, most fervent American political rising on the left side of the spectrum in decades, galvanized by the political detonations from the radical right in power. If, in the end, the rising failed to avert defeat, it offered at least a partial template for eventual victory. The defeat of 2004 was the beginning of a recovery.

When I asked Steve and Jackie Grumbacher, retirees who had never before considered themselves political activists (they had marched and petitioned in the sixties, over civil rights and Vietnam but hadn't so much as put up a lawn sign "since Gene McCarthy") why they had decided to get involved in the 2004 campaign in the nearby rural, heavily Republican Lebanon County, Steve said unhesitatingly, "George Bush. The war and Guantánamo. The idea that we'd invade a country that showed no indications of attacking us. Also the Patriot Act. The arrogance of it all—if you voted against us, we don't care what you think."[3] The same Republican juggernaut that shocked (but did not awe) most of the world when it launched a disastrous war succeeded in convincing many millions of Americans, at least for a while, that politics was not a specialized enthusiasm or a peculiar hobby but a necessity—and not a necessity for somebody else but a necessity for them.

Bush was a danger so clear and so present as to shake somnolent Democrats awake. As the Iraq war grew in destructiveness and the White House claimed more executive power, the Democratic base was seized by a sense of emergency, a sense inflamed, if anything, by the widespread perception that the party was gravely in default of its obligations as either an opposition force or a party worthy of governing and ready for it. Item: As the Florida aftermath of 2000 stretched on for weeks, the party lay slack, inert, its legal and political apparatus unready and part time (unlike the Republicans), its base discouraged from mobilizing (also unlike the Republicans).[4] Item: In the 2002 midterms, the party had tried to dodge undodgeable issues about Iraq and security in favor of pre–September 11 boilerplate, only to find itself slammed into submission by Republicans who accused Democrats of insufficient patriotism anyway.

Came 2003 and the Democratic elite, such as it was, seemed ready to go at the next year's presidential nomination in an equally uninspired spirit, ducking the increasingly grim Iraq war. Enter the obstreperous Howard Dean, a marginal figure who burst from the party's margins by dint of his boldness—indeed, aggressiveness—his persistence, and his pioneering use of the Internet. Oppositional boldness and aggressiveness were what the activists of the so-called netroots were waiting for. Dean as governor had frustrated the party left, but running for president, he played to the liberal side of his record, stressing his opposition to Bush's Iraq adventure. His base—the Deaniacs—was, as later research showed, "strongly liberal."[5] Dean's supporters were better educated (one-quarter had graduate degrees), religiously less observant, whiter, and more prosperous. Seventy percent of them wanted the party to be "more liberal."[6] What they pined for was nothing more or less than an anti-Bush, because what spurred and united them was their conviction that Bush was driving the country toward disaster— combined with a passion to do something about it. Only 7 percent said they preferred Dean for his "electability,"[7] but they were anti's of an interesting sort—realist legions in behalf of the cause of victory, in behalf of the party, not against it.

Dean went down in Iowa, where caucus members, usually considered disproportionately liberal for the state, were far less so than Dean's keyboard legions. But however much the Deaniacs thought the dastardly media were to blame for hyping his infamous scream-heard-round-the-world on television the night of his caucus defeat,[8] they stayed to fight for Kerry without skipping a beat—even though Kerry had supported the 2002 Iraq war resolution that they despised, even though his eventual ballot partner John Edwards had done so as well, even though Kerry's public statements on the Iraq war and his positions on it passed no purist litmus tests.

Adaptable and tenacious, Dean's Internet troops represented a new current of activism—activism chiefly in behalf of the Democrats, not for specific identity or ideology groups. Or rather, the identity group that nourished the Deaniacs consisted of the college-educated as a whole and not a single-issue segment of them. Whereas only 20 percent of Americans identified as liberal, 80 percent of the Deaniacs called themselves by that cobwebbed name,[9] double the percentage among 2004 Democratic convention delegates and triple the percentage among Democrats nationally. Fused by the conviction that Bush was an angel of darkness, they funneled the spirit of a movement into the machinery of a party. Howard Dean, M.D., was their doctor and, they hoped, the country's.

Yet they were defeated in the primaries by voters who disagreed with them about the importance of victory, as well as about the means to win it. Vociferous Deaniacs might scorn "electability" as a reason to vote for one of Dean's rivals in Iowa or New Hampshire—John Kerry or John Edwards—and yet, in the end, they cared about electability, too. It is interesting to note that MoveOn.org, the largest single organization of online activists, did not endorse Dean. In the spring of 2004, it decided that its threshold for endorsement would be 50 percent, but Dean failed to cross that threshold, leading with 44 percent of the 317,000 members who voted. The Deaniacs were the advance guard of a still larger force, the movement-cum-party-base that came to be known as the netroots and included the Grumbachers, who were devotees of Daily Kos and americablog, among other well-frequented left-of-center sites. These wired warriors, deriving news and opinion from the Internet, were activists, relatively speaking, and they were also (to use the word neutrally) opportunists—they wanted above all to drive George Bush and the Republicans from power. They preferred the most liberal possible Democrat whom they thought had a serious chance to beat Bush. Many who didn't support Dean supported General Wesley Clark—as long as he looked like a plausible candidate. When he revealed that campaigning was not his strong suit, they looked elsewhere. They were the party's salvation movement, and they turned out to be the party's salvation.

According to the best available tally, the Internet-savvy Democratic-leaning activists numbered something of the order of 2.25 million Americans in 2004—several times larger than any single liberal interest group, though not necessarily larger than the sum of those groups, and only about one-seventh of the number of union members in the United States. They were activists: two-thirds of these netroots Democrats "either attended a campaign rally, donated money to a campaign, knocked on doors, or worked a phone bank," for a total of roughly 1.6 million adults.[10] More than the particulars of policy on abortion, affirmative action, health care, or the environment, more even than a particular direction in foreign policy or even in (or out of) Iraq, the netroots cared about defeating Republicans because they knew that as long as Bush was president and his allies ran Congress, they stood no chance at all of approximating their desires, let alone realizing them in toto. They understood deeply the concept of necessary conditions—that retaking the White House was the necessary condition for a live and decent politics. And this meant that they were Democrats first.

It makes sense to call the Democratic netroots a movement because, by 2004, they moved—they acted, they attracted, they sprawled, they made themselves up as they went along. It was one of their strengths that they were hard to pin down—they were not an ideological tendency or an organization. They were not even consistent. What united them was energy and a certain arrogance—they laid claim to opposition. They felt responsible for the Democrats' course and, not least, saw themselves as a movement. "We are at the beginning of a comprehensive reformation of the Democratic Party—driven by committed progressive outsiders," was a typical proclamation (from Jerome Armstrong and Markos Moulitsas Zúniga, the founders of the liberal sites mydd.com and dailykos .com, respectively).[11]

The netroots' most electric aggregation of activists was MoveOn .org (together with its spin-offs under various names, required for legal reasons), started online by Wes Boyd and Joan Blades, a Berkeley husband-and-wife team of software entrepreneurs, as a counterreaction to the Republicans' impeachment campaign of 1998. (*Censure Bill Clinton and move on*, was their petition-to-Congress notion.) Boyd and Blades consider themselves expediters, not traditional leaders, and with good reason. When I visited their comfortable but modest (no dishwasher) brown-shingle house in the Berkeley hills in 2004, Boyd told me he took inspiration from James Surowiecki's just-published book *The Wisdom of Crowds: Why the Many Are Smarter Than the Few and How Collective Wisdom Shapes Business, Economies, Societies, and Nations*. In the spirit of nonleading leadership, MoveOn would frequently poll its members and adopt priorities—even slogans—accordingly. Members were those who signed up to be members. Boyd and Blades were serious about the virtual nature of their organization—they were not averse to hiring staff without meeting them face-to-face. Boyd considered the Microsoft campus model of Internet organization a throwback to college bull sessions: too many meetings were time-wasters.

By 2004, MoveOn counted 3 million members who donated millions of dollars, sometimes overnight, for candidates and for ads, subsidized campaign workers, and made hundreds of thousands of phone calls into twelve swing states. (In 2006, with more advanced software and a still-growing membership, MoveOn claimed to have instigated 7 million phone calls and spent $25 million supporting House candidates.) Throughout 2004, MoveOn ran anti-Bush ads in selected states, arguably opening up the space for a vigorous opposition; its pollsters thought these ads alone had, early on, put a sizable dent in Bush's approval ratings. In the get-out-the-vote phase, MoveOn claimed to have netted 470,000 Kerry voters. In New Hampshire, for example, MoveOn claimed to have turned out 11,000 Kerry voters who otherwise would not have voted—and Kerry won the state by 9,274 votes. The organization also claimed more than the margin of victory in Wisconsin. "We took people who were registered but hadn't voted in the last four or five elections," MoveOn's twenty-five-year-old wunderkind Eli Pariser told me, "and who had various other demographic traits that made them likely to vote for Kerry but not likely to vote. We had our volunteers going to their doors and talking to them, and giving them information, and checking back in, and phone calls, and so forth." But for all that MoveOn claimed credit for good results, Pariser did not need prompting to acknowledge that other associations could make equivalent claims.[12]

Pariser put in his time in a single technology-choked room in Manhattan[13] before stretching out, in 2004, into a Brooklyn apartment he shared with his girlfriend. He worked long hours. He was intense. He had given himself a political education in a hurry. He knew his information technology. He also knew his management jargon. Both came into play when he thought about the future. What would the organization do next? What did it stand for? MoveOn had come a long way in a short time, and instead of a theory to guide it, it settled for a method: consult the members. The organization was both eminently democratic and programmatically elusive. This marked it as a group of the left, not the right. Pariser's faith in his members' collective wisdom sounded at once passionate and vague. Vagueness and passion combined: it was hard to tell what this brew portended. Was it indecision and airiness? Or the mysticism of a popular movement that brings something new into the world while fumbling for a language that honors precedents without being drowned in them?

The netroots would be an integral part of Democratic campaigns for the foreseeable future, and they would cut across political lines. Howard Dean was only the first politician to pay attention. Wesley Clark followed suit—his lame campaign only going to show that online organization was no route to automatic success. In 2006, with Bush's bankruptcy clear to independents and even Republicans who had not noticed before, the netroots passionately promoted the antiwar primary campaign of Ned Lamont against Joseph Lieberman in Connecticut. But the bathrobe brigades included more than the party's left wing. As the well-informed blogger Mark Schmitt pointed out in 2006, "The centrist Democratic Senate candidate in Missouri, . . . Claire McCaskill, is backed by almost as impressive a group of Show-Me-State blogs as Lamont is by Nutmeg blogs."[14] The political scientist Henry Farrell wrote, "[W]hile many netroots bloggers describe themselves as progressive, they are generally not leftists in the conventional sense. Certainly they aren't committed to any program of fundamental political and economic reform."[15]

One perceptive activist, Matt Stoller of mydd.com, saw the netroots this way:

> I don't really see us as either the New Left or the New Right, though if I had to pick I'd say we're more New Right in terms of our structural orientation. . . . We're much more pragmatic and politically cautious, eschewing stupid and counterproductive attention-grabbing protests, somewhat similar to the way the New Right took Barry Goldwater's extremism and made it palatable. . . . [T]here's a pluralistic element to what the progressive movement is doing that is quite populist and democratic. We are fundamentally arguing for a tolerant and pluralistic society, and we're doing it aggressively and somewhat viciously. That's why it's so hard to pigeonhole.[16]

During the summer of 2006, when the netroots were alternately being lionized and demonized for Ned Lamont's victory in the Democratic primary against the prowar Connecticut senator Joseph Lieberman, Stoller was one of many bloggers who defined themselves as "a movement in behalf of the party." So did Henry Farrell:

> For too long, the Democrats have been less a political party than a process of painstaking triangulation between the competing demands of different interests. The netroots are pushing the Democrats to become a party again, less beholden to interest groups and more willing to actively, vigorously oppose the Republicans.[17]

When insider journalists criticized the blogging legions as unruly outsiders, some of the latter criticized back with pronounced indignation as if they were veritable '68ers, though the revolution they heralded, if they heralded any revolution at all, was nothing more or less than forthright opposition to the right. Thus, when in the summer of 2006 the *New Republic*'s Jonathan Chait fulminated that "to be in the good graces of [Daily Kos's Moulitsas and other bloggers], one must believe not only that the rise of Internet activism has some potentially positive ramifications, but to signal that one accepts a Manichean battle between virtuous people-powered activists and corrupt Washington insiders,"[18] the liberal blogger who goes by the name of Digby responded that any nastiness on the part of the netroots

> reflects the frustration of millions of politically active progressive citizens who have been scapegoated and derided for decades by the political insiders who now find themselves on the other end of the attack. *These people are the base of the Democratic Party.* . . . People in Washington need to wrap their minds around the fact that this stuff really is bubbling up from below and it's real. Bloggers are merely in the vanguard of a rising leftwing populist sentiment around the country. . . . Liberalism has been moribund for some time now. This is a chance to at least begin the process of resuscitation and could be used by the political establishment as a

useful counter-weight to help drag the country back from the
brink of rightwing extremism. [Emphasis in original.][19]

Digby used the language of movements: "bubbling up from
below," "vanguard," "rising," "populist." She was unabashed
about "leftwing" and "liberalism," but she didn't mean "populist"
in the old sense of an uprising of the poor or the working class, but in
the current sense of *popular, enthusiastic, grassroots, anti-elitist*.
However hyperbolic she might have been about the import of the
netroots, she was enough of a realist to recognize that there needed
to be a political establishment and that a crucial measure of the
netroots' importance was the degree to which they move that
establishment.

One could easily exaggerate the significance of the netroots—
certainly some of the big-name bloggers did that. They hyped the
numbers of readers who were paying attention to them. They
obscured the narrowness of their class base. Like all political
insurgents, they sometimes rose to heights of bravado—as if their
ability to draw Harry Reid, Mark Warner, Bill Richardson, and
other top Democratic politicians to a Las Vegas netroots convention called YearlyKos was the equivalent of nominating a candidate. They were no exception to the rule that every insurgent
movement of the last four decades and more stands for "people-
powered politics," for "the decentralization of power from the
elites in the media, political, and activism establishments to regular
people."[20]

Fund-raising prowess sometimes led to rhetorical overreach and
consequent backlash, as against Eli Pariser, who caught flak for a
December 9, 2004, MoveOn e-mail to supporters: "In the last year,
grass-roots contributors like us gave more than $300 million to the
Kerry campaign and the DNC, and proved that the party doesn't
need corporate cash to be competitive. Now it's our party: we
bought it, we own it, and we're going to take it back."[21] If the online
networks could raise money quickly for primary congressional
challengers such as Stephanie Herseth in South Dakota (2004)
and Paul Hackett in Ohio (2005), they could hardly claim to have
put Howard Dean on top of the Democratic ticket, let alone into the

White House.[22] They seemed to be most effective where there was already a progressive movement on the ground—as in Connecticut.[23] "Let's credit the netroots for what they do well," wrote Mark Schmitt, "generate enthusiasm, force the big questions onto the agenda, generate a new definition of what it means to be a Democrat. But by themselves they can't create a viable candidacy or bring down a popular three-term incumbent. Only organizing and the incumbent's own mistakes can do that."

Digby's readers seemed to share his indignation. One of the 160 commenters who chimed in within twenty-four hours on his piece against Chait declared, "[I]t's not the angry left, you elitist prig. It's the ANGRY CENTER." A second: "Maybe this is the beginning of the revoloution [sic], when the People decide that the elites are steering their party onto the rocks and they refuse to let them keep hold of the wheel. Who knows? Maybe there is an awakening starting in Connecticut. Let's fan the flames." A third: "For me the revolution started in 2000, as seems to have been the case with a lot of people I know . . . with the election theft, I realized that American politics is too important to be left to the politicians."[24]

Like the rank-and-file, the netroots' chief left-of-center superintendents were also Democrats first. They were, for the most part, men in their thirties, such as Markos Moulitsas Zúniga of Daily Kos.com, Jerome Armstrong of mydd.com, Joshua Micah Marshall of talkingpointsmemo.com, and Glenn Greenwald of his eponymous site, or in their late twenties, such as Matt Stoller of mydd.com. They were not of the generation that remembered the sixties or assumed that progressive politics had to be rooted in post-sixties interest groups. Their freedom from such attachments was a product of their experience. They had never lived under Democratic hegemony and therefore never assumed, in the bedrock of their politics, that identity groups prevail by putting pressure on a government apparatus that might bend if they clamor loudly enough. The president when they were in grade school was Ronald Reagan, and they had lived their entire political lives with the Republican Party the presumptive majority party and the radical right a huge force in American life. Even if many of their contributors were graybeards—a fact much noticed by journalists who

covered the YearlyKos convention in Las Vegas in June 2006[25]—
these were precisely the baby boomers who had grown weary of
segmented movement politics. Neither were they beholden to, or
especially impressed by, post-thirties labor unions. They were, in
fact, willing to buck the unions in primary endorsements.[26]

They were angry about the Iraq war and in some sense generally
liberal, but they were not ideologues, exactly. They were not
exactly outsiders, either: both Armstrong and Moulitsas worked
as political consultants. (In 2006, Armstrong signed up with former Virginia governor Mark Warner, scarcely the liberals' dream
candidate.) Their 2006 book *Crashing the Gates* would make
resoundingly clear that they were as hostile to the party's doctrinal
factions as was any Democratic Leadership Council cadre.[27] If they
were liberals—"progressives" was their term of choice—it was
loosely so:

> [B]y and large, the netroots are bonded not by their allegiance
> to any single issue, but by their belief that only a broad-based
> progressivism will save the nation from the destructive influ-
> ences of the current administration. The netroots activist,
> much like the new generation of grassroots activist, is fiercely
> partisan, fiercely multi-issue, and focused on building a
> broader movement. It's not an ideological movement—there
> is actually very little, issue-wise, that unites most modern
> party activists except, perhaps [sic] opposition to the Iraq
> War. . . . [W]e are pragmatic and believe the Democratic
> Party has room for a lot of different viewpoints."[28]

They were crashing the gates not in order to melt them down but in
order to get inside.

In firing up this practical opposition, George W. Bush accomplished
something remarkable: he coaxed divergent Democratic elements
into the same insurgent republic and opened up the prospect of a
historical resurrection of no mean proportions. At least for the
moment, he convinced pre-sixties Democratic stalwarts and post-
sixties activists, old pros and young amateurs, union faithful and
do-good volunteers, generalists and concentrators on single issues

that if they did not hang together, they would most assuredly hang separately.

I have been arguing that parties and movements are both indispensable and always to some degree uneasy with each other, for they work by opposing principles: movements aim to force or midwife something transcendent—something not-yet-existent—into existence, to convert energy into mass, say, while parties get results by converting existing mass into energy. Left and right alike incorporate both forces, and for each side, political success hinges on both a division of labor and a certain collaboration.[29] Sometimes the movement side leads and the party side lags; sometimes it's the other way around: sometimes one is smarter, stronger, more gifted in leadership, or luckier than the other, but when they operate at cross-purposes, their common fate suffers.

One way to summarize the plight of the Democrats is as follows: through most of the seventies, eighties, and nineties, the enfeebled Democratic Party and the sectoral liberal movements encountered each other—if at all—with acrid suspicion. The rupture was a large and fateful legacy, if that is the right word, of the fabled sixties. One short answer to the question of what happened to American politics after the sixties is that the right harnessed its movement to its party while the left did not do the equivalent.

As the Republicans built themselves a base of messianic Christians and antitax enthusiasts, traditional small-town Republicans and white working-class converts, the orthodox liberal Democrats and the movement left painted themselves into a corner: a culture of defeat. They seethed with resentment against their only victorious presidential candidates, Jimmy Carter and Bill Clinton. Each movement magnified its distinctness and indispensability for the progressive cause. Each took umbrage at the accusation that its cause—the cause of women, of African Americans, of Hispanic immigrants, of reproductive rights, of environmentalism—could be described as the cause of an interest group. Each of their causes was, movement activists devoutly believed, the cause of humanity. Their sincerity was undeniable. Each made a substantial case. Rarely were they arbitrary. They were not the demonic Valkyries vilified by the bitter enemies of "political correctness." And still the sum of their strong cases was less than the sum of their parts because they nourished their differences more than their commonalities. Some liberals and leftists so deeply prized their purity as to swallow the tempting Kool-Aid of Ralph Nader.

It came to pass that the unified, hierarchically organized, well-funded, technically sophisticated Republicans, who for all their antigovernment passion devoutly believed in disciplined power, conquered every single national political institution in the country, and most of the states, and vast reaches of the national agenda. While tactically (though often sincerely) whining that "the liberal media" were rigged against them, they boasted a kept media of their own—a reliable, comfortably upholstered radio, television, print, and Internet apparatus (multiplatform, in the new jargon) for focused, pugnacious propaganda.[30] They spurred themselves by insisting that they were recovering the people's lost power, since they did not control the *New York Times* or Hollywood or Madison Avenue or Ivy League universities. They built their party around a fierce, mobilized base convinced that Democrats were plotting to vanquish them by illicit means—a useful projection of their own desires. They had vast treasuries to draw on.

For Republicans who wished to be an effective opposition, the election debacle of 2000 proved an instructive and transformational trauma. It smacked the opposition between the eyes, showed them definitively that there was a method, or several methods, to the mauling. After the first cousin of the loser of the popular vote, on a network owned by a partisan of that loser, led the media charge to declare that his cousin was the winner in Florida and therefore the winner of the electoral college vote, creating the presumption that all subsequent legal actions by his opponent were dilatory and illegitimate; after renowned custodians of national news repeatedly urged the winner of the popular vote to step aside in order to prove his statesmanship; after Republican mobs interrupted vote recounts in Florida (while the Democratic winner of the popular vote dissuaded another prominent Democrat, Jesse Jackson, from being so bold as to organize protests); and politicians waived the rules for counting overseas ballots; and the Republican secretary of state, Katherine Harris, a Florida cochair of the Bush campaign (and a

Bush convention delegate who had campaigned for him in New Hampshire), the official who had supervised the purging the voter rolls, made decision after decision to Republican benefit; and, if there was any doubt, after the Supreme Court decreed who was president in an incoherent decision apparently arguing that the rights of George W. Bush and his voters trumped the rights of everyone else to have their votes counted—with this cascade of raw power, the opposition understood that it had to play catch-up on every practical front.

When they recovered consciousness, Democrats, progressives, liberals, even many of those who had cast ballots for Ralph Nader, understood viscerally what they were up against. Even intellectuals (some intellectuals, anyway), who had a stake in believing that ideas were the alpha and the omega of politics, began to acknowledge that there was a great deal about the workings of the United States of America that they did not understand; that politics was concrete, not abstract; that, to paraphrase Donald Rumsfeld, you conducted politics with the people you had, not the people you wished you had; that political life was a matter of strategy as well as ideals; that political infrastructure mattered; that politics was more than an election here or there, but a mobilization to be measured in decades.

And so, both sides of a polarized politics came to converge on one banal but primal lesson: in a deeply divided country, power accrues to those who successfully organize to get it and hold it. The Bush usurpation of 2000 began to convert many liberals (and even those further left) to the party of practicality. As Miles Rapoport, who leads the think-tank Demos, put it, "It's hard to hear many people [on the left] say it doesn't make a dime's worth of difference who's in office anymore."[31]

The trauma of 2000 multiplied as Bush entered the Oval Office and began to govern from the hard right, as movement conservatives had longed for decades to see a Republican president do. That trauma only multiplied with the compounding trauma of the September 11 massacres and the unwinding catastrophe of the Iraq war. Think-tankers, fund-raisers, get-out-the-vote activists, unions, campaigners for the environment, for women's and gay rights, and various and sundry others in the vast terrain of the left-of-center began to grasp that the Bush machine that had commanded America for four years represented the triumph of more than cunning, more than deception, more than money and congenial media, though it had all those in spades. It represented, on many fronts, the culmination of forty years of the right's effort to take power. The corollary was: there was no alternative to winning but losing, and the alternative to power was not freedom but powerlessness.

So, in 2004, a ragged regeneration movement met a Democratic Party straining to be reborn, and the two forces, instead of wondering how best to pulverize each other, decided to buddy up, not only to reinvent their politics—no small task in itself—but to "take back" America, really to redeem it (although this movement's language, unlike the other side's, was rarely comfortable with that sort of religious lingo). And if you needed any proof of the fusionist nature of the new mobilization, here was John Kerry, a near-caricature of the privileged movement stereotype of the sixties (itself a half-truth in its time), with his upper-class origins, his Yale education, and his wealthy wife, "reporting for duty" to represent a Democratic Party hell bent for victory. To try to put him over the top in Scranton, Pennsylvania, were antiabortion working-class Catholics collaborating with pro-choice middle-class liberals, many of them Jews. After 2004, the two most prominent analyses produced by Democratic factions agreed that white working-class and Catholic voters were the two largest categories that the Democrats had forfeited.[32] Scranton was a good place to find these two categories overlapping.

I started visiting Scranton on weekends in September 2004. My wife had bused there on a day trip from New York, volunteering for Kerry, and decided to stay and do whatever needed to be done, which pretty soon meant that she was helping to run the Lackawanna County Democrats' storefront office, in the Chamber of Commerce Building a few blocks from the courthouse, for six weeks. The place looked like its nature: "Scranton the All-American City," proclaimed the fading paint on the side of the building.

Addressing the canvassers who shipped in each weekend as the mobilization revved up, Dave White, the Kerry campaign's twenty-five-year-old regional field coordinator, liked to say, "This year the road to the White House leads through northeast Pennsylvania." (A hard-working politico named Margi Cowley, who came from a long line of local politicians, preferred an earthier metaphor: "You are at ground zero in the ground war.") They weren't blowing smoke, though there were plenty of other places that could claim an equivalent status. Full of conservative working-class Catholics, an antiabortion hotbed for years, with a newspaper that would begin its coverage of a John Edwards rally by featuring a single antiabortion counterdemonstrator, Scranton is the kind of town that brings up adjectives compounded of gastronomic staples: salt-of-the-earth, meat-and-potatoes. It has a neighborhood bakery where you can order a birthday cake in an Army camouflage pattern. It also has a lesbian bar, one excellent coffeehouse, several Catholic colleges, and a fair assortment of metallically adorned young faces.

In Scranton, an eighty-five-year-old man said to me on the phone, when I called to find out his intentions about John Kerry, "Are you telling me to vote for Jane Fonda?" and a high school student walked into Democratic headquarters one day to get Kerry-Edwards supplies—he'd just started a Democratic club. Scranton also features the Casey Laundry Building, an annex to Hotel Casey: it is the base of the former governor Robert P. Casey, and his son, Bob Jr., the state treasurer, who in 2006 would defeat the right-wing Republican senator Rick Santorum and become the first Democratic senator elected in the state since the Republican land-slide of 1994. The father was a devoutly antiabortion Democrat, famously so, having been prevented from speaking at the 1992 Democratic convention because he refused to endorse nominee Bill Clinton (as he refused to endorse all other pro-choice politicians) and because he wanted to give an antiabortion speech.

In Scranton, residents who had never so much as put up a political lawn sign streamed in. Some sat down in a volunteered legal office next door, punched phone numbers nonstop, and read questions from a script. Some asked for Kerry-Edwards signs. Some pledged their time to canvass, phone, register new voters, arrange for rides to the polls, fire up on-again-off-again Democrats, enter phone results into statewide data banks—whatever. Union members were visiting every union household in town. Kerry-Edwards canvassers grazed past canvassers from Americans Coming Together, MoveOn.org, and other groups—not always well coordinated, and forbidden, by law, from being so. Likewise, the Democrats who made cold calls often encountered people on the other end of the line who were irritated because they thought the Democrats had already called them, when, in fact, earlier calls to them had come from soft-money groups.

Into this old-fashioned Democratic stronghold, out-of-towners poured down by the hundreds, most of them from New York City. One man drove four hours down from the Berkshire hills of Massachusetts, canvassed for five hours, then drove home that night. Whether these volunteers were there strictly to express their pure hatred for George W. Bush or whether they loved John Kerry enough to share the proverbial beer with him, let alone take a bullet for him, was unknowable, but in a way was also beside the point. This was more than a campaign. It was a cause. To the volunteers, this was, in its own way, a salvation movement in behalf of truth, virtue, and the American way.

What struck me in conversations with several dozen volunteers, carpetbaggers and locals alike, was the almost uniform answer when I asked if they had ever worked on a national political campaign: no. A few had worked in local campaigns. I met one who had worked for George McGovern in 1972. If they had any political background, it was in support of single-issue political causes.

The volunteers came in all shapes, sizes, ages, and cultural dispositions. Say what you will about the culture war and the unbridgeable class divide, locals named Mary Beth and Tony had no trouble working with a visiting canvasser from New York named Pagan. Scranton Democrats, many of them resolutely anti-abortion, were willing to live with a pro-choice candidate because they recognized without much trouble that he stood, however imperfectly, for egalitarian values that they shared—and the outsiders felt no need to wear their pro-choice positions on their sleeves. No canvassers from anywhere expressed any objection to going out door to door with little yellow ribbons pinned to their jackets. At pre-canvassing briefings, New Yorkers gasped as loudly as Scrantonians did upon being told of the volunteer who, on a previous canvass, had knocked on the door of a woman whose son was stationed in Iraq and told her that he was fighting for oil. No explanation was required—the volunteers understood that they were not there to proselytize for left-wing positions. A single warning sufficed—there were no sequels.

Volunteers tended to fall into distinct issue camps. Locals, many of them from the working class, tended to care most about jobs seeping away. Visitors were more preoccupied with the Iraq war. But during canvassing expeditions, they all stuck to instructions for efficiency's sake—don't get involved in heavy discussions on the block; figure out which way people are leaning and move on. There were predictable office tensions between party pros and outsiders, but the only bad vibe I witnessed came from a Kerry campaign public relations specialist from Los Angeles who swooped in with snakeskin boots and an insulting hauteur—but she offended the outsiders as much as the locals.

Purple Pennsylvania in 2004 was a magnet for activists, but it was not only importing outsiders to work alongside locals, as in Scranton. Local activists came forward even in the absence of a local machine, activists who were not so much bound to single issues as outraged by Republican power personified in George W. Bush, and convinced that they had to put together a contrary power—a party with movement passion. In such an important swing state, there were counties where Democrats were not only a distinct minority but dysfunctional, almost defunct. There, volunteers who yearned to put in long hours to defeat George W. Bush had nowhere to go— unless, as in rural Lebanon County, a hundred miles west of Philadelphia, where Republicans outnumber them two to one, they turned themselves into functioning Democrats.

Steve and Jackie Grumbacher are baby boomers whose careers had been in nonprofits; they had retired to a small town in Lebanon County a few years earlier, from Washington, D.C. They are in the habit of completing each others' sentences. That May they told me,

"We called up the Democratic headquarters hoping we could lick envelopes. We discovered they weren't doing anything. They thought they would start cooking around the fall. The Democrats were only using the office once a month. We were extremely unhappy and decided to hold a meeting every week and spread the word. A lady in the party office asked the chairman, who said we could have meetings there. The meetings would get us toward action. A big plus: at least the party didn't get in our way."

"The party's never done anything here," Steve said. "People like us felt alone. If they put a bumper sticker on their car, they would get stoned"—they meant with rocks, not drugs. "A lot of the Democrats were really supporting Bush. They said things like, 'Don't criticize the commander in chief.' They were supposed to manage the party, but not to win. We started with ten people, by word of mouth. We said, 'That's respectable.' In the meantime, the Republicans had twenty phones in their headquarters. A lot of churches were for Bush. People told us that. There was pressure to vote for Bush. People went to the polls with ballots already made out for Bush."

They pushed the Democrats to play catch-up. "We played the Democrats and the Kerry campaign against each other to get help. We were sort of inventing the wheel. None of us had any experience with politics." The office had a single computer, dating from the eighties. Their small database was disconnected from the Democrats' statewide database. Lists of previous voters were stuffed in a file cabinet, unconsulted. "We recruited volunteers. Our big task was to get enough people to call at home and get them to come in to the office in shifts, so we could find out who were the shaky voters and so on. We got voter lists, found out how many times they'd voted. We strategized. We had to manage a lot of people—find out who's already been called, what are the results, and so on. We have been supervisors of lots of people in our time."

"We went to the county fair," Jackie said. "We set up a booth, showed a videotape of Kerry. It's very red there, country farmers. I was amazed to see them taking the material. All you see usually is Republican stuff here. When they saw other people saying what we were saying, they were glad. Some of them would look around on the sly, to see if somebody's watching. The Republicans had a huge booth with six-foot figures of Ronald Reagan. Somebody said anybody who voted for Kerry would go to hell." By mid-October the Grumbachers' Democratic group was pulling in seven hundred volunteers a week.[33]

Yet here was the rub: for all the Democrats' upsurge, when the ballots were counted, it turned out that the Republicans surged higher. From 2000 to 2004, Democratic registration in Lebanon County increased by 942 while Republicans went up by 1,781, almost twice as many voters. (Independents went up by 1,523.)[34] The Democratic percentage of registered voters stayed the same, at 29 percent, while the Republicans declined by a single point, to 59 percent. From Election Day of 2000 to Election Day of 2004, Bush's vote climbed from 62 to 67 percent, while Kerry's vote percentage fell below Gore's, from 35 to 33 percent.[35] In a word, the activist Democrats were out-organized.

When I spoke to the Grumbachers several months later, they were on fire. I asked them about the sequel to the election. "We were dead with disappointment," Jackie said. "We decided a few days later we would just pull ourselves together. A lot of people came together and we decided we just weren't going to give up. People missed having other people to talk to. We got together in December to bare our souls. We said we cannot meet every week but since then we've been meeting every month, in a coffeehouse. We have a pretty stable core group of thirty to forty. We got people to run as election judges and inspectors in 97 percent of the precincts."

They kept on. They attended a weekend training session in Gettysburg, one of several organized by Democracy for America, a group made up initially of Deaniacs and headed by Howard Dean's brother, Jim. "The idea is to keep a progressive voice alive— to keep a progressive community alive," Jackie said. They would do the equivalent of what conservatives did during the wilderness years when they were on their way to winning control of the Republicans: they would maintain their own esprit de corps while moving into the heart of the party. With what political views? Ninety-five percent of the Lebanon County volunteers consider themselves "progressive," with the rest "just anti-Bush," or in the center—"they know they're not on the right." What they share is realism. "There's no such thing as a non-pro-gun, non-pro-life person around here," said Jackie. "But we still have to start by taking back power."

In 2006, the Grumbachers, like many of the Scranton volunteers, carried what Jackie called "the Kerry spirit" into the Senate campaign for Bob Casey Jr. against Rick Santorum, who had held the seat for eighteen years. Jackie was fired with the movement sense of insurgency. At the 2004 county fair, she recalled, she had contrasted the "massive" Republican display, festooned with banners, with her group's "folksy booth." "I had this moment," she recalled, "in which I thought, the old Democratic Party died. It's ossified—it's caught in a time warp. We're alive. This is the future. This country's got to be saved. The whole top-down structure of the Republicans, with their talking points—we're the reverse of that. We're not hypnotized. It's not unlike the American Revolution. It's in our court now."

And the party? "The party's been slouching along to Bethlehem as usual." "If you went down to Democratic headquarters," Steve chimed in, "you'd see a picture of FDR." In the twenty-first century, the Democrats had become the party of nostalgia.

The Democratic mobilization of 2004 was huge, it was unprecedented, it succeeded in linking machine organization with movement verve—and there wasn't enough for victory. It turned out numbers that may well have been decisive in Wisconsin and New Hampshire—and that fell short in Florida, New Mexico and, crucially, Ohio.

This is only to speak of turnout. If we turn to outcomes, the central social problem with the Democratic vote becomes clear. For as surely as narrow defeat has many mothers—it may be attributed to various combinations of votes going the wrong way—surely the most dramatic way to state the Democratic shortfall is this: whites without a four-year college degree, who went for Bill Clinton by a single percentage point in 1992 and 1996, went to George W. Bush by 17 points in 2000 and 23 points in 2004. As the

Democratic analysts John Halpin and Ruy Teixeira wrote in an influential essay on party strategy in the spring of 2006,

> Democrats did especially badly among white working-class voters who weren't poor, but rather had moderate incomes and some hold on a middle-class lifestyle. Among working class whites with $30,000 to $50,000 in household income, Bush beat Kerry by 24 points (62 percent to 38 percent). And, among working-class whites with $50,000 to $75,000 in household income, Bush beat Kerry by a shocking 41 points (70 percent to 29 percent).

As Halpin and Teixeira understated the point (perhaps with unintentional drollery), "Clearly, these voters do not see progressives as representing their aspirations for a prosperous, stable, middle-class life." And how important were white working-class voters? They accounted for 52 percent of the 2004 vote.[36]

When the votes were in, commentators across the board agreed that the Republicans in 2004 appealed to these big brigades with their own deeply fused combination of movement and machine. According to the right-wing journalist Fred Barnes:

> Roughly 1.4 million Bush volunteers were recruited [in 2004], stayed active through election day, and now constitute a permanent party cadre. Political reporters missed another Bush breakthrough: they were admiring of Howard Dean's success in collecting 600,000 e-mail addresses of supporters. But with little fanfare, the Bush campaign amassed an e-mail list of 7.5 million names.[37]

While Democrats streamed from out-of-state into Pennsylvania, Florida, Ohio, Nevada, and New Mexico, the Republicans ran their own equivalent operations—less noticed by the press because they tended to cluster in rural and exurban areas, beyond the reach of metropolitan media. In New Mexico, to name one important swing state, Republican volunteers poured in from West Texas, winning votes among Hispanics, exurbanites, and rurals, counterbalancing Kerry's increases over the Gore vote in Albuquerque, Santa Fe, and Taos.[38]

Dwell for a moment, too, on fatal Ohio, which Bush won by 118,457 votes, according to the official tally. Halpin and Teixeira argued that in such a close election, the ground game did matter. Comparing 2004 with 2000 results in Ohio, they maintained, the Democrats' "gains were mostly cancelled out by Republican mobilization in conservative rural and emerging suburban areas. So Ohio, in the end, was only slightly closer (2.5 percentage points) than it was in 2000 (3.5 points)."[39] Americans Coming Together head Steve Rosenthal agreed up to this point: "We added 554,000 votes to our totals, but the Republicans countered with 508,000, enough to keep the state in their column."[40]

But was it the Republican mobilization that was decisive, or did they have other logistical advantages as well? In Ohio, the Republicans did well in all three areas that contribute to electoral success: the ground rules (registration, the provision or nonprovision of voting machines, and so on); the ground game (microtargeting and turnout); and the message (the candidates' lines of argument and their persuasiveness). Apropos the ground rules, as in the Florida of 2000, the Republicans were not bashful about suppressing as many Democratic votes as possible under the supervision of an unscrupulous, partisan secretary of state. The Katherine Harris of 2004 was Ohio's Kenneth Blackwell, who pulled out many stops to restrict the franchise.[41] In the recount, too, they benefited from evident violations of laws and rules.[42] Second, the Republicans benefited from the difficulties faced by minority and other liberal voters, though there is a heated dispute about who exactly was responsible. Halpin and Teixeira observed that John Kerry prevailed in Franklin County (Columbus) by 41,000 votes, much more than Gore's margin of 4,000 in 2000, and took Cuyahoga County (Cleveland) by 218,000 votes, well over Gore's margin of 166,000 in 2000. Kerry won the bellwether Stark County (Canton) by 4,354 votes, whereas Gore had lost it.[43]

But after an exit-poll study of rural and exurban voters in heavily pro-Bush counties, Steve Rosenthal argued that the superior ground game did not account for Bush's Ohio margin. For one thing, religious voters did not account for Bush's victory—in fact, "in Ohio, the share of the electorate represented by frequent churchgoers actually declined from 45 percent in 2000 to 40 percent in 2004." Second, "turnout in Democratic-leaning counties in Ohio was up 8.7 percent while turnout in Republican-leaning counties was up slightly less, at 6.3 percent." Third, Democrats and unions were actually more successful in reaching new voters than Republicans and conservative groups (right-wing churches, pro-life groups, and the NRA) were.

In 2004, as in 2002, the Republicans ran pell-mell to the right. Whatever credit Karl Rove received for campaign innovation, this stark reversal of conventional wisdom about running toward the center at election time was no innovation, but rather a resurrection of Spiro Agnew's strategy of 1969, "positive polarization." In Agnew's time, the Republican rhetoric was even more lurid. "It is time to rip away the rhetoric and to divide on authentic lines," said the vice president then, heralding a righteous majority that would overpower rowdy minorities and, indeed, "separate them from our society—with no more regret than we should feel over discarding rotten apples from a barrel."[44] Over the intervening years, the Republicans learned to soften their Kulturkampf on state occasions. But in the rhetoric of the Rush Limbaughs, Pat Robertsons, and Ann Coulters, in the campaign battering rams wielded by Lee Atwater and Karl Rove, the GOP harked back to Agnew's hard edge. In contemporary terms, they Swift-Boated the domestic evildoers and dressed them up as ambassadors of Osama bin Laden.

This campaign strategy extended the logic of George W. Bush governing as "a divider, not a uniter."[45] Republican strategists calculated that their base was bigger than Kerry's, that genuinely undecided or moderate voters were shrinking as a proportion of the electorate, and that their money was better spent and effort better invested in turning out that base than in trying—as in the past—to win moderate voters. As Thomas Edsall put it, "[T]he basic function of the campaign became to activate voters' 'anger points.'"[46] The Republicans spent their money accordingly: "Instead of putting the customary 80 percent of campaign cash and staff into persuading the undecided—the traditional amount—only 50 percent went to that task in the 2004 Bush campaign. . . .

The amount of money going to voter registration, mobilization, and turnout of the already-committed increased by 150 percent, from 20 percent of available resources to 50 percent."[47]

Mindful of the desperate closeness of the 2000 race, the Republicans set out to pluck votes from conservative niches—and such votes might well have added up to more than the Republican margin of victory. They not only turned out their reliable base from 2000, supplemented by some 4 million evangelicals who, Rove believed, had failed to vote for Bush,[48] but enlarged it with microtargeting—finding pro-Bush voters wherever they might be found, whether in swing states, blue zones, or the tiniest demographic slivers. "Rove's team had a critical advantage: a substantially better computerized system for pinpointing small but significant pockets of potential supporters and even individual voters," the *Los Angeles Times* reporters Tom Hamburger and Peter Wallsten wrote. They deployed a massive database as well as consolidated marketing data, then organized house calls to prospects who otherwise might have fallen through cracks:

> Russian Jews in Cleveland . . . thirty-something whites in Midwestern exurbs . . . Puerto Rican barrios in Orlando . . . new immigrants in New Mexico . . . middle-class, churchgoing black suburbanites in Pennsylvania . . . business-oriented Asians in the Pacific Northwest . . . second-generation Indian Americans in the South, and . . . hopeful young entrepreneurs everywhere.[49]

The Republicans' early investment in database consolidation permitted them to hit "anger points" with pistols, not shotguns. By merging commercial data on subscriptions, hobbies, television favorites, and so on, they could target direct mail, precinct walks, and phone banks with tailored messages on late-term abortion, trial-lawyer fees, estate taxes, and other Bush issues.[50] Such preparations also enabled them to pick away at the Democratic base, as Hamburger and Wallsten wrote: "The Republicans' ability to send custom-tailored messages to relatively small numbers of voters inside Democratic precincts in swing states enabled them to slice away pieces of the enemy's base. Each slice might seem inconsequential standing alone, but taken together the slices might add up to something very consequential."[51] Using needle-in-a-haystack techniques, Republican media buyers were able—for example—"to send pro-gun messages to NRA members within the United Automobile Workers."[52] They invested in targeted media. In Edsall's words:

> The Bush campaign concluded that many of their voters did not trust the networks and the establishment press, and therefore did not trust messages transmitted through them. [RNC chair Ken] Mehlman said that talk radio and cable television "are more credible" to potential Bush voters. Ultimately the Bush campaign invested an unprecedented $20 million in narrowly targeted advertising on cable and in radio, with a heavy emphasis on religious, talk and country and western stations, and such specialty outlets as golf and health club channels.[53]

The Republican Party benefited from brute efficiencies. It enjoyed "a major logistical advantage: its highly centralized control over data, targeting, and strategy."[54] Campaign finance reform was one reason. Since the Democratic Party had relied on soft money more than the Republicans had (Republicans could count on better-heeled donors), the McCain-Feingold reform of 2002 saddled Democrats with an asymmetrical burden. Once the soft money channel to parties was closed, liberals had to set up so-called 527 groups such as Americans Coming Together ($135 million), the Media Fund ($59 million), and MoveOn.org Political Action ($11 million) to funnel soft money into technically nonpartisan on-the-ground activities like voter registration and turnout. These groups were permitted to raise unlimited sums, but coordination between officially partisan and officially nonpartisan groups was legally forbidden. Moreover, Bush raised much of his money before Kerry had won his nomination and was able to spend millions to establish hostile images in advertising by the time Kerry began running against him. In the end, both liberal and conservative money was split between the party and the 527s, but the Republicans raised a much higher proportion of their total in hard money. The Democrats and their allies spent more money on advertising ($344 million to $289 for the Republican counterparts), but coordination gave the Republicans a better return on their investment.[55]

The splitting of money between the party and the 527s was also damaging at the local level. It led to duplication of effort on the ground, as volunteers discovered in Scranton, when people told party canvassers and phone-bankers that they'd already been visited—understandably, individuals who had been phoned or visited by the 527 groups didn't distinguish between them and the Democrats proper. "These groups did a lot, but much of it was redundant and unconnected," Minnesota's former Democratic-Farmer-Labor chairman told Hamburger and Wallsten. "The day after the election, many of these groups leave the state, and their voter files and experience leave with them."[56] The Democrats also outsourced much of their own get-out-the-vote operation to labor. By contrast, a far greater percentage of total conservative funds poured directly into the Republican Party apparatus, which took maximum advantage of data coordination and faced far less confusion. Once again, the Republicans benefited from funneling movement energies directly into their party.

Bush's margin of victory in 2004 came not only from the Republican apparatus's ability to suppress hostile votes, not only from Kerry's inability to sound like a convincing alternative on economic policy, but from Bush's formidable advantage on security, boosted, most likely, by Osama bin Laden's eleventh-hour intervention, most likely calculated to help Bush over the top, on the plausible theory that Bush's Iraq invasion had (1) tied down American troops, (2) confirmed the al-Qaeda view of American wickedness, and (3) generally raised al-Qaeda's stock in the Muslim world, benefits that Kerry would rescind by withdrawing.

But the data do not support the claim that Bush won with a mobilization of his evangelical base—which, in fact, seems not to have grown from 2000. According to the political scientist Philip A. Klinkner:

> [T]here is little evidence that religious whites surged to the polls in 2004. Whites who said that religion was important in

their lives and whites who interpreted the Bible literally saw a small 2-point increase in their Republican performance between 2000 and 2004. Because Bush's overall vote increased by 3 points over 2000, these religious voters were no more (and perhaps a bit less) supportive of Bush in 2004 over 2000 compared to the rest of the electorate.[57]

Moreover, "Bush did not, as first speculated, run any better in states with anti-gay marriage referendums on the ballot. Political scientist Alan Abramowitz found that Bush's vote increased by 2.6 percentage points in states with gay marriage ballot measures, lower than the 2.9 percent in states without such measures."[58]

The 2004 election was a referendum on terrorism and war, and more voters were willing to give Bush a pass on Iraq than were willing to give Kerry a pass on terrorism. When the National Election Survey asked the open-ended question "What do you think has been the most important issue facing the United States over the last four years?" Klinkner wrote:

> [F]ully 43 percent of voters cited terrorism as the most important issue. Coming in a distant second was the war in Iraq with 17 percent, followed by the economy at 15 percent. . . . [T]he last time that an issue was cited by this many voters was in 1968, when 44 percent said that the Vietnam War was the most important issue. . . . Not only did the terrorism issue dominate the election, but President Bush dominated on the issue of terrorism. Among those who cited terrorism as the most important issue, 70 percent voted for Bush. . . . Bush's performance advantage on the terrorism issue far outstripped his advantage on moral issues, 18 percent versus 1 percent.[59]

By contrast, those who said Iraq was the most important issue voted as strongly for Kerry (69 percent) as those who said terrorism voted for Bush.[60] In other words, those who said Iraq was the most important issue knew there was a difference between "Iraq" and "terrorism." If they knew there was a difference, they were likely to vote for Kerry.

A critical mass of voters were more impressed by the fact that the United States had not been attacked by jihadis since September 11,

2001, than by the fact that Bush had failed to avert the September 11 attacks in the first place. (Never mind the attacks in Tunisia, Indonesia, Turkey, Jordan, Madrid, London, and the myriad daily assaults, bombings, and kidnappings that turned Iraq, intended to be the beacon of a Middle East insulated from terrorists, into a living hell.) The security edge helped Bush slice off slivers from the demographic groups that might otherwise have tilted Democratic.

The rising of 2004 was the best that the American left-of-center could put up against George Bush's radical rule, but Bush won nevertheless, along with a Republican Congress. The unexpired residue of September 11 still worked for a commander in chief who, however bogged down in Iraq, exuded reality-defying "strength." To make such a race close was a near miracle. The right's lock on the old Confederacy, the prairie, and the mountains, combined with its mastery of the attack campaign, seemed insuperable.

Could a different Democratic candidate (an actual, not a hypothetical one) have won? Unlikely. For all John Kerry's evident shortcomings as a candidate—his upper-class habits, his inability to come forth with a vigorous riposte to the Swift Boat attacks, his maladroit statements, his inability to set out a compelling idea of how he would govern, the last minute (and arguably intentional) intervention of Osama bin Laden—Howard Dean or John Edwards would probably have done considerably worse against the charmed and sufficiently charming Bush. Dick Gebhardt would have gone into the race with some geographical advantages and a certain appeal to white working-class voters, but he would not have had the military-security experience to make up for Bush's immense (if unearned) edge. There are times when the nature of the candidate matters, even decisively—more on this subject further on—but in 2004, history would have reared the same obstacles in the way of any imaginable Democrat.

Still, the movement-party mobilization of 2004 continued into 2006, aroused now not only by the sense of continuing emergency but by the whiff of possible midterm victory. No sooner did Bush claim a mandate from his 2004 victory than his charm ran aground and his popularity sank. He invested his political capital in a campaign for Social Security privatization, only to run into a singularly unified Democratic opposition (galvanized in part by a netroots campaign). With news of quagmire and deadly chaos arriving daily from Iraq and no good news flowing to counter it, only Bush's most faithful base could go on thinking that the occupation of Iraq retained much promise of "victory," whatever that might mean. The incontrovertible evidence of Hurricane Katrina and the Gulf Coast flood washed away whatever reputation for competence the White House still enjoyed. There ensued the indictment and resignation of Tom DeLay, the profusion of Abramoff-inspired financial scams, and, last but not least, the Mark Foley congressional page affair, which not only dented Republican claims to "clean up the mess in Washington" but implicated Republican moralists in one more embarrassing cover-up.

In short, the Republicans were revealed to be the party of unabashed executive power, but their power was revealed to be impotent in the world. Abroad, in the midst of a lengthening war, it did not bring results besides negative ones. A flood of facts washed away the Republicans' reputation. Governing from the right was no longer smart politics. Having consolidated their party into a pyramid of top-down discipline, Bush's Republicans could not shield themselves from the rot at the top. The midterm election turned into a referendum on Bush.

In Scranton, the local activist core threw itself into Bob Casey Jr.'s Senate campaign against Rick Santorum. Unlike in 2004, the get-out-the-vote volunteers were local this time: New Yorkers were not thrilled about traveling to Pennsylvania to work for the anti-abortion Casey, never mind that he had the right name, the right credentials, and the right assortment of views for a winning campaign. Technologically, the Democrats finally caught up. Using new software,[61] they devoted themselves to phoning only "drop-off Democrats"—Democrats who ordinarily voted only in presidential elections, not in midterms. The point was to focus all available energy on mobilizing voters who didn't have to be persuaded to vote Democratic in the first place, on the premise that the calamity of one-party Republican rule was itself so compelling as to have energized the passionate Democrats who ordinarily vote in midterm elections. The logic was strong, even if, in the end, there was no proof that it made any difference in the outcome.[62] Statewide, Casey won handily, 59 percent to 41 percent, with Lackawanna County landsliding for the local favorite by 70 percent to 30 percent.[63]

Via MoveOn and other such groups, netroots activists threw themselves into the campaign. In the weeks leading up the election, MoveOn's own upgraded software enabled them to identify likely Democratic voters; in the final days, they made get-out-the-vote calls in unprecedented numbers. As in 2004, they parachuted into promising districts. Robert Snyder, a fifty-one-year-old journalism and media studies professor at Rutgers University's Newark campus, volunteered in Pennsylvania's Eighth, a hybrid district that included a white segment of Philadelphia and moderate suburbs with an environmentalist bent, where Republicans had held the seat since 1992. (The incumbent, Mike Fitzpatrick, was endorsed by the Sierra Club.) The Democratic candidate was Patrick Murphy.

Snyder had worked in Democratic campaigns intermittently since the McGovern days, when he was in high school, but he had a particular reason for gravitating to Murphy. His old friend Frank Carville, a New Jersey National Guardsman and a supporter of John Kerry, had died in an ambush in Iraq on June 4, 2004.[64] At a Veterans for Kerry rally, Snyder had met the thirty-three-year-old Murphy and been impressed by his eloquence. The son of a Philadelphia policeman, Murphy had joined the ROTC at King's College in Wilkes-Barre, had become a prosecutor, and had seen military service in both Bosnia and (as a captain in the 82nd Airborne) Baghdad. Two years later, he was the sort of dream candidate savvy Democrats had been scouring the country for. He was young, eloquent, energetic, and accomplished, with an open smile and a damp-behind-the-ears look. He was also a liberal Democrat, pro-choice, and deeply critical of the Iraq war (he favored withdrawal of all but some Special Forces within one year).[65] That he was a passionate Philadelphia Eagles fan and had voted for George W. Bush in 2000 did not hurt him. Neither did it hurt, in the end, when the Republicans Swift-Boated him with a Fitzpatrick ad saying that in Iraq Murphy had served only in convoys and hadn't seen *real* action. Murphy came roaring back with an ad saying that since he had seen Iraq's violence up close, "Mike Fitzpatrick's lies and smears don't bother me too much."

Murphy mustered a thousand volunteers on election day.[66] Some were outsiders like Snyder, but many were mainstream local Democrats, people of modest means, deeply sympathetic to the armed forces, who felt the war in Iraq to be a betrayal by Bush.[67] MoveOn.Org claimed to have mustered 106,691 phone calls into the district in Murphy's behalf.[68] He won by 1,521 votes.

As for Jackie and Steve Grumbacher, the activists who had ignited the Democrats in rural Lebanon County, Pennsylvania, in 2004, their flame still burned intensely in 2006. "We've gone a little mainstream," Steve e-mailed me. "We crashed the gate," was the way Jackie put it, referring to the title of the netroots manifesto by Jerome Armstrong and Markos Moulitsas Zúniga. The Grumbachers were elected to the county Democratic committee, with Jackie as vice chair. (The chair was a local businessman—a former Republican who left the party in 2004.) They ran Bob Casey Jr.'s Senate campaign in the county, hopeful that the anti-incumbency mood would help, since Santorum "is married to Bush." They worked with one of the three Democratic staffers that DNC chair Dean had inserted into their state—the one responsible for central Pennsylvania.

As for their post-2004 Democratic group, it evolved into an officially nonpartisan discussion group, Lebanon Exchange and Dialogue, with a mailing list of four hundred, meeting biweekly to discuss state and local issues. LEAD included "Republicans who got sick of the party becoming a party of exclusion," said Jackie. In 2005, the group supported a moderate Republican district attorney who, after being defeated in the Republican primary, ended up running as a Democrat and losing narrowly—a sign of how rampant disillusion was among the majority Republicans. A local reporter, John Latimer, told me, "LEAD gave moderate Republicans a way to support Democrats like Casey, and non-endorsed Republicans, without jumping ship to the Democrats. That is a very valuable outlet to have in a community where to be a success you almost have to be a Republican. If you are not, you risk losing business ties and certainly will not be invited to join the country club, etc."[69] In short, LEAD and the Grumbachers learned the art of forming majorities. They were makers of big tents.

In 2006, the Grumbachers upped their diet of activist blogs and fronted the money to rent a storefront for the midterm election. The moral, said Jackie in July 2006, was: "Do something. Get people involved. Look bigger than you are. Don't sit around gnashing your teeth, lamenting."[70]

They remained "pragmatists." Some other Democrats for America activists were refusing to get involved in party activity— indulging, the Grumbachers thought, in "a kind of purity." Having campaigned for a more progressive candidate than Casey to run against Santorum and having been defeated badly, these people were "sitting on their hands" in the Senate race. (Some eventually supported a Green Party candidate whose funds came primarily from Republican donors.) The purists had no time for a man of such conservative views as Casey's. "With his position on abortion," John Latimer told me, "Casey is as close to a Republican as a Democrat can get and that is what it takes to win in Central PA."[71] Bush dragged Santorum down with him. In November 2006, in a county still registered 2 to 1 Republican, Santorum won only 55 percent of the vote.[72]

"It's a conservative state," Jackie said. "I know that. But the goal for me is to get Santorum out and get a majority in the Senate." The point was to drive the extreme right into a corner—the corner where the left used to find itself during its long exile from power. "What is progressive now is what used to be the center," said Jackie. One could take this statement as reflective of the realism that is requisite after the Reagan revolution. One could also take it as sad commentary on liberalism's self-limitations—how the luminous ideals of freedom, equality, and community have fallen!

Before Election Day of 2004, on one of those incandescent days when the stream of volunteers was steady and strong and the prospect of President Kerry did not seem hallucinatory, I asked a number of out-of-town visitors to Scranton whether, if Kerry won, they could imagine turning out to lobby for health-care legislation in a recalcitrant Congress, say, or to work for some other pro-gressive cause. A few said yes, but many more thought not. Politics was not really their thing.

In the lives of most citizens, movements are episodic adventures. We—and I mean the vast majority of citizens, even activists—are freelancers, dipping in and out of activity as we like, improvising our political lives as we go along, making ad hoc judgments about our next moves. External events intrude; so do private ones. We make political forays and—lacking clear formulas to measure success—assess the results as best we can. Not being pure products of political conscience, we gauge the quality of our experience. The rest of life has its lures.[73] Most historical moments do not galvanize vast numbers, do not make unconditional demands, do not feel like emergencies for the people who live through them. By contrast, the specialists who practice politics as a profession haven't the luxury of coming and going. Even as the amateurs rise and subside, there is always some politics for professionals to do.

In 2006, as in 2004, the movement and the party of the center-left converged in common cause, but this time the Democrats triumphed. This was in no small part because under severe stress the Republican movement-party relationship came unstuck, with many movement conservatives deeply disillusioned by Bush over Iraq, corruption, and government spending, while growing num-bers of independents and rank-and-file Republicans went into revolt against Bush's alignment with precisely those movement conservatives. Republican candidates went out of their way to cut and run from the taint of Bush, but even their sudden show of independence did not avail their national prospects.

In the event, voters seized the midterms as a no-confidence moment. Despite the Republicans' redistricting conquests, the Demo-crats won a majority in the House and also retook the Senate. At the same time, a net twelve governorships changed hands from Republican to Democrat, putting the Democrats in a 28–22 major-ity, and the Democrats gained a net 637 state legislative seats, leaving them in charge of both chambers in 24 states, as against 16 for the Republicans—a strong start toward dominating the redis-tricting that will follow the 2010 census. According to exit polls,

Democrats won the popular House vote 52 to 46 percent, and the Senate vote by 55 to 42 percent.[74] In a poll taken just after the election, a bare quarter of those surveyed, 24 percent, called themselves Republicans, while 35 percent identified themselves as Democrats, and a whopping 40 percent called themselves independents.[75] These, Democrats won by 18 percentage points.[76] By March 2007, fully 50 percent either identified with the Democrats or leaned toward them, as against 35 percent who sided with the Republicans.[77] Plainly, at this moment, the operating majority was—not Republican. The non-Republican big tent was open for business. Democrats of all stripes felt relieved, indeed *lightened*— they were evidently not doomed forever!

What with Democratic gains in every region, among voters under thirty, among nonevangelical white Protestants, Catholics, Hispanics, men and women, the demographics suggest that the time is nigh for the "emerging Democratic majority" anticipated prematurely by John Judis and Ruy Teixeira in 2004. But one vivid fact and one vivid contingency should quash any premature celebrations. The fact is that there will never again be an election that can so readily be converted into a direct referendum on George W. Bush. He will never again serve in person as the negative pole who delivers electric shocks into all quarters of the electorate. The prime contingency concerns matters that are out of American hands— specifically, terror attacks. Whatever actual damage they may do to life, limb, and property, terror attacks in general do accomplish what they were intended to accomplish: they generate terror, evoke a panic reaction, in the short run (at least) driving much of the public into the arms of the more authoritarian, militaristic party. Still, in 2008 there would be no incumbent Republican to take advantage.

If the GOP's short-term prospects are diminished, the damage Bush did will endure to arouse the antagonism of his opponents. Democrats may well run against Bush for years to come, as they ran repeatedly against Herbert Hoover well after 1932. The movements that cultivated, loved, and honored Bush will strive onward, even as his would-be successors strive to shirk responsibility for the ways in which he truly did represent them. In Bush's twilight, new

Republican leaders will emerge, aiming to catapult the party out of the Southern corner into which it has painted itself. Against them, movement conservatives will rededicate themselves to purification. They may or may not succeed in their artful dodges and rededications, but one way or another, liberals will face, yet again, their enduring problems of self-definition and strategy.

One thing is certain: if liberals—and other Democrats—are to continue their fitful recovery, the sort of party-movement hybrid that materialized in 2004 and 2006 will have to remain at its core. Again, a disciplined, no-nonsense movement-party relationship was at the heart of conservative growth after the Goldwater debacle of 1964. The conservatives' discipline deepened as Ronald Reagan knit together the moralist and antigovernment conservatives, the amateurs and the professionals, into an enduring coalition. For the Democrats to become and remain the next governing majority, the veterans of the 2004 and 2006 risings, all those small-d democrats and small-r republicans, supplemented by fresh recruits, will have to mobilize and remobilize, taking politics into their hands, calling the meetings, knocking on doors, making the calls, collecting the data, passing out signs and buttons, and performing all the other chores of on-the-ground politics. This ensemble will have to harness an on-the-ground party, with all its complexities of geography and policy, to the moral force of liberals.

A movement is not a sum of marquee names and spectacular mobilizations, though the names can help and the mobilizations are markers. A movement is organized, and its soul is made up of the organizers—and not just the names who convene, make declarations, and issue pronouncements. A movement is a sum of moral acts undertaken by people who, one at a time, feel called in a thousand little ways to *do something*.

One Saturday night in October 2004, a Scranton man named Joe Viola called Democratic headquarters to say that he was incensed. At evening mass at St. Anthony's church in Dunmore, a suburb of Scranton, he said, the deacon, the Reverend Mr. Carmine Mendicino, had told the parishioners—not once but three times— to vote against John Kerry.

Such worldly interventions by clerical personnel were taking place throughout the United States. A number of Catholic bishops said publicly that they would deny communion to politicians—it was hard to obscure the fact that John Kerry was one of them—who did not vote against abortion. Perhaps under Vatican pressure, at one point they declared judiciously that while they would not endorse such virtual excommunications as mandatory church policy, they would not forbid local clerics from making their own decisions. Kerry professed himself against abortion personally, but as a civil matter he upheld a woman's right to abortion. His opponents were horrified by such distinctions.

Joe Viola said that not only he but others were seething and shocked, for the Catholic Church in this very antiabortion corner of Pennsylvania had never resorted to such declamations before. The next day, Viola called back to say that he had fired off a letter to the pastor, Monsignor Anthony C. Marra, telling him the deacon's exhortation was not only morally wrong but could cost the church its tax exemption. Marra called him back and apologized. The deacon approached Viola at his place of work, apologized, said he wanted to do penance, and asked Viola what he should do. Viola told him to get up next Sunday and say he was wrong to do that. The deacon said he would.

Some fine day, the Democrats might figure out how to stay on the right side of the value divide. They would define America as a commons belonging equally to all citizens, not a playground of the strong. They would get used to putting themselves forward, undefensively, as patriots, not outsiders. They would concentrate their minds on composing a vital majority, and they would be rigorous about making the effort to maximize their own strength and minimize their opponents'. Should they get to that point, some would recall that during the bitter and hopeful and then again bitter year of 2004, at least for some moments, they breathed a spirit that not only touched them deeply but made them feel, for a while, giddy—a culture of winning.

11

Frames, Demons, and No-Longer-Silent Majorities

How to recover from the Bush calamity? How to revive an intelligent version of the common good? How to consolidate and extend the midterm victories of 2006? How to further such auspicious dynamics as are in play and hinder the retrograde ones?

The supply of Ways Forward these days matches the demand for them. Proposals for tactics and strategies, new ideas (or less-or-more stirring *calls* for new ideas) about governing principles and policies, and—not least—new candidates go on display, online, for Democrats, liberals, progressives, or what-have-you with every passing week. Professional party strategists and come-latelys, inside and outside the Beltway, as well as troubled software tycoons of a liberal bent, engagé social scientists, bloggers, and local and national activists launch proposals that quickly metamorphose into scrimmage, even debates, via the Internet. Among the more important questions: Do conservatives outnumber liberals, implying that Democrats must run toward the center? If the Democrats *should* run toward the center, just where is that elusive place to be found? Doesn't it shift as issues and passions arise and decline? Can progressive economics trump culture wars? Are the Democrats fatally tainted by their dependency on fat-cat contributions, and, if so, isn't the public financing of elections a sine qua non of serious reform, and, if *that* is so, how is such reform possible when sitting politicians, by definition, have no need of it—they may even need to reject it—and meanwhile the federal courts seem unlikely to back such a radical change, however worthy? Should Democrats take heart from having won the popular vote in three of the last four presidential elections, or lose heart from the fact that they won't have Bill Clinton on their ticket again? Was the 2006 election a sign that a new political majority is busy being born or only the thumping repudiation of a disastrous president?

Robust debate, even vociferous scrimmage, is a sign of live politics. If the conflict were not intense, this could only be because a political elite was making all the decisions behind closed doors, which could be healthy only if the party elite could be trusted to make its decisions well. Neither of these conditions obtains. So a profusion of notions about the future of a political party is a precondition for vitality. Best, of course, if the notions come equipped with logic and evidence.

Two prologues to a where-do-we-go-from-here agenda. To start with, what about reforming the way we speak? There has been a great deal of talk in the last few years about the question of how to "frame" media messages and "brand" the party. There is so much reference to "narratives," it is as if the gates that the activists crashed belonged to the English Department. Not surprisingly, linguists have taken the lead in scolding liberals for their linguistic malfeasance. The linguist George Lakoff has written indefatigably that progressives have succumbed to a conservative trick by granting the right the power to frame issues. We are always answering the question of whether we're going to stop beating our wives. When we accept conservative metaphors, we accept conservative frameworks, their ways of posing the questions; then even people who disagree with conservatives are predisposed to their answers. At a deep psychic level, we are held in their thrall. Once we let conservatives define the estate tax as "the death tax" or abortion rights as a "culture of life," we lose, for where is the robust American who will stand up for a death tax or against a culture of life? Progressives leaped to Lakoff's call, hoping that the proper reframing offered a short-cut to voters' hearts.

Without doubt, it is better to use stirring slogans than flat ones, and it is wise to dispute the feel-good loading in phrases like "No Child Left Behind," "Clean Skies," "Healthy Forests," or, for that matter, the Patriot Act and "family values."[1] So much is elementary. But to say that slogans should engage affirmative emotions is not to say that linguistic differences are direct transcriptions of deep value differences. One problem with Lakoff's linguistic hyperbole is that he assumes that ideologies clump together—that positions on the Iraq war, for example, automatically group together with positions on, say, abortion, Social Security, taxes, and deficit spending, which are, in turn, rooted in divergent models of good family structures. He promotes the theorist's assumption that casual language is a revelation of deep belief, so that when people hear a slogan, they automatically place it within a deep structure, a fundamental "narrative." Moreover, Lakoff goes so far as to insist that the ideological clumps stem from profound feelings about family structure. Conservatives adhere to a "strict parent" assumption on the premise that children are ill-behaved by nature and must therefore be disciplined strictly in order to succeed. (If one follows the evidence that conservatives disproportionately have authoritarian personalities, one could go further and say that they *desire* strict parents because, at some level, they want to be spanked.) Progressives, Lakoff proposes by contrast, believe in a family led by nurturing parents: consensual, democratic. In order to convince citizens to change their political preferences, progressives must activate the nurturing frame.

But Lakoff's arguments are strictly a priori. He offers no evidence that policy positions clump, let alone that the clumps are aligned with people's views of, or experiences with, family life. He underrates the variety of mix-and-match possibilities.[2] Moreover, if the family structures that are the roots of political views are sunk as deep as Lakoff proposes, it would seem unlikely that a campaign of sloganeering could dig deep enough to unearth them. Lakoff's counsel would then be fruitless.

Rhetoric that makes your side look golden and the other side look like bums surely conveys advantages. Democrats ought to get used to defining themselves as a moral force, so that the right to health care is a *value*, the right to a living wage is a *value*, more equality of opportunity is a *value*, the preservation of clean air and water and the phasing out of fossil fuels are *values*. It suits a party that aims to carve out an enduring majority to find candidates who, when they talk about community and mutual reliance, do not sound as though they are speaking foreign tongues. But perhaps the Democrats are already willy-nilly speaking the language of values when they stand for an increasing minimum wage, sustainable energy, and so on. Does a party win "value voters" by stamping its feet and insisting it likes values?

In general, the linguistic fetish is more a mark of desperation than a solution. It smacks of a search for shortcuts, rhetoric being easier to alter than principles, party organization, or the quality of candidates. If only language were so important! Then professors, writers, and bloggers could win by the strokes of their keyboards. But it should not be surprising that university professors are prone to exaggerate the importance of correct speech.

And the professors have influence outside the academy, too. A couple of generations of university graduates have imbibed the so-called linguistic turn that hit the social sciences in the seventies, an ensemble of intellectual moves that emphasized—often enough for good reason—the importance of "discourse" in securing social power.[3] No elaborate linguistic theory is necessary to recognize that the Republicans benefited from braying that any plans for troop withdrawals from Iraq amounted to "cut and run," or that Democrats would do better to speak of investing in new energy jobs than tree-hugging. Nifty phrases on bumper stickers would be dandy, but it is the well of principle from which slogans are drawn that concerns me more. Somewhere in the obsession with framing is an assumption that the United States would be a progressive nation if liberals tinkered better against the forces of evil. About this assumption, I will have more to say later in this chapter.

A second prologue concerns the quality of the present debate about the next moves for the liberal left and the Democrats. This debate borders on the acrimonious and frequently crosses the line into nastiness. But even if the heat-to-light ratio stays high, the fervor is a price of democracy. Nobody ever promised that open discussion would be the utmost in tranquility or rationality. Public debate (not least its latest carrier, Internet chatter) is rife with insult, laced with obscenity, dense with shoddy argumentation. It does not warm a heart committed to reason as a core principle of public life. Moreover, bear in mind that for all the vigor of the online debate about progressive strategy, the netroots, whether at their best or not, are not the entirety of the Democratic Party—far from it. The largest single bloc of the party faithful consists of members of labor unions, and even in the unions' debilitated state, their number totals at this writing *many* times more (possibly ten times more) than the sum of all netroot activists.[4] Moreover, there is no guarantee that the grassroots discussion about strategy, however intense, will bite—will sway the thinking of players who operate more or less professionally in the arena of political life. Still, without the discussion there is very unlikely to be any smart, combative, victorious party at all. On the other hand, if what emerges from the netroots is nothing more than a collective gnashing of teeth, then the Democratic default will play before a larger audience than ever before, but a default it will remain.

One elementary principle of progressive life is that the so-called conservative movement must be roundly defeated if America is to be capable of equitable and reasonable policies. The big tent of the Democrats must include the practical left and all others who understand that whatever affairs of state they care about, whatever burdens weigh most heavily with them, whichever policies strike them most urgently, the right stands in their way. This right will seize the offensive whenever it can. It can shift shape, emerging now as "neoconservatism," now as "compassionate conservatism," now as "old-fashioned conservatism," now as the incarnation of Burke, now of Hayek, now of Newt Gingrich. It can endure waves of unpopularity—it has done so before. But it is also, in fact, a great uniter—of its opposition. George W. Bush, Dick Cheney, Donald Rumsfeld, Jack Abramoff, Tom DeLay, Mark Foley, Pat

Robertson—these Republican poster children unite all those who recognize the disasters these men stood for.

This is true in the short run because George Bush chose to govern through knife-edge polarization. Ronald Reagan harbored this tendency, too, in foreign policy most of all, but it was muted by the Democrats' dominance in the House and their skill in congressional opposition. For six years, though, Bush's take-it-or-leave it politics commanded not only the White House but the Republican congressional elites and the media of the right, driving their party further rightward. Bush furthered (though he did not begin) the identification of the Republican Party with its most radical elements—the evangelical-fundamentalist Christian-based right and the big business bloc that subordinates the interests of the majority to the interests of the wealthy. Having chosen to govern from the hard right, to centralize power within the executive branch and even more tightly within a small circle there, to mobilize and reward his base accordingly, and to avoid the need for compromise by resolving to win elections by small majorities, Bush squeezed more moderate elements out of the party. Having no need to compromise on specifics, he resolutely refused to do so. Bush and his lieutenants did not need to take into account anyone's positions or arguments but their own. His 50-percent-plus-1 approach to strategy invigorated the cadres. They were invested in more than a strategy, but an identity as well: the party as fighting force. Yielding was out of the question. If push came to shove, they believed they could win—and mainly, they could.

And then, in his second term, as Bush's public support slumped, they couldn't. As the Iraq war looked increasingly bleak, Bush drove wedges into his own party, forfeiting part of the center, thus inviting Democrats to pick up more independents and Republican moderates—the opposite of what the Republicans accomplished in the South when the Democrats' support for civil rights cost them their old solid base there. Bush lost traction on issue after issue. Much of his base deserted him on Social Security privatization. Republican dissenters on Iraq, surveillance, torture, immigration, stem cells, Terri Schiavo, and executive power in general were emboldened. Where once, in the shadow of the Southern Strategy,

Democrats were shedding their donkey skins to reinvent themselves as Republicans (Senators Strom Thurmond, Phil Gramm, Richard Shelby, and Zell Miller), in 2005 and 2006 most of the traffic was running in the opposite direction.

The former Reagan administration navy secretary James Webb, who opposed the Iraq war, won the Democratic nomination for a U.S. Senate seat in Virginia and went on to win the election against right-wing reliable George Allen. "Thirty years ago, the Republican Party embraced people like me," Webb told the *American Prospect* before the election. "Today, however, the Republicans' extreme wing has pulled the party so far outside the mainstream that a lot of people who share my basic beliefs are looking for new leadership."[5] The head of the Republican Party of Kansas—Kansas, alleged to be the heartland of right-wing false consciousness—quit the GOP, declared himself a Democratic candidate for lieutenant governor, and denounced the Republicans as "fixated on ideological issues that really don't matter to people's everyday lives. What matters is improving schools and creating jobs. I got tired of the theological debate over whether Charles Darwin was right."[6] He won. Another former Kansas Republican ran for attorney general—as a Democrat—and won, too.

This seepage might be arrested if the Democrats moved too far left on hot-button issues such as immigration and gay marriage, or if the Republicans produced yet another in their long line of rough-rider leader-heroes. In principle, many of the Democrats' close victories in 2006 might well be reversible in 2008, once the Bush albatross is unwrapped from Republican necks and tossed overboard. But it is beyond dispute that the Republicans will continue to face disagreeable divisions. Their libertarian wing revolts against Bush's big-government moves—"No Child Left Behind," growing deficits, congressional earmarks, subsidized agribusiness. Most of the party revolted against Bush's immigration reforms. Senator Lindsey Graham of South Carolina, an erstwhile John McCain supporter who was later at odds with the Bush White House on torture and the handling of Guantánamo prisoners, said in July 2006—directly contrary to Karl Rove's line—that Republicans must move beyond mobilizing their base "because our base isn't big enough to propel us to victory 10 years from now."[7] In a Gallup poll published the same month, some 41 percent of Republicans said they would find Senator John McCain an "unacceptable" presidential candidate in 2008[8]—even though McCain gamely made his pilgrimage to Jerry Falwell's Liberty University in order to demonstrate that if not quite willing to kiss the ring of a man he had labeled an "agent of intolerance," he was willing to shake the hand that wore it.

As I have argued throughout this book, the Republicans have for decades benefited from leaders of stature, men who radiated an aura of strength and shelter that warmed the hearts of more than true believers and gave them the feeling that they, or the people they thought themselves to be, would be properly represented. They may, temporarily, at least, have reached the end of that line. With Bush's popularity stuck in a trough, serious conflict within the Republican coalition resurfaces unavoidably. The jockeying for the 2008 nomination may well exacerbate divisions that the party kept muted as long as Bush was riding high.

After Bush, no successor is obvious. With George Allen gone down to ignominious defeat, Jeb Bush succumbing to family fatigue, Bill Frist discredited—indeed, driven out of politics altogether—and Sam Brownback narrow in his capacity to inspire, the religious right has no natural candidate. On Iraq, even if John McCain succeeds in convincing the Christian right that he has made his peace with it, he has carved out a deeply unpopular position by calling for more troops in Iraq and provided his adversaries an unforgettable Dukakis-in-a-tank moment by strolling through a Baghdad market in body armor, accompanied by helicopters, sharpshooters, and a detachment of one hundred troops, having just declared that "many parts" of the city were safe for Americans. Chuck Hagel departs from Bush (as well as from fellow Vietnam veteran McCain), which could attract centrists and independents, but he did not win important friends on the evangelical right when he said, "You cannot have a foreign policy based on divine mission. We tried that in the Middle Ages, that's what the Crusades were about."[9] Rudolph Giuliani will try to distract from his gay-friendly, pro-choice politics with pugnacity, while his opponents remind female voters that he has been married three times and that he announced his intention to leave his second wife *on live television* before telling her face-to-face. (How would his post–September 11 reputation for "strong character" weather a campaign against a strong opposition? I wonder.) If the Republican coalition were issuing a casting call, its most plausible candidate might be the glib, businesslike, commonsensical-seeming Massachusetts ex-governor Mitt Romney, a man with a square jaw and an easy smile who denounces taxes and presses all the right buttons for evangelicals (if he supported abortion and gay rights in the past, he can always claim to have been born again, which appeals to the religious right). He is, however, a Mormon.

For practical reasons, despite the scruples of their McCain-Graham wing, the Republicans will probably remain a radically conservative party for the foreseeable future. Precisely to overcome their electoral weaknesses on domestic policy, they will have to rely on their mystique of toughness, their popular edge in the "war on terror," and a friendly relationship—even a negotiated one—with the hard-edged Christian right. Republican politicians of a moderate bent on social issues will find it hard to win primary support over the confirmed opposition of movement conservatives who are quick to spot an Antichrist in Northeastern clothing. In tough elections, panic stratagems remain the Republicans' strongest gambits. And this is another reason that it is very likely true in the long run as well that the Republicans must be defeated if progressive movements are to have a chance.

In other words, with Republicans in power, all the progressive movements, as well as moderate Republicans, are choked off from influence. The practical left will have little or nothing to say about what is to be done about Iraq or Afghanistan or Israel-Palestine, about abortions or contraception, about the draining away of jobs, about the melting of icecaps, about departing from fossil fuels, about stagnating wages and whether wages will continue to be taxed more heavily than wealth, or about whether government is to be turned over to self-seeking cronies whose attentiveness to the common good is consistently sidetracked by their pursuit of the exceedingly private interest. As long as the Democrats are confined to the outside peering in, almost all progressive labors are blocked. With Democrats in power, they have a solid chance. Not a guarantee, but more than a sliver of power. They are represented inside the big tent. They can stoke up debates. They can clamor. They can prospect for new policies, policies that are not dictated by industry and lobbyists from the far right. They can propose policy A or B and object to policy X or Y and have a nonzero chance of getting results. With the Republicans in power, on most issues of central interest to their constituencies they can make nothing but noise.

The only way to displace the right is to pour energy and treasure into a party that combines the energies of all those who are throttled by the hard politics of the Republican right—from the hard-core constituents who make up the Democratic Party's interest groups (African Americans, Hispanics, union members, gays and lesbians, social-liberal professionals) to the citizens who want something done about jobs and universal health care, to the independents and the principled conservatives who want a modest foreign policy and a solvent government. The right will not be displaced by street demonstrations, though some might be useful now and then, or by digging interest-group chairs more deeply into the sand or by table-pounding protest against new styles in empire or the benighted racism of the white working class or the general virulence of American history. There is no shortcut around political power, which means there is no shortcut around coalitions, which means there is no shortcut around tradeoffs. The party capable of driving the Republicans into well-earned retirement will not be strictly a liberal party—there aren't enough across-the-board liberals in the country. It will be a coalition. It will be a party of reason and it will also be a party of several reasons, not just one.

For generations, the right has built up energy, clarity, and unity through demonization. The demon is not really government in the abstract, for the right finds government congenial when it is ordering up and deploying the machines of war and surveillance, and even, under George W. Bush, when it is imposing uniform tests upon American schoolchildren. The demons are you, readers. From the Bush-friendly point of view, you are likely to be overly educated and insufficiently devout, and you have hijacked the authentic American mission. You are soft, if not swish; tender-minded, not tough-minded; wishy-washy, not resolute. You promote trivial liberties that undermine national strength. You practice "the soft bigotry of low expectations." You shackle the primal forces of investment. You appease barbarians abroad and at home, those termite forces always at work to undermine Western civilization. Whether the subject is abortion, terrorism, education, gay marriage, foreign policy, school prayer, affirmative action, taxes, welfare, secularism, court appointments, sex education, obscenity, or immigration, the right's underlying message is that you liberals are, as Newt Gingrich said about Bill Clinton, "the enemy of normal Americans." The Christian right was willing to take a back seat in its coalition, at times, because it knew how crucial it was to lay you low—toward which end it knew it would have to defeat the Democratic Party across the board. When the right was out of power, it concentrated its collective mind on defeating you. When it was in power, it consolidated—even at the cost of overreaching badly.

Through the vicissitudes of recent decades, the movement of Goldwater, Reagan, and their heirs has thrived on intense combat against a common enemy. In politics, a shared antagonism accomplishes a great deal of work in holding a coalition together—and in a modern society, especially one as complex as the United States, there is no scheme of political power that does not require a coalition of elements. Tax-cutters and home-schoolers, upholders of school prayer and opponents of euthanasia, Catholic pro-lifers and militant unleashers of universal democracy had to be bound together to win political power, and this was more than a matter of fitting together compatible and overlapping interests. There had to be an emotional cement.

The emotion came from naming the collective enemy. The enemy was, in the words of Myron Magnet, a writer who influenced Bush, "the majority culture . . . [l]ed by its elite institutions—the universities, the judiciary, the press, the great charitable foundations, even the mainstream churches."[10] In other words, it was an elite of overeducated, *New York Times*–reading, endive-nibbling, wine-tasting, latte-swilling, Volvo-driving, gay-loving, and would-be flag-burning blue-staters, secular or (at the least) too busy for church, denizens of the "three coasts" (the North Atlantic, the Pacific, and the Great Lakes)—in brief, Manhattan and Massachusetts, Harvard and Berkeley, the *New York Times* and Dan Rather, Michael Dukakis and John Kerry.

More affirmative versions of what the Republican-conservative combine stands for emerge from time to time. In 1960, Barry Goldwater himself couched his faith this way: "[T]he people's welfare depends on individual self reliance rather than on state paternalism."[11] In the spirit of the Puritans, Myron Magnet spoke of "personal responsibility, self-control, and deferral of gratification."[12] The Social Darwinist theme—every man for himself and the devil take the hindmost—is a perennial, though it tends to be muffled nowadays by the pleasant alliteration of "compassionate conservatism." Contemporary conservatives, of course, add a traditional culture spin: this rugged individual who is to make his (or, less likely, her) own way requires family shelter and succor. From the other side, Jared Bernstein of the Economic Policy Institute has dubbed the Republicans YOYOs: You're On Your Own.[13] This is not unfair, except that the compassionate conservative spin would be: if you fail, throw yourself on the mercy of family and charity, but do not look to cold, inept government for help.

All of these formulations emphasize the Republicans' libertarian appeal, the notion that Republicans are, in essence, freedom lovers, in the deep American grain, and that their brand of freedom-loving is what made the country great. This appeal overlaps with the tough-guy mystique that positions them as the party to trust against terrorists, potential terrorists, regimes that harbor terrorists, and all other regimes that rule tyrannically and are unimpressed by American interests and values. Bush attempted to repackage the self-reliance motif as "the ownership society," emphasizing the economic dimension of every-man-for-himself. The tough guy and the ownership guy have this in common: they are rugged individualists. They despise safety nets. Those are for dependents—that is, weaklings. Tough guys and owners—they are the freedom fighters who live on Ronald Reagan's "city upon a hill." No wonder white men have been the bulwark of the Republican vote for decades.

But nearly half of Republicans during the years of George W. Bush had a different priority, at least one tilted at a somewhat different angle. They were cultural and moral traditionalists. According to the political scientist Gary C. Jacobson, "45 percent of Republicans are religious traditionalists ['defined by fundamentalist beliefs, regular participation, and identification with religious movements'] or LDS [Latter-Day Saints]."[14] These voters—largely antiabortion, anti–stem cell research, anti–sex education, anti-contraception, antigambling, antiobscenity, pro–school prayer, and so on—could not be called core members of Grover Norquist's "leave-us-alone coalition." They are government interventionists when it suits them to be. They believe that they, and the institutions they prize, need and deserve a helping hand from the strong arm of the law. Their passion is not to leave other people alone. They want to bend the resources and the rhetorical powers of government to shore up the values that they believe are the core of America's purpose.

The genius of the Republican leadership—when it works—lies in its ability to convince all the believers in this coalition that they are at war against the same resolute enemy; that the next election, bill, judicial nomination, talk show, or Fox newscast is yet another momentous battle against that enemy; and that their leaders look after their vital moral interests even as they are forced to compromise and postpone some of their aims. They are both visionaries and gradualists, proprietors and insurgents. They may not abolish abortion tomorrow, but they will chip away at late-term abortions and insist on parental notification. One judge at a time, they will reclaim the federal courts. There is nothing wrong with their coalition that more power cannot solve.

Thus the importance to them of a "war on terror" in perpetuity. For their coalition, war without end is a uniter, not a divider. Since the massacres of September 11, 2001, the Republicans have drawn heavily on the panic dividend. Obviously, Americans have real enemies among the jihadis of al-Qaeda and its franchises and allies. It is equally true and obvious that the Republicans have been adroit at cashing the dividend. It is their strategists' recurrent theme. In the run-up to the 2002 midterm elections, Karl Rove well understood that Republicans needed to "focus on the war"—that is, run as the party best (or uniquely) equipped to defend the country against terrorists.[15] In 2005, as we saw, he accused liberals of "want[ing] to prepare indictments and offer therapy and understanding for our attackers."[16] In January 2006, speaking to the Republican National Committee, he was still beating this drum: "At the core, we are dealing with two parties that have fundamentally different views on national security. Republicans have a post-9/11 worldview, and many Democrats have a pre-9/11 worldview."[17]

The better part of wisdom, as we try to dig out of the Bush disaster, is to think of the Democratic Party as the ensemble of all those who, whether they belong to liberal movements or not, understand that a right-wing Republican Party is the enemy of all they aspire to. If they want a rational energy policy and a foreign policy that works better than raw military power; if they want health care and growing wages; if they want some right to abortion (even to contraception); if they take their Christianity from the Sermon on the Mount and not from Pat Robertson, or if they're steadfastly secular; if they want a more balanced budget—then they must isolate the Republicans as the party of the Iraq debacle, embrace the Democrats as the party of everyone else, and evict the Republicans from the seats of power.

It is for good reason that Will Rogers's saying of 1935 became a perennial: "I am not a member of any *organized* party—I am a Democrat." But heretical as this may sound, a Democratic ensemble that is serious about power cannot afford to be too loose. The Republican bulldozer will look to smash its way through the big tent. As the right did when its traditionalists, anticommunists, and libertarians decided, in the early sixties, to put their differences aside in favor of a common loathing for liberals and the left, the Democrats must rediscover the virtues of unity as a matter of principle. Within the party, liberals should surely fight for their values. When they dissent from the more procorporate wing of the party on bankruptcy legislation, trade policy, labor legislation, or foreign policy, they should push. They should not give up. But they should be willing to lose battles in order to win wars. And when they are in power, they should not regard the Democratic Party simply as a hollow vessel to lobby.[18] They must be committed to it as their party—their imperfect party, but their party nevertheless.

12

Is the Tent Big Enough?

The hard, plain, unblinkable evidence is that for the foreseeable future, there are not enough consistent liberals to elect a majority party—that is, a party capable of governing, playing a sizable part in governing, or even effectively opposing the ruling party. A party of the practical left must be a party of the center-left.

Does this mean that, as Barry Goldwater put it in 1960, "America is fundamentally a Conservative nation"?[1] Or, to put it another way, are Americans generally committed to conserving an ideal of themselves as rugged individualists? Has anything changed since 1948, when Richard Hofstadter published the following words?

> Although it has been said repeatedly that we need a new conception of the world to replace the ideology of self-help, free enterprise, competition, and beneficent cupidity upon which Americans have been nourished since the foundation of the Republic, no new conceptions of comparable strength have taken root and no statesman with a great mass following has arisen to propound them.[2]

And if more than fifty years have passed since Hofstadter's observation, can there be any doubt that Americans by and large enter politics with the assumption that government ought to be, while competent, still minimal (at least, when the military is not concerned)? Is there any reasonable way to spin the known facts about the American disposition to deny that Americans overall come to public life with a conservative temper?

To deny the country's conservative bias, I think, requires a definite wishfulness—a cherry-picking of evidence eerily reminiscent of the Bush-Cheney administration's notoriously selective use of prewar intelligence about Iraq. It is not a mere surplus of political caution that drives the more cautious Democrats to worry aloud about the practical consequences of driving the party too far to the left—as, for example, William A. Galston and Elaine C. Kamarck wrote in their 2005 article "The Politics of Polarization": "When American politics turns into a shootout between liberals and conservatives, conservatives almost always win."[3] The exceptions consist of the bluest states, but there aren't enough of those to win and hold either the Senate or the House, let alone the presidency.

Galston and Kamarck are the strategists whose earlier article "The Politics of Evasion," written in 1989 for the Democratic Leadership Council, was an influential manifesto promoting, in effect, the candidacy of someone very like Bill Clinton. Seeing their names on a new manifesto, some liberals may be inclined to turn the page, so resoundingly does the DLC speak to them of corporate toadying, but that would be small-minded: one should pay acute attention to the evidence and the line of argument that Galston and Kamarck bring to bear. Facts, as best we can ascertain them, are stubborn things.

People who follow the numbers know that, consistently, when pollsters ask voters to label themselves liberal, moderate, or conservative, almost five call themselves conservative for every three who call themselves liberal. According to the compilation by Galston and Kamarck, the average percentages, looking at the seven presidential elections from 1976 to 2004, are as follows:

- Liberal: 20 percent
- Conservative: 33 percent
- Moderate: 47 percent

In other words, there were 65 percent more self-described conservatives than self-described liberals. The 2004 election was just about typical, with 21 percent calling themselves liberal, 34 percent conservative, and 45 percent moderate—an excess of 62 percent self-described conservatives over liberals.[4] It then follows, Galston and Kamarck argued (following their similar conclusion of 1989), that Democrats have to "appeal successfully to the center of the American electorate."

Now comes the harder part. What do people mean when they call themselves conservative, moderate, or liberal? Where is the center, anyway? From a liberal point of view, the numbers might be challenged or prettied up if you suppose that the center has moved leftward, so that to call yourself a conservative in 2004 means that you're actually rather liberal, but either because the term *liberal* has become taboo, you don't like labels in the first place, or you're unaware that your definitions are shifting, you call yourself "moderate" or even "conservative," or refuse any label at all, when the pollsters call up and give you three choices and three choices only.

Scott Winship, a graduate student at Harvard who conducted research for Galston and Kamarck, probed various survey results precisely to see whether these things have been happening.[5] Winship's work is the most sophisticated exploration I know of these matters, and it offers at least some lukewarm comfort to liberals. In late 2004, the National Election Survey (NES), which presses people to choose either "liberal" or "conservative" rather than "moderate," found 22 percent of voters who called themselves *liberal* as against 36 percent who called themselves *conservative* and 32 percent who called themselves *moderate*.[6] So far, then, the Galston-Kamarck analysis seems to hold into 2004. Liberals are outnumbered.

The question remains, what do people mean by the labels? Plainly, the norm, the prevailing sense of the normal, moved sharply right during the years of the Republican ascendancy. Consider, for example, the astute political analyst Paul Waldman's observation that when the NES asked respondents how liberal or conservative the presidential candidates were, self-described conservatives in 1992 and 1996 called Bill Clinton more liberal than self-described conservatives had called Hubert Humphrey in 1968, Walter

Mondale in 1984, Michael Dukakis in 1988, or even George McGovern in 1972.[7]

And regardless of what Americans call themselves, what do they actually think and feel? Has liberalism become the ideology that dares not speak its name, and is it this reticence, or fear, that accounts for the fact that conservatives outnumber them? Might people who call themselves conservatives actually hold positions that political analysts consider liberal? Moreover, which issue positions actually determine how people vote? In other words, might some people claim to be conservative, whereas the survey results show that their liberal positions are actually determining their votes, or vice versa?

To answer these questions, Winship analyzed the 2004 NES data to see what positions the respondents, *regardless of what they called themselves*, took on issues. He broke the results into four issue areas: moral values; foreign policy and national security; economic and social policy; and fiscal policy. To take account of how important their policy preferences were in determining how people actually voted, he weighted each issue in accordance with "how well it predicted the presidential vote." Then he "categorized everyone as a liberal or conservative in each [of the four] domain[s]" by taking the weights into account and seeing whether, de facto, liberal outweighed conservative or vice versa. The terms could be defined in different ways, of course. In fact, Winship used two different schemes for classifying people as operationally liberal or conservative. Depending on which definitions he used, the data pointed to either an even split or an edge to the operational liberals.

Whether people were *operationally* liberal or conservative, regardless of what they called themselves, depended on the issue area. Only 38 percent of adults were liberal on values, 46 percent on foreign policy and national security, 54 percent on economic and social policy, and 58 percent on fiscal policy.

Winship's analysis offers evidence that the "liberal" label has, to put it mildly, decayed. The best predictors of whether people called themselves *conservative* or *liberal* were their culture war views and the presence or absence of authoritarian values, as reflected in their child-rearing preferences. Whatever people might mean by the term, even people with liberal views were reluctant to use the label. *Operational liberals—people with liberal positions on issues— were as likely to call themselves moderate as liberal.* Interestingly, 13 percent of the population (and 10 percent of the electorate) refused to choose any label at all—even "moderate." (More than two-thirds of these, in the general population, were operationally liberal, as were 80 percent among voters.) On the strength of this survey, it would seem that the term *liberal* has been definitively tainted.

Winship classified eight distinct populations among the voters:

- Self-identified conservatives who were also operationally conservative: 30 percent of the electorate
- Self-identified liberals who were also operationally liberal: 20 percent
- Self-identified conservatives who were operationally liberal: 6 percent
- Self-identified liberals who were operationally conservative: 2 percent
- Self-identified moderates who were operationally liberal: 19 percent
- Self-identified moderates who were operationally conservative: 13 percent
- People who refused to self-identify but were operationally liberal: 7 percent
- People who refused to self-identify but were operationally conservative: 2 percent

Totaling the percentages of those who were *operationally* liberal or conservative—who voted one way or the other regardless of how they labeled themselves—Winship arrived at the conclusion that the 2004 electorate consisted of more *operational* liberals (52 percent) than conservatives (48 percent)—almost exactly the opposite of the Bush-Kerry vote. Among adults overall, the figures were 53 percent liberals to 47 percent conservatives.

In 2004, at least, a majority of adults were well disposed toward progressive government. They wanted greater social spending. So much was good news for liberals. However, one question and one question alone in 2004 was so powerful in predicting how people actually voted that it drowned out their positions on health care, job creation, even abortion, gay marriage, any or all of these. The best predictor of how people voted—stronger than any specific positions in the four issue areas—was whether, in an open-ended response, they approved of Bush's "handling of the war on terror."

In 2004, 43 percent of voters thought terrorism was "the most important issue facing the United States over the last four years"— overwhelmingly their top choice.[8] As long as terrorism is so salient to voters, as long as fear is the dominant emotion in politics, Democrats will be staggering uphill. Raw fright ignites a primal confidence in Republican leadership, even if much of what passes for said leadership consists of bravado, gestures, and counter-productive wars laced with blind faith. (In this light, it is striking that the citizens of the states most endangered by Islamist jihadis are *least* likely to be flooded by an unreasoning fear that leads them to support the Iraq war and other Bush operations as remedies for the threat. The *less* endangered you are—if you live in Mississippi or Wyoming, say—the *more* likely you are to support Bush's macho approach to defeating terrorists.) Knowing this, why wouldn't the Republicans go on beating the terror drum in the run-up to *every* election, just as they did in 2002, 2004, and 2006? Since Osama bin Laden seems to prefer Bush-style Republicans in power, the expected October surprises write themselves. For the foresee-able future, such a campaign is the likely GOP version of "nation-alizing the election"—a Contract with America promising fright, preventive war, and vast presidential powers.

On the other hand, fright is not always equally marketable, reactive clenching not always equally attractive. In 2005, Bush advertised Iraq as "a central front in the war on terror,"[9] but with the American position there deteriorating steadily, this is not a card that's easy to play in the future. Had John Kerry offered a clearer alternative in 2004, the Democrats might not have succumbed to the panic dividend. Which is only to say that the center shifts as times goes by, and that as the center shifts, so does the meaning of shifting tactically in order to win votes there.

In polarizing American politics and running pell-mell rightward, Bush's Republicans jammed themselves into a corner—a Southern corner, at that—leaving the Democrats free to pitch a tent big enough to hold a national majority. Some sort of realignment may well be in the works wherein the Democrats become the political home for all those who do not want to be ruled by the radical right—or the remains of the Confederacy. Indeed, the most striking feature of the 2006 election results was their geography. The Republicans were isolated—had isolated themselves—in a Southern redoubt. Harold Meyerson wrote, in apt summary:

> They've become too southern—too suffused with the knee-jerk militaristic, anti-scientific, dogmatically religious, and culturally, sexually and racially phobic attitudes of Dixie—to win friends and influence elections outside the South. . . . Democrats decimated the GOP in the North and West. Twenty-seven of the Democrats' 30 House pickups came outside the South. The Democrats won control of five state legislatures, all outside the South, and took more than 300 state legislative seats away from Republicans, 93 percent of them outside the South. . . . In all, 45 percent of Republican senators come from the Greater South (the Confederacy proper plus Kentucky, Missouri, and Oklahoma).

Bush, who had tried to look like a Westerner while governing like a Southerner, ended up being cast as a Southerner after all, his party a Southern party even when Bush's own policies (as on immigration) were not—at a time when the dominant Southern values and policies had cut themselves off from the rest of the country. The Southern formula no longer played on the national stage. As Meyerson wrote, "most of the Republican message" came from the Greater South as well.

> Following the gospel according to Rove (fear not swing voters but pander to and mobilize thy base), George W. Bush and the Republican Congress, together or separately, had already blocked stem cell research, disparaged nonmilitary statecraft, exalted executive wartime power over constitutional niceties, campaigned repeatedly against gay rights, thrown public money

at conservative churches and investigated the tax status of liberal ones. In the process, they alienated not just moderates but Western-state libertarians.[10]

The West was now cut loose, if not to make its lasting home under the Democrats' tent, at least to leave the Republicans behind.

In this scenario, the Democrats' big tent makes room for thoughtful conservatives, independents, and self-proclaimed moderates who ought to welcome a post-Bush era. The prospect of a humble foreign policy—precisely the foreign policy promised by George W. Bush in 2000—ought to gladden their hearts. So should the prospect of a decent respect for government—for civil servants chosen for their knowledge and skill, not for their crony connections and campaign contributions; for decision making that is rational, based on evidence and realistic appraisals, not on the fitful workings of a president's viscera and a vice president's dogma. That is to say, even conservatives, if they are honest about the rule of law and not quasi-monarchical power, about modest government and not the farming out of public powers to corporate interests, about equal opportunity and not plutocracy, about the conservation of the good things of the earth and not the squandering of its finite but marketable resources—if they are serious, in other words, about conserving, ought to gravitate toward a center-left party that makes room for them, even if most of it disagrees on abortion, gun control, and other fronts in the culture wars.

Liberals may enter the big tent, where the rostrum is in place, the microphone ready, the crowd gathered, and the silence beckons them to make their case. This is not to say that they are guaranteed success: far from it. But guarantees of success are for promotional brochures and matchbook covers, not for serious Democrats with work to do. In 1953, the barbed-tongue Bertolt Brecht sarcastically urged the East German government to dissolve the people and elect another one. Democrats and progressives might now learn to cross Brecht with Rumsfeld, however unlikely the pairing, and conclude that you fight for political power with the people you have, not the ones you wish you had.

13

Narratives and Values

To win in the long run, liberals must be as disciplined and ingenious as the right has proved to be. This does not mean that they must be as authoritarian or deceptive, dredging the depths of demagoguery for equivalents of Willie Horton, "Swift Boat Veterans for Truth," or the 2006 Republican commercial that featured a sexy blonde wiggling her bare shoulders, winking, and simulating a phone call ("Harold! Call me!") to the African American Democratic candidate for a Tennessee Senate seat, Harold Ford. It does mean that they must maintain a fruitful tension between the affirmative and the negative.

Ronald Reagan taught the Republican Party to appreciate uplift—and the party elevated him, rewarded him, and loved him for personifying it. Under Reagan's symbolic tutelage, the party mastered a division of labor. The poster face smiled while, offstage, the attack dogs snarled. This dual appearance was integral to the party's discipline. The negativity didn't cancel the smiley face: it made it more welcome. The smiley face didn't cancel the negativity, which was free to do its work. In fact, the coexistence of promises and warnings is a hoary recipe for political success. Franklin Roosevelt well understood it: the jaunty warrior who proclaimed that "the only thing we have to fear is fear itself" also made time to denounce "economic royalists."

In 2006, it sufficed for the Democrats to take the advice offered them, in an unguarded moment, by Newt Gingrich: "What they should do is say nothing except 'Had enough?'"[1] Observing the Republicans mired so deeply in scandal, identified so closely with a dead-ended war and domestic malfeasance, a voting majority had indeed had enough. But George W. Bush has run his last campaign. Now what does the party-as-movement stand for? When Democrats come to mind, what principles ought they to summon up?

Let us stay with Gingrich for a moment, since he and other leading Republican ideologues have answered the question for their own party. Shortly after coming to power in the House of Representatives in 1995, he told an interviewer that American history breaks in half in the sixties. From 1607 through 1965, he said, "there is a core pattern to American history. Here's how we did it until the Great Society messed everything up: don't work, don't eat; your salvation is spiritual; the government by definition can't save you; governments are into maintenance and all good reforms are into transformation." Gingrich went on with his remarkable account: "From 1965 to 1994, we did strange and weird things as a country. Now we're done with that and we have to recover. The counterculture is a momentary aberration in American history that will be looked back upon as a quaint period of Bohemianism brought to the national elite." This countercultural-Clintonian elite, he continued, "taught self-indulgent, aristocratic values without realizing that if an entire society engaged in the indulgences of an elite few, you could tear the society to shreds." The new House majority leader Dick Armey of Texas agreed: "To me all the problems began in the '60s."[2]

Say what you will about a short course in American history that omits slavery and Indian wars from the "core pattern" of "how we did it." Gingrich's tale is still, to use today's buzzword, a *narrative*. It is reasonably coherent as long as nobody asks persnickety questions. It tells a story complete with heroes—the righteous, hard-working, entrepreneurial American people—and, of course, villains. It includes stirring moments and turning points. The plot thins, but it has the simplicity of a primitive cartoon.

As for the progressives' party-as-movement—what is its story? It should be something like the following. The main line of American history is the story of widening circles of people seeking liberty and pursuing happiness by challenging the authorities who would tread on them. In the American Revolution, they toppled the British crown. The Declaration of Independence declared that it was legitimate to eject the king because Americans were a people of unalienable rights, including "life, liberty, and the pursuit of happiness." The Constitution enshrined a system of balanced government that was intended to secure those rights by limiting the dominance of any elite. At every turning point in American history, rights have collided with privileged interests, whether religious, governmental, or economic. When the country was beset by slavery, by monopolies and oligopolies, by abusers of power of all sorts, whenever limits were clamped upon the freedoms of ordinary people and the whole society's democratic potential, one out-group after another fought to secure its rights by turning America's unfulfilled promises to its benefit. The un-propertied, the landless, the enslaved, women, African Americans, Native Americans, Hispanics, homosexuals, immigrants—all fought for full citizenship and dignity. Eventually, for the most part, sometimes haltingly, always against fierce resistance, they came some distance, even a considerable distance, to winning majorities over and making reforms.

Now, this narrative is not without its seams, hurdles, detours, and cross-pressures. Liberties for some people collide with liberties for other people. The happiness of some is purchased with the unhappiness of others. In order to increase liberties for the many, it may well be necessary to enlist one powerful force (generally, the state) against others (corporations, say, that must be deprived of their liberty to abuse those who work for them and swindle those who buy from them). Moreover, large numbers of Americans interpret "the pursuit of happiness" as strictly a private matter, a substitute for the pursuit of the common good—or rather, they assume that America can be properly handled by a social version of Adam Smith's invisible hand in which the sum of private pursuits is sufficient to generate a public good. Up against this doctrine of providential social grace, the common good has a difficult time trickling down.

But no political narrative is without its internal contradictions. The more power Democrats gain, the more opportunities arise for fracases to break out under their big tent. Distinct interests will vie, all under the banner of "the common good"—for, after all, who in a modern society does not claim to embrace the common good? ("We're the elite!" "Vote for our special interest!"—such slogans do not have the right political ring. Those who want to eliminate the estate tax for billionaires claim to be defending small business and family farms.) All factions will stomp their feet and demand priority, and all will have their reasons to do so, to declare their positions principled to the point of nonnegotiability. As some problems were more or less successfully addressed, others will come to the fore. That's politics.

The party-as-movement needs a convincing rhetoric of the common good, but—or therefore—it must also face demographic reality. Even as non-Hispanic whites shrink as a proportion of the population, whatever victories the Democrats win in the years to come, it would take a miracle for a permanent new majority to form unless the Democrats win over a significant portion of the white working class (or call it the middle class, as most of those who are white and work for wages prefer). The core Democratic principles need to be embraceable by what are sociologically the two largest segments of the existing Democratic base—the roughly 40 percent who are professionals and the roughly 60 percent who are lower income[3]—*as well as* a significant segment of the white working class who have mainly deserted the Democrats since 1968.

Analysts of various political persuasions agree that a cross-class cement must be found. Galston and Kamarck put it this way:

> Today, a majority party must hold together a coalition representing citizens of vastly differing economic circumstances. Republicans have become adept at deploying a social populist agenda of national strength and traditional values to weld the denizens of corporate boardrooms and NASCAR race tracks. The Democratic Party has not yet found a comparably effective formula for bringing its post-McGovern surge of educated

professionals together with the average families who continue to hope for some relief from the burdens and uncertainties of the modern economy. Until it does, national Democratic candidates will remain vulnerable to Republican efforts to portray them as elitists, which has always been the kiss of political death in this viscerally egalitarian nation.[4]

The more liberal John Halpin and Ruy Teixeira, in their rebuttal document "The Politics of Definition," agree on the importance of making inroads in the white working class, which they define as whites without four-year college degrees. This population is shrinking, but they make the "reasonable guess" that in 2016 it "will still be around 46 percent to 47 percent—a very large group among which to be doing very poorly. In fact, a progressive majority coalition is simply not possible if that poor performance continues." Halpin and Teixeira calculate:

> If Democrats can simply keep the Republican margin among white working-class voters to the low double digits (say 11 to 12 points), and maintain their margins from 2004 among college-educated whites and among minority groups (note that we assume no improvement from 2004 in the Democratic performance among Hispanics, though we strongly believe that is likely to happen), our estimates indicate that the Democrats would win the popular vote in the next presidential election by 3 points. That would be an exact reversal of the 2004 popular vote, which Bush won by around 3 points. And if the Democrats can keep the Republican margin among working-class whites to single digits? Then it should be possible to start building a solid majority coalition for progressives in very short order.[5]

Over the din of the Democrats' internal battles, a consensus may be emerging: that the party's prospects rest heavily on its ability to stand for an ideal of the common good, one that transcends the beggar-thy-neighbor ruthlessness of today's Republicans, their trickle-down inequity, the sectarianism of the Christian right, and the recklessness of neoconservative foreign policy. Halpin and Teixeira, and Michael Tomasky of the *American Prospect*,[6] are among the strategists who have been promoting the ideal of "the common good," an affirmation that a national purpose cannot be reduced to the simple affirmation of leave-us-alone at home and our-way-or-the-highway abroad. The premise is that after the Bush years of rampant self-seeking, Democrats now rise or fall on their ability to evoke a spirit of high and shared purpose against the party of Halliburton and Falwell. It has become the conventional wisdom—and high time, too—that opponents of abortion and gay rights have, and deserve, no monopoly on the word *values*.

A liberal politics of commonality would be comfortable speaking the language of morality but would also happily cross the line dividing religious voters from seculars. (We are already hearing from prominent evangelicals who do not believe that Christian piety requires an unending spew of greenhouse gases from fossil fuels into the atmosphere.) As Democrats have already been doing, this liberal politics of commonality would be willing to jettison gun control, a definite nonstarter in swing states such as Pennsylvania, Ohio, and Colorado—even Montana, where the populist Democratic governor Brian Schweitzer, elected in 2002, is a proud hunter. It would *not* jettison a woman's right to choose abortion—a majority view—but neither would it demonize its pro-life standard-bearers or those who, while subscribing to abortion rights generally, disagree at the margins. Such common-good politics would also have the virtue of speaking to all the constituencies that the Democrats must blend if they are to assemble a working majority. Perhaps the debacle of the Bush years can coax Americans to prove Richard Hofstadter wrong about what is at the core of their traditional character. Perhaps they have indeed had enough.

If the Democrats are to do more than creep into office at emergency moments, if they are to build mandates for major policy shifts, they must know how to unite around certain themes even as they diverge on others. They have to presume the public mature enough, discerning enough, far-sighted enough to pay attention to the general shape of its signature programs. The populace is unlikely to be satisfied for long with incantations about "new ideas"—it deserves to be honored with actual ideas, not the nebulous suggestion that new ideas would be a good idea.

The party should evolve toward an identity—a "signature"—that can be recognized as more than anti-Republicanism. Slogans are always welcome, but first and foremost come common themes. In politics, the words matter, but the music matters more. The music consists of values. Various party factions will promote changes that offend other party interests, but the common themes should endure.

The moral should also be practical. Fortunately for liberals, they are the proud possessors of several possible themes with the capacity to unite the party, win elections, and, if implemented, produce substantial and constructive change toward the common good. If the public still does not recognize these programs as the party's signature, the party should make sure that this is the fault of the media for paying scant attention, not the fault of the party for failing in clarity and boldness.

What would the resonant music sound like? All sorts of social programs might be desirable and politic at the same time, but the emphasis should be on universal programs of the order of Social Security and Medicare, entitlements that (in principle) fused the common good and the private interest in the New Deal and the Great Society.[7] Both their symbolism and their material rewards were undeniable, and as a result, they became fixtures of progressive achievement—as George W. Bush discovered to his chagrin when he essayed, essentially, repeal of the first and expansion of the second (to prescription drugs, albeit in a form that coddled the pharmaceutical industry). As a matter of justice as well as politics, two domestic priorities seem especially promising themes:

1. *Universal health care.* The core principle is elementary: health care is a human right. If American wealth is supposed to serve a human purpose beyond the accumulation of wealth itself, what purpose is more sensible than the health of the citizens? Is it anything less than disgraceful that in 2005, 48 million Americans spent part of the year uninsured? The consequences are evident. More than half the uninsured who had chronic conditions reported skipping their medications. More than half skipped medical

screenings and dental exams.[8] And the present forms of insurance do not by themselves solve the problem. In 2001, medical expenses were implicated in half of all bankruptcy filings, affecting a total of about 2 million Americans, *three quarters of whom were actually insured.*[9]

Is a strong government role in health care still taboo? Conservatives would insist so. But both the Veterans Administration and Medicare, for all their deficiencies, have better reputations than for-profit hospitals and HMOs do. Their administrative costs are lower—4 percent in Medicare as against 15 percent in the for-profit system. The VA has kept its costs stable for a decade despite double-digit inflation in medical expenses.[10] In 2003, two-thirds of Americans supported a "universal health insurance program, in which everyone is covered under a program like Medicare that's run by the government and financed by taxpayers," according to an ABC News poll.[11] In 2005, the Pew Research Center found a strong majority in favor of "government guaranteeing health insurance for all citizens, even if it means raising taxes."[12]

Of course, on the subject of ways and means there are thorns everywhere. How to finance universal health care is a thorny problem. How to contain rising costs without damaging the practice of medicine is a thorny problem. How to outflank the health insurance industry, which has a great deal to lose if universal provision deprives it of its ability to cherry-pick the healthier customers, and which can be expected to pump up the propaganda should Washington experience another groundswell for reform as in 1993, is a thorny problem. Still, now that managed care has superseded individual arrangements as the chief means for arranging medical provision, the charge that universal health care would deprive Americans of their sacrosanct right of choice—a charge that proved devastating in the industry's propaganda counteroffensive against the Clinton health plan—should have lost its sting.

2. *Massive investment toward the intertwined goals of energy conservation, environmental sustainability, and manufacturing jobs.* In the language of the Apollo Alliance for Good Jobs and Clean Energy, a labor-environmentalist coalition that advocates a

ten-year effort of this sort, all political bets would be covered: the program would "rejuvenat[e] our nation's economy by creating the next generation of American industrial jobs and treating clean energy as an economic and security mandate to rebuild America." The aim is to address, at once, global environmental disruption and "an economy hemorrhaging its highest paying and most productive jobs, cities falling apart with over a trillion dollars in unmet public investment in crumbling schools, transportation, and infrastructure," and a "middle class . . . increasingly insecure as career ladders are broken and not replaced in new service sector jobs."[13] Public funds would be invested in hybrid cars, more efficient factories and electrical plants, "green buildings," renewable energy, new transportation, and so on. In an era of soaring oil prices and heightened awareness of environmental dangers, this would seem a no-brainer—not only "the common good" in earnest but an adventure with verve.

Such programs would not only do what they promise to do, "to form a more perfect Union, establish Justice, insure domestic Tranquility, provide for the common defense, promote the general Welfare, and secure the Blessings of Liberty to ourselves and our Posterity," in the language of the Constitution's preamble, but they would also do precisely what the Republicans fear they would do: impress and consolidate new constituencies devoted to their maintenance.

To such programs, Democrats should add a deep commitment to smart government—government that accomplishes its ends. Could it be that—in the wake of New Orleans drowning and post-tyranny Iraq melting down—government that works emerges as an indispensable element of the common good? The lamented Michael Dukakis reaped much scorn in progressive circles for declaring, on accepting the nomination for president in 1988, that "this election isn't about ideology. It's about competence." But the twin fiascos of Iraq and Katrina lend that once dull noun *competence* a bright luster, at least for a while. After the Bush years of rampant neglect, malfeasance, secrecy, and deception, it does not sound empty to embrace Dukakis's "old-fashioned values like accountability and responsibility and respect for the truth."[14] Competence in government becomes a cause, even a crusade, in its absence—when ideological fidelity and personal cronyism tear it to shreds and millions palpably suffer as a result. Looting, profiteering, and flagrant negligence in Iraq, the thick web of high-level Republican connections with Jack Abramoff's bagman-lobbying operations, the appointment of Michael Brown as head of FEMA—these were not incidental scandals but the by-products of doctrine: deregulation and private outsourcing at work.

Radical conservatism in the Bush vein had no standard of governance to deploy against cronyism or doctrinal purity because it favored corporate power and didn't believe in government. When the American president is an inattentive, ignorant, vacation-hungry man who, on being given a CIA briefing titled "Bin Laden Determined to Strike in US," says to his briefer, "You've covered your ass now"[15]—when this is the president of the United States, then the fate of union, justice, tranquility, defense, welfare, and liberty veers toward abandonment. Whether addressing birth control, climatic convulsion, infrastructure security, Iraq, evolution, or the Israel-Palestine showdown, the Bush administration (if it can indeed be said to administer) felt no evident qualms or embarrassment when it breezily neglected scruples, logic, and evidence. A government devoted to the welfare of private corporations is not going to place rationality first. In this setting, competence in government is not a technical matter, a fetish of concern strictly to the holders of advanced university degrees. Neither is competence an abstraction when images of Americans waving for help from the rooftops of their flooded houses remain fresh. When reason is driven out of government, competence is a positive good worth fighting for.

Finally, it may well be asked, with all this talk of the common good, what becomes of the interests of post-sixties movements? Would a big-tent party, in its own defense, muzzle the interest groups that make up much of its base? In a word, that would be rampantly self-destructive. Just as the Republicans can ill afford to smack the Christian right around, Democrats of all stripes, including the Democratic Leadership Council, must know that much of the party base (with their energies and their dollars) comes from the ranks of labor, environmentalists, feminists, and racial, ethnic, and sexual minorities. More conservative Democrats who detest Howard Dean, MoveOn, the Reverend Al Sharpton, and "angry bloggers" would be ill-advised to organize purge trials.

How the party and the movements should manage their marriage is a matter of emphasis and proportion. The party needs the interests, and the interests need the party—they need, in fact, a party that doesn't wholly belong to interests, that may even require Sister Souljah moments when the party distinguishes itself from the interests. For their own good, the separate interests need to relearn the lesson that a foundation of Democratic power is necessary for interest-group politics. If environmentalists and defenders of abortion rights have not learned as much from the Bush years, what are they waiting for? The interests are most of the time worthy, their passions formidable, but the party, like an engine, must regulate those passions. Only such a party, putting the common good first, might drive the wedge further into the Republican coalition. Only such a party can appeal—as it must appeal—to independents, moderates, and rational conservatives, inviting them to free themselves from the prison cells of their petty (or, to use their word, *special*) interests, so that they recognize the party of the center-left as their party, too.

As Republicans hurl wedges at Democrats, Democrats need to make a habit of hurling them back. They need to foreground what holds them together—secularists and moderate evangelicals, budget-balancers and Keynesians, fair traders and free traders, defenders of civil unions and defenders of gay marriage who are willing to live with civil unions, displaced manufacturing workers and university graduates, defenders of the human rights of immigrants, amnesty advocates, guest-worker advocates and opponents alike. It is likely that from time to time, they may need to shift the boundaries of the tent—to move the pegs one way or the other, to alter the silhouette, to raise the pole, as the wind direction, the ground waters, and other elements may require. Proposals may be disputed. Decisions may be unfortunate. Still, discipline will be indispensable. The denizens of the tent will need to remind themselves that outside there dwell barbarians.

Is such thinking practical? In politics, there are no certainties. But consider that in 2006, in spite of congressional gerrymandering, in spite of big-donor advantages, in spite of the rural tilt of the electoral college, in spite of voting machine breakdowns, in spite of Republican turn-out-the-vote operations, in spite of cleavages between the Democratic center and left over such crucial questions as Iraq and trade, and over which candidates to back, in spite of turf wars between Howard Dean's fifty-state organizing plan and the party's congressional focus on winning key swing districts—in spite of all this, Democratic discipline held, and paid off.

14

Enemies, Bogeymen, and the Limits of American Power

Is there any question about whether the United States must protect itself against mass murderers who devoutly believe that brutality is their ticket to paradise? The question is silly, or worse. When addressed strictly to progressives, it amounts to a calumny. Why should such a question be asked of liberals alone and not of the party that presided over the country and ignored warnings when the al-Qaeda plot to massacre thousands was well underway and the country's defenses were down? The only serious debate is about *how* to fight the movement composed of al-Qaeda and its allies. Resolutely, of course—that goes without saying—but there is also a moral obligation to fight mass murderers intelligently. Breast beating about war is not actual war against enemy states and movements. It is certainly not a foreign policy. It is not even a military policy.

There can be no precise blueprint for a long fight against terrorists with apocalypse on their minds. Blueprints imply that enemies stand still. But they metamorphose. They react to America's moves and the moves of its allies and enemies. Surely, however, as details change, there are guidelines and orienting principles.

Liberals will not, and ought not, be permitted to duck the genuine problem of how to defend the United States.

It is a given that the country must protect itself intelligently, must fight and defeat its real enemies. The intelligent use of power must be, as conditions require, both hard and soft—military *when necessary*, and then in a focused, intelligent, and collaborative manner; police-minded in a coordination of intelligence, penetration, and disruption; diplomatic in order to spare life and make any use of force legitimate; and ideological in order to combat the appeals of jihadism. Anyone who doesn't think we have a grave fight on our hands is morally frivolous and in intellectual default. But anyone who thinks that today's jihadis are the military equivalent of the Wehrmacht is profoundly ignorant. And anyone who thinks that the struggle against the jihadis can be waged with blithe indifference toward how a billion Muslims see the United States of America is ignorant to the point of stupefaction. Today's global interdependence, like the eighteenth century's struggle for independence, demands that the United States be guided by "a decent respect to the opinions of mankind."

Blinded by a willful faith indistinguishable from stupidity,[1] George W. Bush's ideology-heavy Republicans have compiled a staggeringly unimpressive record defending the country. The 2001 war in Afghanistan against the Taliban and its al-Qaeda allies was the sum total of their intelligent initiatives overseas. The intervention in Afghanistan was just and, at first, an efficacious war properly justified on national interest grounds, as well as on liberal principle. It had multilateral sanction. Its errors were errors of incompleteness—for Bush, who despised "nation building" from the start, was entranced by the glimmering vision of "regime change" in Iraq followed by dominoes gaily falling throughout the Middle East. He cut and ran from Afghanistan. He withdrew troops, failed to invest in Afghani restoration, and as a result, at this writing, more than five years after launching the war, still has a war on his hands—and not a war closing to victory.

In foreign policy as in medicine, we do well to begin with the Hippocratic injunction: *Do no harm*. Is it not evident at last to a growing majority that Iraq, in its miseries, had enormous harm done to it? This avoidable war is—and can lastingly be—proof that Republican rule is disastrous. (Despite the maneuvers of stab-in-the-back theorists blaming Democrats, who had not the slightest power over the war, and inevitably, in the Nixon-Agnew tradition, the press, which escorted the country into the war without an abundance of qualms, a powerful future slogan might be: Who Blew Iraq?) It deserves to become the Republicans' definitive albatross, as emblematic for them as corruptions of welfare proved for the Democrats before Bill Clinton. For the war was the Republican personality in action, the product of movement conservatism at work.

Americans ought to learn from the debacle that, first of all, wars ought to be wisely chosen and scrupulously fought. Roping together disparate adversaries with rhetorical lassos like "evil-doers," "axis of evil," and "the terrorists" was bravado and sloppy thinking masquerading as resolve. After September 11, it was crucial to strike at and wipe out actual enemies—not a tyrant who had been successfully contained, and not in defiance of allies, and not on false pretenses. In 2002 and 2003, it would have been sensible to maintain the multilateral sanction that had contained Saddam Hussein—indeed, to pursue it more wisely, and not to abandon it for the reckless course of a near-unilateral war and the fantasy of a movement for democracy in the Middle East promoted by American occupation. As it is, the war infuriated far more people—and not Muslims alone—than it impressed. After 1945, the island of West Berlin behind the Iron Curtain advertised the American way of life of elections and prosperity. After the "shock and awe" of 2003, the nightmarish sequel of the American occupation inspired more terrorists than it killed and advertised the recklessness and haplessness of American power.

Is the Iraq misadventure the "root cause" of anti-Americanism? No. Terrorists were plotting mass murder years before the United States went to war to depose Saddam Hussein. Republicans (and Tony Blair) are right about this. But it should go without saying that intelligent warfare must weaken the enemy more than it weakens our own side. To the contrary, with the Iraq war and the preventive war doctrine that accompanied it,[2] Bush hurled the United States into a morass of sectarian violence and, indeed, terrorism, and then had the audacity to maintain that Iraq had become "a central front in the war on terror."[3] To the extent that Iraq did become that, it was strictly because of Bush's actions. Without doubt, Bush's proud exhibition fit nicely on posters for recruiting Muslim jihadis throughout the world. The names Guantánamo and Abu Ghraib provided precisely the illustrations that America's enemies would have commissioned on their own.

How does America stand vis-à-vis the jihadis? It may turn out that, as American officials were reported to believe early in 2007, "as Al Qaeda rebuilds in Pakistan's tribal areas, a new generation of leaders has emerged under Osama bin Laden to cement control over the network's operations. . . . Although the core leadership was weakened in the counterterrorism campaign begun after the Sept. 11 attacks, intelligence officials now believe it was not as crippling as once thought."[4] Or it may turn out that al-Qaeda has, in a sense, peaked: that, in the words of the journalist James Fallows, whose prewar perspicacity about the likely consequences of the Iraq war was second to none,[5] "because of al-Qaeda's own mistakes, and because of the things the United States and its allies have done right, al-Qaeda's ability to inflict direct damage in America or on Americans has been sharply reduced." In 2006, Fallows surveyed some sixty national security experts, half of them in the government, and found them agreed that al-Qaeda was weakened—its Taliban base in Afghanistan badly damaged, its finances and communications disrupted, its ability to mount centralized attacks disputed.[6]

The consensus was that al-Qaeda's "hopes for fundamentally harming the United States now rest less on what it can do itself than on what it can trick, tempt, or goad us into doing. . . . [T]errorists, through their own efforts, can damage but not destroy us. Their real destructive power . . . lies in what they can provoke us to do." Thus the *double* blunder of the Iraq war. Whereas the war on the Taliban had only incidental boomerang effects, greatly outweighed by the justice of the war overall and the benefits accrued to the Afghanis themselves, the misplaced American-British expedition in Iraq turned that miserable country into a recruitment zone and a remoralization center for the jihadis. Along with Bush's refusal to expedite an Israel-Palestine peace, it sapped American moral authority and offered new waves of recruits—European and Pakistani Muslims in particular—fresh reasons to take inspiration from Osama bin Laden. It tied down the American military.

The Iraq war sparked deadly terror attacks in Madrid, London, and elsewhere. (Or do neoconservatives want to deny that Madrid and London, the capitals of our presumably devoted allies, are "over here"?) It raised the prestige of the jihadi movement, confirming its propaganda, helping to persuade many Muslims that the United States was in fact devoted to an anti-Muslim crusade. As Fallows wrote, "The United States is immeasurably stronger than al-Qaeda, but against jujitsu forms of attack its strength has been its disadvantage. The predictability of the U.S. response has allowed opponents to turn our bulk and momentum against us."

One of Fallows's sources told him, "America's cause is doomed unless it regains the moral high ground." This was not Noam Chomsky or Michael Moore but Sir Richard Dearlove, the former director of Britain's secret intelligence agency, MI-6. The damage the Iraq war has done to America's reputation may well take the better part of a generation to dispel, for across the Middle East and Pakistan, and among the Muslim populations of Europe, there are abundant prejudices to fan into flame, and the jihadis are no amateurs at propaganda. And, of course, they have availed themselves of passionate anger directed not only against Israel—for both good and bad, honest and dishonest reasons—but against Bush's cavalier abandonment of America's honest-broker role in favor of the policies of Israeli hawks, including virtual carte blanche for disproportionate Israeli air attacks in Lebanon during its clash with Hezbollah in 2006.

Still, let there be no illusions about what the United States is up against. Britain's government and public opinion have been far less favorably disposed toward Israel in its fight with the Palestinians than are America's government and public opinion, but this has not prevented British terrorists from planning and executing mass murders in Britain.

The military correspondent Fred Kaplan has written of one source of "liberals' vacillations on national-security policy—the tension, which nobody seems to know how to resolve, between the protection of American interests and the expansion of American ideals. Bush pretends that there is no tension—that our interests and our ideals are synonymous."[7] But for the United States to "stand for" ideals of democracy and freedom by overthrowing autocracies in disregard of the cost (in esteem, stability, and treasure) is folly. For the United States to assume that it is fated to an eventual military collision with China is equally folly. Humanitarian interventions are defensible, as in Bosnia and Kosovo, when they are self-limiting, when there is a genuine attempt at *collective* security, and when there is a substantial chance of success. The sovereignty of states is not a sacrosanct principle. In extreme circumstances, when powerful nations can protect the unprotected against the depredations of governments, they are permitted—even obliged—to do so. Thus was the Vietnamese invasion of Cambodia to overthrow the Khmer Rouge justified in 1979. So would an African, United Nations, or (come to that) American intervention have been justified to avert the Rwanda genocide in 1994.

The principles of collective security and the shrewd use of diplomacy will speak to many foreign policy conundrums in a Hobbesian world of states—a world rendered yet more dangerous by murderous jihadis moving around in the interstices of states. It should go without saying that an America in a mood to collaborate with a world of nations on global warming, missile defense, the control of nuclear trafficking, the control of poverty and disease, and so on, would be in a stronger position to win global support for mutually advantageous campaigns than the muscle-bound thrashings of George W. Bush have permitted it to be.

This is not the place for more detailed proposals, and the details are not what will win American voters, in any case. It's the thrust that counts. The important point is that progressives should not try to wish away the subject of national security—even if that were possible, which it is not. The obvious first reason is that this is no less our country than it is any other American's. The secondary reason is that Republicans will not let the subject go away. Fair enough. Let's argue about the best means of defense—that is, let's "play politics" with it. Surely Republicans have not shrunk from doing so. Regularly since 2002, and into the foreseeable future, Republicans have played and will play their strongest suit, which is fright, scanting all the evidence of their stark negligence in office, from the Bush administration's sweeping aside of counterterrorist warnings from Clinton administration holdovers such as Richard Clarke on up to the CIA warning that bin Laden was "determined to strike" inside the United States. Why would they stop?

15

The Human Face

In anxious days, when facile and boisterous optimism barely conceals huge, if unacknowledged, doubts about the capacity of American institutions to address the prevailing troubles, we hear a clamor for leadership—perhaps in inverse proportion to the amount of that mysterious quality in actual evidence. If it is not altogether clear what leadership means, it is at least the name of a longing.

Americans long for personal rescue so intensely in large part for the structural reason that we lack a tradition of coherent parties that can stand taller than singular personalities. This structural reason is certainly powerful by itself. In a parliamentary system, when parties are more or less consistently ideological, and the voting public is used to such a system of politics, they vote for the party, not the person. If one leader is deposed, they take it in stride and vote for the next. The American system is obviously different, all the more so in the course of the twentieth century, as the parties "wasted away," in James McGregor Burns's evocative phrase.[1] From 1932 on, emergency succeeded emergency, and accordingly the executive branch swelled in centralized power, from the Depression through World War II into the Cold War. War of one sort or another, actual or symbolic, proved to be not only (as Randolph Bourne understood during World War I) "the health of the state" but also the health of the strong man, the man of the hour, the commander in chief, the decider.

The American president came to approximate Hobbes's one-man "sovereign," and for Hobbes's reason: to rescue the fearful from the state of nature. Parties waned in authority. Personal organizations popped up. Candidates pressed forward, dialing for dollars, becoming household names—nominating themselves, in effect. Radio and then television were, and remain, their indispensable allies, resources, pipelines. The personal political franchise became normal—all the more so as Americans grew accustomed to being plunged, daily, hourly, minute by minute, second by second, into a media torrent, the psyche—perhaps the soul—looking for recognizable faces to thrill or at least anchor them.

Even as Americans have withdrawn from political life in the course of the last century, then, one thing the leftover half, more or less, wants from politics is guidance by celebrated figures who are in some ways like ourselves but in other ways not—Americans who appear able to master what we ourselves cannot; who not only offer rewards but radiate comfort, embody authority, promise to shape the unknown, put names on the unnamable, and grab hold of destiny. Even in a more or less democratic society we need such presences in charge (or we need to believe that they *are* in charge) because whatever the utilitarians thought, we are not just creatures of rational calculation. Collectively, we are lost souls. So we long for someone to trust. In a world of concocted images we crave—my oxymoron is deliberate—the appearance of authenticity.

The democratic age was born breathing an Enlightenment spirit that celebrated both individual and collective self-determination, but it has shown no sign of indifference to the personal qualities of its leaders. In truth, these imperfect democracies—and not just America's—choose leaders, not policies. (More precisely, from among a range of impressions of leaders they choose this one and not that.) Even the smiley-face nostrums of American culture fail to cancel our inner knowledge that we are, in Auden's words, "Lost in a haunted wood/Children afraid of the night/who have never been happy or good." The wood is vast and tangled, and we see very little of it firsthand. So we turn for clarity and comfort to someone who, we believe, or trust, or at least hope, will see farther than we do, will know how to make his or her way through the thickets. Even popular ideologies must be personified: Theodore Roosevelt's macho nationalism tinctured by a rhetoric of reform, Franklin Roosevelt's patrician warmth and improvisational touch, Ronald Reagan's buoyant alloy of Cold War confrontation and deregulatory zeal, George W. Bush's four-square casual style.

Politics is part theater; theater invites identification, and identification requires characters. Ideologists of all sorts need to see their faces and hear their voices; Americans are not unique about this. What is Leninism without Lenin? Trotskyism without Trotsky? Fascism without Mussolini? Nazis without Hitler? Baathism without Saddam Hussein? Nonviolence without Gandhi? Antiapartheid without Mandela?

What goes for societies under severe stress also goes for less afflicted societies where the pressure of ideology is muffled. America's anti-ideological ideologies want faces, too. The citizens imagine themselves as part of a larger community because they behold its symbolic presence—its story in the shape of a person. A presidential system like that of the United States places exceptional weight on personality (though in the televisual age, even the more ideological parliamentary parties of Europe and elsewhere have discovered that the images of their leaders are distinct and indispensable forces). Even if we have an ideology, we know that ideology by itself is no guarantee of good judgment. Ideology is nothing without the people who deploy armies and cast votes and vetoes. The buck stops in front of identifiable human beings with names and faces.

And therefore—I say this at the risk of belaboring the obvious—the presence or absence of compelling candidates will continue to be a huge factor in liberal success and failure. Never mind that the candidates are filtered through media images. It is an ineradicable oddity of our age that the people are willing to—or wish to—entrust immense powers to human beings whom they have never met and of whom they have no direct experience. We are willing to entrust them with (no exaggeration) the future of life on Earth. The saturation of media makes this trust both possible and necessary: possible because we can harbor the pleasing illusion that we know our leaders by their lights, their images and sounds, their auras; and necessary because, when everyday life is clogged with media, the expectation from politics—which is, after all, offered to the public via media—is that it will also offer what media are expected to offer for other purposes: emotions and sensations.[2]

But this is not to say that the key images will be engineered by television's gatekeepers all on their own. Candidate images are coproductions. Candidates perform. They gesture, wear costumes, drop phrases, and strive to look and sound like living incarnations of voters' values. Handlers advise. Media select, aiming to attract eyeballs. Empty suits get filled—with something. Pundits pronounce conventional wisdom—with occasional influence. Constituencies adopt favorites—and blinders. Ineffable qualities come to the fore, others recede. Some politicians acquire reputations as "authentic," others as wildly ambitious. So George Bush, dynast, joshing fraternity boy, failed oilman, and military shirker, becomes the amiable amateur, "a uniter, not a divider," and Al Gore, the intelligent veteran, becomes a serial liar and a corrupt egotist. Yet it is not always clear in advance which personal qualities will rise to the surface and prove "defining." Michael Schudson has shrewdly pointed out that almost every president since Eisenhower has been declared by some pundit or other—at least once safely in office—to be the definitive "television president," (Gerald Ford and George H. W. Bush might be the exceptions) though what quality was shared by the witty John F. Kennedy, the stiff Richard Nixon, the beaming Jimmy Carter, and the folksy yet dignified Ronald Reagan is not easily discernible.

The larger point is this: the qualities that people intend when they speak of leadership are, to put it mildly, elusive. What they want from a leader may be unclear even to themselves. They'll know it when they see it—and they may be quick to think that they see it because the media so easily convey an impression of intimacy, posing before each election the less than penetrating question, Are you ready to let this person into your living room for the next four years? They may want inspiration, but they have to make inferences on the basis of doubtful knowledge if they want to conclude that the candidate who inspires them will also inspire others.

Such psychological uncertainties may be compounded by a sociological fact: the strangely complicated styles and tastes of a modern society. Any victorious chunk of the electorate must be remarkably diverse. It is doubtful that there was ever a time when political choices did *not* hinge on personal qualities and impressions—today blithely lumped together as matters of "character"—but never before have the requirements been so elusive. The candidate must send more signals than a forest of beacons. The candidate must not *seem* to be all things to all men and women—that would be hopelessly wobbly, waffly, or wussy. He or she must *seem* sharply defined—but in fact must be a projective screen for a multitude, especially insofar as political parties are weak and uncommanding. The candidate must speak through many microphones at once, convincing each constituency that he or she is worthy of affection, entitled to have shortcomings overlooked, and worthy on grounds of both principle and self-interest. Bill Clinton must be both New Democrat and Old. George W. Bush must be a compassionate conservative and a crusading war president.

Who arises as an apt leader at a particular moment, of course, depends on the moment, and moments do not always shout out in chorus with their demands. Times change, and therefore the public's expectations from its leaders, the nature of its bonds with its leaders, and even the identity of those who feel bonded change. Whoever thinks they see the changes coming has been watching too many talking heads. Whatever George W. Bush and his entourage may think, the mind of God is not so easily read, and even the mind of the people, democracy's next best thing, does not always know what it thinks, and certainly not in advance. Democracy is moody. Moods turn. All the talk in the world about "tipping points" and "defining moments" cannot decree when they will turn. History, in short, cannot be outdone as an upsetter of apple carts.

All the more reason that leadership cannot be ordered up by formula. Leaders do not come emblazoned with haloes. Voters are fickle (or, if you like it, flexible) and no less is required of leaders. Impressive (and idiosyncratic) personal qualities are more likely to trump ideology than the other way around, and unimpressive candidates are defeated by their deficiencies even when their positions happen to coincide with the views of a critical mass of the electorate at a certain instant in time. Effective leaders are opportunists with style. At an early White House press conference, Franklin Roosevelt—who had campaigned for a balanced budget and attacked Herbert Hoover for spending too much—likened himself to a quarterback whose planning is flexible because "future plays will depend on how the next one works."[3] In politics, as in war, business, and even love, the tests of pragmatism take place in real time, depending not only on one's own moves but on others'. This sort of political pragmatism can fairly be criticized for short-sightedness—obsession with tactics, not strategy, let alone principle. But it remains the quintessential political skill.

The question arises why, since Lyndon Johnson, Democrats have produced so few national leaders gifted with both this cast of mind and the skills to bring it off. The exception, of course, is Bill Clinton—an anomaly in his political generation in that, in his early twenties, he was already mindful of his desire to maintain his "political viability within the system . . . to prepare [him]self for a political life characterized by both practical political ability and concern for rapid social progress."[4] This sort of straddle would later earn Clinton the loathing of the fundamentalist left without shielding him from the contempt of the right. But his desire to be "practical" in his means while "concerned" for "rapid social progress" in his ends is precisely the sort of movement-party amalgam that has proved so rare in the center-left politics of our time. Call this circle-squaring disingenuous or doomed, but in hazarding the attempt Clinton is thus far unique among Democrats during the entire past half century.

Adroit politicians are in short supply at the best of times, but I am inclined to think that this particular shortfall has a generational aspect. Consider first the pool of political activists that included, at the practical end, Bill Clinton. The sixties and the seventies were rich in activists of the left with political passions, but poor in the sort of large personalities who could lead a practical left.[5] The New Left and its offshoots were purists with a low threshold for disgust—this is partly the luxury of a youth movement. The politics of elections was a choice between corruptions. To feel the moral passions of the time was to despise compromise—this was visceral. Compromises were signs of having joined a compromised world. The important thing was to be good, and one measured one's goodness by the state of one's conscience—a matter of keeping internal books. A respect for lost causes was yoked to a certain romance of lost causes. That a cause was lost might even be proof that it was good, and winning—even the ambition to win—therefore equivalent to selling out.

The sense of disgust in the later sixties and forward should not be minimized. The moral loathing for established institutions may have been rooted in a sweeping alienation, cultural as well as political, but it was wrenchingly reinforced by experience. The betrayals of public trust by Lyndon Johnson ("we seek no wider war") and other leading Democrats were not the invention of activists swaddled in anti-American diapers. Since Democrats, even liberals, had dominated American politics all our lives, but America was nevertheless falling short of its promise, we had some reason to think that the question of who precisely held formal political power was, as we liked to say, "irrelevant."

So the political structure of the time reinforced a moral predilection. We were moral individualists in the American vein, straight out of Thoreau. It didn't matter if our formal ideologies decreed that we were supposed to think about ourselves in terms of class, race, sex, or whatever—in our hearts of hearts we knew we stood alone. That is why we were existentialists. Whatever our commitments to the Enlightenment, we held our inner natures to be sacred, inviolable. (I once heard the master civil rights organizer Bayard Rustin defend civil disobedience with Martin Luther's words: "Here I stand. I can do no other.") Curiously, this spiritual force was masked by a hand-me-down intellectual vocabulary. The New Left was prone to blame contemporary evils on deep structures and lasting ideologies—imperialism, capitalism, racism, militarism, sexism. Scratch a contemporary issue, and you quickly got to profound evils. If the war in Vietnam, say, was nothing more than a current manifestation of an imperialism that was the country's original and besetting sin, then to many of us it seemed to defy reason to believe that the war could be usefully confronted at the ballot box—especially when the party of most of the movement's constituents was the party in power, responsible for the war in the first place.

Moreover, we were disgruntled by hierarchy and order. Indiscipline was a badge of honor, a proof that autonomy was alive, conscience was flourishing, one's inner depth and complexity were getting their due. One was devoted to movement politics but also resisted its demands: one had personal needs, after all. Meanwhile, class privilege was a mark of Cain, professionalism made us uneasy, and it was worthy to see virtue in regular people. To be seen hobnobbing with elites, on the other hand, was to court suspicion. Political ambition—like other forms of ambition—was tainted. Therefore, about political power in a dirty world we were, to put it mildly, ambivalent.

Across the left-of-center this mood suffused the air—part of a general distrust of authority, even of one's own. Teachers were exploring open classrooms; psychiatrists, antipsychiatry; urban planners, community values; doctors, patients' rights. Sometimes the very idea of a profession struck New Left activists as a violation of their commitment not to violate the prerogatives of the non-professional by purporting to know more than he or she did. Sometimes Maoist formulas were adopted: "expertise" had to play second fiddle to "redness."

And it wasn't just New Left activists who were curiously ambivalent about political careers, even their own semisuccessful ones. Mario Cuomo was three times elected governor of New York, but when it came to national ambitions, he stalled. (The reporter Jack Newfield, a confidant of Mario Cuomo, told me that Cuomo mused to him, while deliberating whether to run for the Democratic nomination in 1992, "Do I really want to be awakened in the middle of the night and told that the American ambassador in El Salvador has been taken hostage?") Not only did he decide not to run, flashing a green light to Bill Clinton to run without strong liberal opposition, but he later turned down Clinton's invitation to nominate him for the Supreme Court.[6] Jerry Brown, twice elected

governor of California—no small achievement during a period
when the conservative tax revolt was gathering steam—prided
himself on personal idiosyncrasies (for example, refusing to live
in the governor's mansion) and let it be known that he disdained the
give and take of vulgar politics. In California and New York,
at least, the two largest concentrations of Democrats, even rank-
and-file party activists approved of their semi-oddballs.

Eventually, once the millenarian mood disbanded, some sixties
activists did launch political careers. By design or default, they
became local: state legislators, mayors, a handful of members of
Congress. This was the extent of this generation's achievements
in practical politics (again, with the singular exception of Bill
Clinton). As expected, activists who did make careers in politics
found their experience confirming their fears. Miles Rapoport, the
SDS veteran who was several times elected to Connecticut state
office, described the legislature as

> an incredibly atomizing and compromising environment. I
> would say every day in the Democratic caucus, you had to
> make three or four decisions about whether something was
> worth fighting for or not. I used to say when I got to the Con-
> necticut legislature that it was worse than my worst leaflet—
> you know, in the level of influence that the corporate lobbyists
> and business lobbyists, and the trade association lobbyists,
> and lobbyists in general, had. X bill was always referred to by
> the name of the lobbyist who was pushing it, as opposed to
> by the title of the bill. And when it came time to do fundrais-
> ing, the leadership would take out the lobbyist list and divvy
> them up for who was going to hit up who.[7]

Today, thanks to George W. Bush, there are probably more party
activists at work than the Democrats have seen since 1968's short-
lived insurgencies of Eugene McCarthy and Robert F. Kennedy.
They think of themselves as a movement, and the Internet gives
them a sense of magnified numbers. They have few illusions. Democratic weaknesses are widely known, the commitment to overcome
them widely shared. They are not shrinking violets. Having taken it
upon themselves to clean the Augean stables, they expect to find
excrement there.

So progressive activists have been beating the bushes for candidates and training them to run for local and statewide office. Wellstone Action is one such undertaking, operating in twenty-five states since the senator's untimely death in 2002. Progressive Majority recruits, cultivates, trains, and supports local activists in Arizona, Colorado, Pennsylvania, Washington State, and Wisconsin. It claims to have backed 75 local candidates in those five states during 2005, and to have elected 53 of them.[8] In 2006, it claims to have elected "102 new progressives . . . in eight states."[9] Progressive Majority wants "to fill the political pipeline for decades to come." Not incidentally, it aims to affect statewide redistricting, with its large implications for the House of Representatives.[10] Such efforts likely paid off during the 2006 midterm elections, when, for example, one Pennsylvania candidate backed by Progressive Majority won a state House seat by twenty-three votes, putting Democrats in charge for the first time since 1994.[11]

There are sundry related efforts afoot—think tanks, Internet sites and linkages, research undertakings, all churning out smart reports, strategies, tactics, and policy treatises—not to mention fund-raising and get-out-the-vote schemes. Reviewing such developments one by one would be pointless unless the present book were to be published in a loose-leaf edition, and even then it would require daily, sometimes hourly, blog updates. But this much is worth saying: surely, all such efforts, driven by the desire to harness movement spirit to organizational force, are promising—late but promising.

How much or how little so? I am not in the prophecy business. There are too many contingencies. Politics is fluid. The targets move. Events intervene and sometimes change the rules. So do singular human beings. The science of politics does not resemble chemistry. In a closely divided country, a single terror attack could panic enough voters to flip the majority. A seat won by twenty-three votes could be lost by twenty-three votes the next time. But I can speak in conditionals—in effect, I have been doing so throughout this entire book. If the Democrats take up long-term residence in a big tent; if the course of the Republican Party in power continues to be self-evidently calamitous, bogged down in Iraq, in the eyes not only of Democrats but of a sufficient number of moderate independents and serious conservatives (especially in the white working—or, if you like, middle—class); if the public resists being stampeded by Republican threats that people court terrorist bombardment unless they vote for the party that blundered into Iraq; if the Democrats' infrastructure continues to improve, attracting stronger local and statewide candidates and long-haul activists and closing the fund-raising gap; if, all in all, movement energies go on flowing through party channels; if national candidates emerge to make a plausible showing for the view that the Democrats are the antiextremist party and the Republicans are extremists, however strenuously their future candidates strive to wriggle away from the shadow of George W. Bush—then the prospects brighten for a post-Bush recovery, as do the prospects for a liberal or progressive revival.

The Republican base was not built in a day and it will not unravel in a day. The damage that Bush's juggernaut has done to American life, to the country's material well-being, its reputation, its law, its veracity, its moral claims, its treasure, its share of the earth's vitality—really, to the American soul, spirit, and reason—all this damage is immense and the work of remedying it and prevailing over his legacy will be likewise immense and not easily reparable, if it is indeed reparable at all. Campaign bands like to play "Happy Days Are Here Again," and winners like to pretend that they have started the world all over again, but history is not a blackboard and tragedy is not erased.

There will be setbacks. Years after all the reputable authorities everywhere have conceded that Saddam Hussein had no weapons of mass destruction, significant proportions of the American public persist in believing that he had them, and even that they were found; and in other ways as well, the grip of delusion on the public mind has not disappeared. Lucidity tends not to flourish in a time when warped minds are further warped by the threat of furious assault by unscrupulous enemies. This country—and it is not the only one— has often preferred to live unhinged than to face the unsavory facts of a grotesque world. (Only a couple of years before what Tom

Brokaw called "the greatest generation" got great, most of them were cheerfully isolationist.) When a significant minority of a population not only refuses to face reality but takes its refusal as a point of pride, all bets are off. Political narratives may be upbeat but will probably not resemble a child's bedtime story.

Americans seem to demand optimism in their politicians and official ideas. Onward and upward runs the national arc. But perhaps (I am not, after all, a politician) I will be permitted an image of future developments rather different from one of unswerving progress toward the light. It is rather too late in history to pretend that America is destined to be a light unto the nations. It is high time to relinquish the hallucination of Manifest Destiny, with America the torchbearer eternally lighting the way for the accursed of the earth as they fall to our feet and strew us with flowers. Were it far wiser than it has proved to be, no power as vast as the United States of America could be exempt from disdain, sometimes warranted, sometimes not. Perhaps it is enough to say that America—the America of widening circles of liberty, where enlightened underdogs fight lawless bullies—is uncompleted but can be renewed; to say, with Langston Hughes: "O, let America be America again—/The land that never has been yet—/And yet must be."

One lives in the time one lives in and does not get to choose another. There are real adversaries who can be relied upon to go on striving to doom the United States to the fate of all empires. There are the jihadis, hoping to draw the United States into Goliath's clumsy overreach, casting themselves as Davids who always told you so—assuring a billion Muslims that the United States is the home of the "far enemy," the Satanic force that it is their sacred duty to bring down by any and all means. At home, there are the would-be monopolists of virtue, the petty despots whose blindness and appetite for power have brought about the long emergency to which we have been subjected. There are the inept government agencies gazing on complacently as the devastated refugees from Hurricane Katrina wait to be restored to their homes; the oil, drug, insurance, and media companies, among others, colluding to keep wages and benefits low, profits sky-high, and ignorance higher.

In this setting, what would constitute recovery? Simply this: to achieve government sufficiently reasonable, sufficiently open, sufficiently bold, sufficiently inspiring, sufficiently clean (and abroad, sufficiently efficacious, sufficiently modest, and sufficiently cooperative) to honor our small-d democratic and small-r republican ideals, to repel faith-based unreason and curb abusive power; and at long last to get on with an adult discussion of how Americans may afford health care and decent housing, win decent employment and fair wages, dampen inequalities, stifle murderous enemies, and sustain a livable earth for generations present and future.[12] There are years' worth of such work to be undertaken inside the big tent. Liberals will need to contend there, winning some, losing some, and go on contending.

Oddly, to think that reason will avail, that Americans will disentangle from the recent reign of follies, one must keep faith. I do not think it is a contradiction—at least, not a discrediting one—to have faith in reason. Reason by itself is not self-sufficient to justify reason. No one lives long enough to see the final consequences—if there are any—of the moves we make in the murk of present time. Reason is not a plot by pinch-brained secular humanists who wish nothing more than to build ramparts against faith, just as morality is not the property of the casters of first stones who glory in their smug anticipation of a saving Apocalypse around the corner.

The sometimes deceptive, sometimes self-deluded movement that bills itself as conservative has fought unremittingly to further its notions of how to predicate reason on faith and thereby save civilization. Liberals have a radically different idea: that all citizens are entitled to live what they consider to be good lives; that, regardless of race, sex, property, religion, ethnic identification, sexual disposition, or disability, they are entitled to equal treatment under the law; that in free pursuit of their happiness, they are entitled to the rock-bottom prerequisites of a decent life; and that government is a human contrivance that can be made to work to further these goals.

Liberals have on their side a resource or two: the Constitution, laws, facts, talents, values, and popular common sense that often enough, given enough time, resists being stampeded. And no small thing, liberals are learning to win—not by repeating the formulas of the glorious thirties (three-quarters of a century ago!) and the sixties (almost half a century ago!), but by building machinery that fuses their strengths instead of magnifying their weaknesses. They need to think freshly, but they do not have to grouse about the state of their ideas. The right's claim to have more and better ideas than liberals do is a sometimes naive, sometimes disingenuous restatement of its faith-based approach to the world. What the right does have are well-endowed ideological cliques (which sound more respectable when they are called think tanks). The right surely has slit the Achilles' tendons of government—partly by putting hack appointees in charge of civil servants—and then proclaimed that government is irreversibly "broken."[13] The right's major, that is, most expensive, ideas (to use war as a primary instrument of foreign policy and to cut taxes always, especially on the rich, even in wartime) matter chiefly not because the right musters logic and evidence to address objections intelligently, not because it has a deeper grasp of world history and the nature of things, but because it has a juggernaut of power. In a fair and honest debate, liberal ideals stand a good chance of prevailing—not for all time, not on every front, but most of the time on most fronts.

The Republicans' radical juggernaut, the product of long-running devotion and unscrupulous will, may have run out of gas, but it leaves carnage and ruination behind. One real-time monument to its delusions is the ongoing bloodbath in Iraq. Another is the massive government debt piled up by dishonest so-called conservatives in order to repay their financiers and puncture liberal hopes. Fortunately, the juggernaut also leaves behind an auspicious sign: the Democratic rollback of 2006, proof that George W. Bush's travesties of liberty and virtue, under the right conditions, can be blocked. But do the results amount to a stall or a stoppage?

If movements and party builders can make themselves at home in the big tent, if independents get off the ride they were taken on, if keen and honest Republicans keep cutting and running, the bullies can be defeated in time, as they were nourished in time. To keep the right corralled inside its stagnant, largely Confederate, base, and to keep order among the unruly populace inside the tent—all this is not the work of a single election, of a single movement, or of a wish or a wing or a prayer, but of generations. Could it be any clearer that the stakes are immense?

ACKNOWLEDGMENTS

Many of my intellectual debts—most, I hope—are recorded in footnotes. Interviews with Jackie Blumenthal, Francine Busby, Robert Edgar, Max Frankel, Trent Gegax, Colin Greer, Jackie Grumbacher, Steve Grumbacher, Harold Ickes, Peter Jung, Dean Nielsen, Eli Pariser, Richard Parker, John Passacantando, Miles Rapoport, Tim Rutten, Wayne Slater, Robert W. Snyder, Howard Thomas, and Michael Waldman were helpful. So were conversations and correspondence with Joan Blades, Yaeli Bloch-Elkon, Sidney Blumenthal, Heather Booth, Wes Boyd, Thomas B. Edsall, Andrew Golis, Michael Janeway, John Latimer, Dotty Lynch, Sidney Milkis, Eric Rauchway, Robert Y. Shapiro, and John Siceloff. Most of all I greatly appreciate the cover-to-cover readings and criticisms of the manuscript administered by Eric Alterman, Michael Kazin, Don Rose, and especially Scott Winship, without whose researches chapter 12, in particular, would have been impossible. Liel Leibovitz was a demon fact-checker and all-around researcher-enthusiast. The usual strictures apply, though—my conclusions are my own.

Brief parts of this book appeared in earlier forms in *The American Prospect*, *Dissent*, *Mother Jones*, and TPMcafe.com.

Ellen Levine represented me nobly. Eric Nelson edited me with an unusual ability to see the lineaments of a case that was at times obscure to me. Laurel Cook, once again, was my light.

NOTES

Introduction: The Bulldozer Stays Its Course

1. Transcript of Bush interview, Washington Post online, www.washingtonpost .com/wp-dyn/articles/A125702005Jan15.html.
2. Robert Pear, "Legal Group Says Bush Undermines Law by Ignoring Select Parts of Bills," *New York Times*, July 24, 2006, p. A12.
3. David D. Kirkpatrick, "Some Backers of Bush Say They Anticipate a 'Revolution,'" *New York Times*, November 4, 2004, p. 1.
4. See Charles Franklin, "Approval of President Bush in 2005 and 2006," Politic alarithmetik.com, http://photos1.blogger.com/blogger/436/1538/1600/Bush Approval20050620060813.png, accessed April 3, 2007.
5. U.S. Senate Web site, www.senate.gov/legislative/LIS/roll_call_lists/roll_call_ vote_cfm.cfm?congress=109&session=2&vote=00206, accessed August 14, 2006.
6. Sidney Blumenthal, "The Emperor's New Veto," Salon.com, July 20, 2006, www.salon.com/opinion/blumenthal/2006/07/20/bush_veto/print.html.
7. My discussion of Election Day 2006 is drawn from my article "Big Tent. Big Plans?" *Mother Jones* (January–February 2007): 28–29.
8. "OnTheIssues," www.issues2000.org/NY/John_Sweeney.htm, accessed December 19, 2006.
9. Paul A. Gigot, "Miami Heat," *Wall Street Journal*, November 24, 2000, http:// opinionjournal.com/columnists/pgigot/?id=65000673, accessed April 3, 2007.
10. Michael Tomasky, "Pol Versus Pole," *New York*, March 19, 2001, http:// nymag.com/nymetro/news/politics/columns/citypolitic/4473, accessed December 19, 2006.
11. Ibid.

12. Brendon J. Lyons, "Congressman's Wife Called Police," *Albany Times-Union*, October 31, 2006, http://timesunion.com/AspStories/story.asp?storyID= 530664&category=&BCCode=HOME&newsdate=10/31/2006, accessed November 10, 2006.

13. Niccolò Machiavelli, *The Prince*, chap. 17, in David Wootton, ed. and trans., *Machiavelli: Selected Political Writings* (Indianapolis: Hackett, 1994), pp. 51, 52.

14. John Mueller, "The Iraq Syndrome," *Foreign Affairs* (November/December 2005), http://fullaccess.foreignaffairs.org/20051101faessay84605/john-mueller/ the-iraq-syndrome.html, accessed May 14, 2007.

15. Caroline Thompson, coauthor of *The Leadership Genius of George W. Bush: 10 Commonsense Lessons from the Commander in Chief*, quoted in "How Bush Leads: Part Patton, Part Dangerfield," Washington Whispers, *U.S. News and World Report* (January 20, 2003): 4.

16. Ralph Reed, "Mr. Right: The Conservative Case for George W.," *National Review* (July 12, 1999).

17. In decline, Bush's ability to rally his base eroded. As the political scientist Philip Klinkner observed (http://polysigh.blogspot.com/2006/05/bush-effect.html# links), a May 2006 CBS/*New York Times* poll divided the sample randomly into two halves. The first half was asked to compare the state of the nation today with the situation "six years ago." The second half was asked the identical question, but the point of comparison was worded this way: "the way they were going six years ago before George W. Bush became president." Among Republicans, mention of Bush did not affect the percentage (a less-than-imposing 31 percent) who thought matters *better* in 2006 than in 2000, but it did slash the percentage who thought matters *worse* (27 percent as against 42) or *about the same* (35 percent as against 24). Loyalty trumped judgment. The personal was indeed political.

18. A careful study of gay marriage ban measures on state ballots in November 2004 shows that they did indeed mobilize evangelical Christians and Catholics ("evangelicals in GMB [gay marriage bill] states had an average level of turnout roughly 5 percentage points, higher than evangelicals elsewhere in the country"), and that in decisive Ohio, the upswing in pro-Bush turnout that resulted from targeted direct mail on the issue "may have mattered." David E. Campbell and J. Quin Monson, "The Religion Card: Evangelicals, Catholics, and Gay Marriage in the 2004 Presidential Election," prepared for delivery at the 2005 Annual Meeting of the American Political Science Association, September 1–September 4, 2005, pp. 6, 19.

19. Rigorous analysis shows that one of the striking features of that election was the proportion of voters who shared a consensus that terrorism was the most important issue—43 percent, the highest number, according to National Election Study, to have agreed on a "most important issue" since 1968, when the issue was Vietnam. Of this 43 percent who cared more about terrorism than anything else, 70 percent voted for Bush, giving Bush a much greater margin of victory than among those who thought "moral issues" most important—an unprecedented preference on a "most important issue." Philip A. Klinkner, "Mr. Bush's War: Foreign Policy in the 2004 Election," *Presidential Studies Quarterly* 36, no. 2 (June), pp. 284, 287.

20. Ibid., p. 289.

21. Professor Klinkner adds (personal communication, May 23, 2006) that what voters thought of Bush's tax cuts also hinged more on what they thought about Bush than on their general views on tax policy. With respect to social issues, however, their views of Bush were "less important than [their] views on social and moral traditionalism."

22. Klinkner, "Mr. Bush's War," pp. 293–295.

23. Robert Y. Shapiro and Yaeli Bloch-Elkon, "Political Polarization and the Rational Public," paper prepared for presentation at the Annual Conference of the American Association for Public Opinion Research, Montreal, Quebec, Canada, May 10, 2006. Some figures were made available to me through the good offices of Professor Bloch-Elkon.

24. I count Condoleezza Rice as a subordinate. Once a protégé of Bush I's adviser Brent Scowcroft, Rice proved pliable in Bush II's hands once she arrived in the White House—an enabler, even if she may have rationalized her pliability as the price of influence.

25. Richard A. Viguerie and David Franke, *America's Right Turn: How Conservatives Used New and Alternative Media to Take Power* (Chicago: Bonus Books, 2004), p. 341.

26. Thomas B. Edsall and James V. Grimaldi, "On Nov. 2, GOP Got More Bang for Its Billion, Analysis Shows," *Washington Post,* December 30, 2004, p. A1.

27. Thomas Edsall, lecture, Graduate School of Journalism, Columbia University, October 26, 2006.

1. The Conquerors

1. I put it this way to take account of the peculiar but revelatory 2000 case, when the Republicans availed themselves of the power they held at various levels of government, from the Supreme Court down to the Florida legislature, to take power without an electoral majority. But this anomalous case confirms the point that power in one segment of the political system is transferable into power at another—all the way up to the White House.

2. They also controlled all three during 1953–1955.

3. David G. Savage, "Judges Battle Transcends Numbers," *Los Angeles Times,* April 17, 2005, p. A1.

4. See www.nationmaster.com/encyclopedia/Political-Party-Strength-in-U.S.-States, accessed April 6, 2007. State legislatures, by contrast, are rather evenly divided.

5. For more on Blackwell's political maneuvers in 2004, see Andrew Gumbel, *Steal This Vote: Dirty Elections and the Rotten History of Democracy in America* (New York: Nation Books, 2005), pp. 281–282.

6. Data on party representation in state legislatures is from the National Council of State Legislatures, www.ncsl.org/programs/legman/elect/demshare2000.htm, www.ncsl.org/ncsldb/elect98/partcomp.cfm?yearsel=2006, and www.ncsl.org/programs/legman/elect/hstptyct.htm, accessed October 1, 2006.

7. Richard A. Viguerie and David Franke, *America's Right Turn: How Conservatives Used New and Alternative Media to Take Power* (Chicago: Bonus Books, 2004), p. 64.

8. Quoted in William Martin, *With God on Our Side: The Rise of the Religious Right in America* (New York: Broadway Books, 1996), p. 89.

9. John Micklethwait and Adrian Wooldridge, *The Right Nation: Conservative Power in America* (New York: Penguin, 2004), p. 281.

10. William J. Bennett, *The Death of Outrage: Bill Clinton and the Assault on American Ideals* (New York: Free Press, 1998); Weyrich quoted in Richard John Neuhaus, "The Public Square," *First Things* (June–July 1999), www.firstthings .com/ftissues/ft9906/public.html#text3, accessed November 17, 2006.

11. Irving Kristol, "Forty Good Years," *Public Interest* (Spring 2005): 9.

12. Ibid., p. 7.

13. Matthew Shugart, "Filibuster Protects the Majority—of Voters," *San Diego Union-Tribune*, May 18, 2005, www.signonsandiego.com/uniontrib/20050518/ news_lz1e18shugart.html, accessed April 6, 2007.

14. Ibid.

15. Jacob S. Hacker and Paul Pierson, "Enter Center," *New Republic* (December 25, 2006): 12.

16. Steven Hill, "Why the Democrats Will Keep Losing," Motherjones.com, www.motherjones.com/commentary/columns/2005/06/why_the_democrats_ will_keep_losing.html, accessed April 6, 2007.

17. See Wikipedia online at http://en.wikipedia.org/wiki/U.S._presidential_elec tion,_2004#Presidential_Results_by_Congressional_District, accessed April 6, 2007.

18. Hacker and Pierson, "Enter Center," p. 12, citing David Mayhew.

19. Tom Hamburger and Peter Wallsten, *One Party Country: The Republican Plan for Dominance in the 21st Century* (Hoboken, NJ: John Wiley & Sons, 2006), pp. 38–46.

20. Steven Hill, *Fixing Elections: The Failure of America's Winner Take All Politics* (New York: Routledge, 2002), pp. 78–94.

21. One thoughtful proposal for overcoming the small-state bias of the electoral college is to amend state constitutions to require states to choose all their electors to support the candidate who wins the national popular vote. If enough states did this, then in effect the electoral college would have been subverted. But the difficulty of arranging this reform is demonstrated by the California experience of 2006, when the state legislature passed the measure only to see it vetoed by Governor Arnold Schwarzenegger.

22. John Cassidy, "The Ringleader," *New Yorker* (August 1, 2005): 46.

23. According to the *Denver Post* (in a revelation unmatched elsewhere in the mainstream news media): "President Bush has installed more than 100 top officials who were once lobbyists, attorneys or spokespeople for the industries they oversee." (Anne C. Mulkern, "Watchdogs or Lap Dogs? When Advocates Become Regulators," *Denver Post*, May 23, 2004, p. A1.) Bush made far more political appointments to top bureaucratic positions than had Clinton. As Greg Anrig wrote ("Excess Baggage," *American Prospect* online, December 15, 2006, www.prospect.org/web/page.ww?section=root&name=ViewWeb&articleId= 12303, accessed December 18, 2006):

> Princeton University political scientist David E. Lewis, reviewing data from the Office of Personnel Management, found that the number of political appointments escalated during the first term of the Bush admin-

istration after declining substantially during Clinton's eight years. From 1992 to 2000, political appointees in the federal government dropped by nearly 17 percent—from 3,423 to 2,845. From 2000 to 2004, that figure climbed back up by 12.5 percent to 3,202.

24. Jeffrey H. Birnbaum, "The Road to Riches Is Called K Street," *Washington Post*, June 22, 2005, p. A1.

25. John C. Green, *The Christian Right at the Millennium* (New York: American Jewish Committee, 2001), p. 5. Typographical error corrected in a personal communication from Professor Green, July 9, 2005.

26. Steven Waldman and John Green, "The Twelve Tribes of American Politics: How They Voted," www.beliefnet.com/story/167/story16763_1.html, accessed April 6, 2007; and John Green and Steven Waldman, "The Twelve Tribes of American Politics," www.beliefnet.com/story/153/story_15355_1.html, accessed April 6, 2007.

27. Barna defines "born again Christians" this way:

> Born again Christians were defined in these surveys as people who said they have made "a personal commitment to Jesus Christ that is still important in their life today" and who also indicated they believe that when they die they will go to Heaven because they had confessed their sins and had accepted Jesus Christ as their savior. Respondents were not asked to describe themselves as "born again." Being classified as "born again" is not dependent upon "church or denominational affiliation or involvement."

28. William R. Levesque, "Quiet Judge Persists in Schiavo Maelstrom," *St. Petersburg Times*, March 6, 2005, www.sptimes.com/2005/03/06/Tampabay/Quiet_judge_persists_.shtml, accessed August 15, 2006.

29. Elisabeth Bumiller, "Bush Remarks Roil Debate Over Teaching of Evolution," *New York Times*, August 3, 2005, p. A14.

2. Centralizing the Apparatus

1. John F. Harris, *The Survivor: Clinton in the White House* (New York: Random House, 2005), p. 84.

2. Ibid., p. 92.

3. Evan Thomas and the staff of *Newsweek*, *Election 2004: How Bush Won and What You Can Expect in the Future* (New York: Public Affairs, 2004), p. xxiv.

4. Associated Press, "Bush: 'Tone Down' Attacks against Gonzalez [sic]," July 5, 2005, available online at www.sfgate.com/cgi-bin/article.cgi?f=/n/a/2005/07/04/national/w210406D60.DTL, accessed April 6, 2007.

5. Newt Gingrich on the subject of Bill and Hillary Clinton, quoted in David S. Broder, "The Good Gingrich and the Bad," *Washington Post*, November 16, 1994, p. A25. Indiscipline and slackness are recurrent themes in conservative jeremiads of the nineties: for example, Robert Bork, *Slouching toward Gomorrah: Modern Liberalism and American Decline* (New York: ReganBooks, 1997), and Myron Magnet, *The Dream and the Nightmare: The Sixties' Legacy to the Underclass* (San Francisco: Encounter Books, 2000).

6. Elisabeth Bumiller, "An Interview by, Not with, the President," *New York Times*, July 21, 2005, p. A1.

7. Michael Walzer, *The Revolution of the Saints: A Study in the Origins of Radical Politics* (Cambridge, MA: Harvard University Press, 1982) p. 1. See also William G. McLoughlin's discussion of what he calls "this driving, unquenchable spirit" in *Revivals, Awakenings, and Reform: An Essay on Religion and Social Change in America, 1607–1977* (Chicago: University of Chicago Press, 1978), pp. 39–40.

8. McLoughlin, *Revivals, Awakenings, and Reform*, p. 43.

9. Lou Dubose and Jan Reid, *The Hammer, Tom Delay, God, Money, and the Rise of the Republican Congress* (New York: Public Affairs, 2004), p. 82.

10. Thomas et al., *Election 2004*, p. 170.

11. Matt Dellinger, "Wednesdays with Grover," New Yorker Online, August 1, 2005, www.newyorker.com/archive/2005/08/01/050801on_onlineonly01, accessed April 6, 2007.

12. Interview with Harold Ickes, June 4, 2005.

13. In September 2006, Ickes launched a new 527 effort to fill the resulting gap. John M. Broder, "Democrats Form New Group for Fund-Raising and Ads," *New York Times*, September 14, 2006, p. A23.

14. Paul Kane, "Liberal 527s Find Shortfall," *Roll Call*, September 25, 2006, citing PoliticalMoneyLine.com's database.

15. David Brock, *Blinded by the Right: The Conscience of an Ex-conservative* (New York: Crown, 2002), p. 66.

16. John Cassidy, "The Ringleader," *New Yorker*, August 1, 2005, pp. 46–47.

17. Interview with Harold Ickes, June 4, 2005.

18. Back jacket flap, Richard A. Viguerie and David Franke, *America's Right Turn: How Conservatives Used New and Alternative Media to Take Power* (Chicago and Los Angeles: Bonus Books, 2004).

19. Ibid., p. 91.

20. Ibid., p. 88.

21. Ibid., p. 97. Emphasis in original.

22. Ibid., p. 100.

23. John Micklethwait and Adrian Wooldridge, *The Right Nation: Conservative Power in America* (New York: Penguin, 2004), p. 82.

24. Viguerie and Franke, *America's Right Turn*, pp. 102–103. Emphasis in original.

25. Telephone interview, Richard Parker, August 25, 2005. Emulating Viguerie from the left, Parker, an editor of *Mother Jones* magazine, and William Dodd, its circulation director, took the magazine's business operation private and set up Parker, Dodd, a for-profit direct mail company doing business with progressives, in 1979.

26. Interview with Harold Ickes, June 4, 2005.

27. *Time*'s Lev Grossman confirms ("What Your Party Knows about You," *Time*, October 18, 2004, p. 38) that "by 2001, the Democrats—the party of would-be overnerd Al Gore—were staring at a data gap. All they had was a few tens of thousands of e-mail addresses stored on a computer so obsolete its monitor was green. So they hired a small firm called Plus Three to build them a database of their very own, which they named Demzilla. Voter Vault and Demzilla currently hold about 165 million entries each." According to *PC World* magazine (Daniel Tynan, "GOP Voter Vault Shipped Overseas," *PC World*, September 24, 2004, www.pcworld.com/news/article/0,aid,117930,00.asp, accessed April 6, 2007): "When the Republican Party clinched close gubernatorial races in

Mississippi and Kentucky in 2003, it relied heavily on its Voter Vault database to get people to the voting booths." According to Tynan, the Democratic version of Voter Vault is called DataMart, and DemZilla is actually "a smaller database used for fundraising and organizing volunteers."

28. Thomas et al., *Election 2004*, pp. 85–86. Thomas notes that, in early August 2004, Robert Shrum, John Kerry's senior political adviser, agreed to forego his advertising fees.

29. Interview with Harold Ickes, June 4, 2005.

30. Jacob S. Hacker and Paul Pierson, *Off Center: The Republican Revolution and the Erosion of American Democracy* (New Haven, CT: Yale University Press, 2005), p. 141.

31. A good summary on House centralization under DeLay's Republicans appears in Hacker and Pierson, *Off Center*, pp. 138–139.

32. Dubose and Reid, *The Hammer*, pp. 87, 134, and 170, where they write: "Everything Tom DeLay has achieved in the leadership derives from the tens of millions of dollars he raised and then contributed to Republican House races." On Johnson, see Robert Caro, *Master of the Senate* (New York: Vintage, 2003), in particular part IV, pp. 519–655.

33. Thomas B. Edsall, *Building Red America: The New Conservative Coalition and the Drive for Permanent Power* (New York: Basic Books, 2006), p. 7.

34. Lou Dubose, "Broken Hammer?" Salon.com, April 8, 2005, www.tpj.org/page_view.jsp?pageid=829&pubid=594, accessed August 16, 2006. See also Jim VandeHei, "GOP Monitoring Lobbyists' Politics; White House, Hill Access May Be Affected," *Washington Post*, June 10, 2002, p. A1. See also Nicholas Confessore, "Welcome to the Machine," *Washington Monthly* (July/August 2003): 30–37; and Edsall, *Building Red America*, pp. 116–118.

35. Dubose and Reid, *The Hammer*, pp. 91 ff.

36. Ibid., p. 6.

37. The extraordinary saga is told in Dubose and Reid, *The Hammer*, chapter 12.

38. The essential moderation of the American public on most issues has been demonstrated repeatedly, as, for example, by E. J. Dionne Jr., in *Why Americans Hate Politics* (New York: Simon & Schuster, 1991), and Morris Fiorina, with Samuel J. Abrams and Jeremy C. Pope, *Culture War? The Myth of a Polarized America* (New York: Longman, 2004).

39. Hacker and Pierson, *Off Center*, pp. 150–162. The quotes are from pages 150 and 151.

40. "Blunt, Boehner Share Broad Network of Lobbyist Ties with DeLay," *Bloomberg News*, January 10, 2006, www.bloomberg.com/apps/news?pid=10000103&sid=a64ZIkmVPv_w&refer=us, accessed August 17, 2006.

41. Jeffrey Birnbaum, "Democrats' Stock Is Rising on K Street: Firms Anticipate a Shift in Power," *Washington Post*, August 17, 2006, p. A1.

42. Patrick O'Connor, "Hastert, Boehner clash," *The Hill*, March 16, 2006, www.hillnews.com/thehill/export/TheHill/News/Frontpage/031606/news1.html, accessed August 17, 2006.

3. The Faithful and the Willful

1. CNN online, "Bush: 'I'm the Decider' on Rumsfeld," www.cnn.com/2006/POLITICS/04/18/rumsfeld/index.html, accessed April 6, 2007.

2. Ron Suskind, "Without a Doubt," *New York Times Magazine*, October 17, 2004, p. 47.
3. If members of Bush's inner policy-making circle harbor a different view of the process, they have not spoken up, with the partial exception of the accounts of White House discussions of Afghanistan and Iraq policy gathered by Bob Woodward in his two books *Bush at War* and *Plan of Attack*.
4. Interview with Brit Hume, *Fox News*, September 22, 2003. Transcript available online at www.foxnews.com/story/0,2933,98006,00.html, accessed April 6, 2007. Whether he actually refused to read newspapers is beside the point. If it is was untrue, he must have been strictly trying to belittle reporters—a sign of his petulance.
5. Lawrence Wilkerson, "Weighing the Uniqueness of the Bush Administration's National Security Decision-Making Process: Boon or Danger to American Democracy?" presentation to the New American Foundation American Strategy Program Policy Forum, October 19, 2005, www.thewashingtonnote.com/archives/Wilkerson%20Speech%20--%20WEB.htm, accessed June 3, 2006.
6. Joan Didion, "Cheney: The Fatal Touch," *New York Review of Books*, October 5, 2006, www.nybooks.com/articles/19376, accessed October 13, 2006.
7. Joan Didion had this to say on Cheney's secrecy: "He runs an office so disinclined to communicate that it routinely refuses to disclose who works there, even for updates to the *Federal Directory*, which lists names and contact addresses for government officials. 'We just don't give out that kind of information,' an aide told one reporter. 'It's just not something we talk about.' " See Didion, "Cheney: The Fatal Touch."
8. Joseph Lelyveld, "The Good Soldier," *New York Review of Books*, November 2, 2006, p. 4.
9. Ron Suskind, *The One Percent Doctrine: Deep Inside America's Pursuit of Its Enemies Since 9/11* (New York: Simon & Schuster, 2006), p. 174.
10. Todd Gitlin, "It's the Stupidity, Stupid," Salon.com, October 26, 2000, http://archive.salon.com/letters/daily/2000/10/26/bush/index.html, accessed April 6, 2007.
11. Examples are legion. For a handy compendium and discussion, see Didion, "Cheney: The Fatal Touch."
12. Ron Suskind, *The Price of Loyalty: George W. Bush, the White House, and the Education of Paul O'Neill* (New York: Simon & Schuster, 2004), pp. 102, 114. Consider, by way of comparison, the decision-making methods of an earlier two-term Republican president, Dwight Eisenhower, himself at the time widely derided as an amiable dunce. Contrary to popular impressions—including impressions created by Eisenhower himself, who deployed a studied vagueness to put up "smoke screens" at his much-derided press conferences—the documents demonstrate that Eisenhower was actually a logical man committed to extensive policy reviews. (On "smoke screens," see Fred I. Greenstein, *The Hidden-Hand Presidency: Eisenhower as Leader* [New York: Basic, 1982], p. 67.) In fact, planning was Eisenhower's forte as a military commander.

Upon entering the White House in 1953, Eisenhower decided to choose a Cold War strategy by commissioning three staff teams to work in secrecy for five weeks, preparing the best possible cases for each of three strategic options: the status quo of containment; a more frontal, aggressive affirmation of containment;

and rollback of the communist empire. When the teams reported back to Eisenhower and the National Security Council, in the recollection of his staff secretary, Andrew Goodpaster: "The President had been sitting and listening to each one of the presentations, not taking a single note. He then rose and spoke for forty-five minutes, summarizing the three presentations and commenting on the specific strengths and weaknesses of each one. Years afterwards, George Kennan . . . recalled that in doing so, the President had shown his 'intellectual ascendancy over every man in the room.'" (Tyler Nottberg, "Once and Future Policy Planning: Solarium for Today," www.eisenhowerinstitute.org/programs/livinghistory/solarium.htm, accessed June 3, 2006. See also Eisenhower to Charles E. Wilson, July 1, 1953, www.eisenhowermemorial.org/presidential-papers/firstterm/documents/291.cfm, accessed June 3, 2006.)

In general, Eisenhower was, as the historian Fred Greenstein wrote (*Hidden-Hand Presidency: Eisenhower as Leader* [Baltimore: Johns Hopkins University Press, 1994], pp. 20ff, 52, 120, 121, 123, 126–127, 129), a "rationalist," weighing the costs and benefits of alternative plans of action. He encouraged debate, using Cabinet meetings as sounding boards to reflect divergences in the Republican Party. Even in his National Security Council, he worked to sharpen disagreements. He sometimes modified his views after hearing contrary arguments. Here is how Eisenhower himself summarized his method, at least in its ideal form:

> I know of only one way in which you can be sure you've done your best to make a wise decision. That is to get all of the people who have partial and definable responsibility in this particular field, whatever it be. Get them with their different viewpoints in front of you, and listen to them debate. . . . You must get courageous men, men of strong views, and let them debate and argue with each other. You listen, and you see if there's anything been brought up, an idea that changes your own view or enriches your view or adds to it. [Greenstein, *Hidden-Hand Presidency*, p. 246, quoting a 1967 Columbia University Oral History interview.]

Eisenhower wrote to his brother Milton, "It is in the combination of . . . various attitudes that we hammer out acceptable policies; enthusiasts for anything go too far" (Greenstein, *Hidden-Hand Presidency*, p. 120).

This is not to say that Eisenhower always operated this way or that his decisions were always wise. In foreign policy, he made two deplorable decisions whose consequences the United States and the rest of the world are still living with: dispatching the CIA to overthrow the elected Mossadeq government in Iran (1953) and the elected Arbenz government in Guatemala (1954). But Eisenhower's account suggests a goal, if not a uniform achievement, worlds apart from Bush's operational method of going out of his way to shield himself from arguments, or patterns of fact, that he had not heard before.

13. Richard A. Clarke, *Against All Enemies: Inside America's War on Terror* (New York: Free Press, 2004), pp. 26, 242.

14. Ibid., p. 243.

15. In April 2006, more confirmation of his approach to the world came, in passing, when his popularity was plunging into the low thirties, and he decided to replace his chief of staff, Andrew Card, with Joshua Bolten. "Josh is a little more overtly demanding," an anonymous former member of the administration told the *New*

York Times's Elisabeth Bumiller ("Not 'the Decider,' but Stirring Anxiety," *New York Times*, April 24, 2006, p. A17). "He's immediately playing the devil's advocate, and he'll challenge you on a lot of things, mostly to make sure it was well thought through and to see if there are any holes in the argument." To put it another way, for the first sixty-three months of the Bush administration, no one in the White House was tending to an orderly, logical decision-making process. (If not Bush himself or his chief of staff, who would it have been?) O'Neill was right to have been shocked when he found Bush indifferent to contrary opinions. Bush hadn't required of his chief of staff that he trouble himself ascertaining whether arguments were "well thought through" or whether there were "any holes" in them. His chief of staff didn't care because the decider in chief didn't care. Only when Bush was mired in disapproval was it time for him to install someone "a little more overtly demanding."

16. "The tendency of American evangelicals, when confronted with a problem, is to act," wrote the evangelical analyst and historian Mark A. Noll in *The Scandal of the Evangelical Mind* (Grand Rapids, MI: Eerdmans, 1994), p. 243.

17. David Frum, *The Right Man: The Surprise Presidency of George W. Bush* (New York: Random House, 2003), p. 30.

18. Elisabeth Bumiller, "For a President at War, Refuge at Camp David," *New York Times*, November 5, 2001, p. A1.

19. William Hamilton, "Bush Began to Plan War Three Months after 9/11," *Washington Post*, April 17, 2004, p. A1.

20. Quoted in George Packer, "Not Wise," *New Yorker*, May 8, 2006, p. 24.

21. See, for example, the Oval Office interview by Kai Diekmann of the German newspaper *Bild*, May 5, 2006, available at www.whitehouse.gov/news/releases/2006/05/20060507-2.html, accessed April 6, 2007.

22. Stuart Stevens, *The Big Enchilada: Campaign Adventures with the Cockeyed Optimists from Texas Who Won the Biggest Prize in Politics* (New York: Free Press, 2001), p. 200.

23. In Diekmann.

24. Suskind, "Without a Doubt," p. 52. The original report appeared in the *Lancaster New Era* of July 16, 2004: Jack Brubaker, "Bush Meets with Amish Group during July Campaign Stop," www.mennoweekly.org/AUGUST/08-02-04/BUSH08-02.html, accessed April 6, 2007. Brubaker wrote in a subsequent column: "Sam Stoltzfus, the Gordonville man who interviewed four people who were present in that meeting with Bush . . . now says he received different wording on that quote from several sources. 'It's very possible that the president didn't say it that way,' Stoltzfus says." But Brubaker went on to note that Bush told Bob Woodward (*Plan of Attack*, p. 379) that in the run-up to the Iraq war: "Going into this period I was praying for the strength to do the Lord's will. I'm surely not going to justify the war based on God. . . . Nevertheless, in my case I pray I be as good a messenger of his will as possible." Brubaker concluded, " 'Messenger of his will.' 'God speaks through me.' The difference seems rather fine." Jack Brubaker, "Did George Bush Really Say, 'I Trust God Speaks through Me'? *Lancaster New Era*, July 23, 2004, p. A8.

25. Bruce Lincoln, "Bush's God Talk," *Christian Century*, October 5, 2004, p. 22. In a 2003 interview for PBS's *Frontline*, Wead clarified that he meant the whole of

this advice for George W. Bush. "My advice to George W. Bush would be, 'Signal early.'" Interview of November 18, 2003, conducted for PBS *Frontline*, "The Jesus Factor," aired April 29, 2004, www.pbs.org/wgbh/pages/frontline/shows/ jesus/interviews/wead.html, accessed April 6, 2007.

26. Wead went on:

> The reason for any political figure to signal early to the evangelical movement is that the evangelical movement is feared and despised and resented by media elites. They don't like them. You take a risk if you're seen with them, if in any way you're associated with them. So if you do it early, when the media's not paying attention, then you don't risk the alienation and the anger of media elites who are offended by that relationship. You do it early, when they're not watching, when it's less important.

27. Interview conducted for PBS's *Frontline*, "The Choice," October 12, 2004 www.pbs.org/wgbh/pages/frontline/shows/choice2004/etc/synopsis.html, accessed April 6, 2007.

28. But here, hard-liners run into limits. In 2003, Bush agreed that AIDS control funds could go to nongovernmental organizations that also counsel women about abortions. "U.S. 'Mexico City Policy': Abortion Funding in Foreign Countries," www.religioustolerance.org/abo_wrld.htm, accessed April 6, 2007.

29. According to Mariah Blake, writing in the *Columbia Journalism Review*, in 2001:

> President Bush invited the [National Religious Broadcasters'] executive committee to join him and Attorney General John Ashcroft for a meeting in the Roosevelt Room at the White House. After the gathering, the NRB's board chairman wrote an exuberant message to members, saying there was a "new wind blowing in Washington, D. C., and across the nation. . . . The President has surrounded himself with a wonderful staff of people of faith."

> Blake noted that the NRB executive committee went on to meet periodically with White House staff, and that, on occasion, "Bush himself attended." Other journalists discovered that writers of apocalyptic Christian persuasions met with White House staff as well, though not necessarily with Bush himself in attendance. At one of these meetings, in 2005, a Jew for Jesus named Joel C. Rosenberg, the author of the novels *The Last Jihad* and *The Last Days*, spoke to two dozen White House staffers (though not to Bush himself) about biblical prophecies of current events. (He also told Pat Robertson that the Bible foreshadowed "the end of radical Islam as we know it." Dan Froomkin, "What's the Motivation?" *Washington Post* online, "White House Briefing," August 4, 2006, www.washingtonpost.com/ wp-dyn/content/blog/2006/08/04/BL2006080400780_pf.html, accessed April 6, 2007. See also my "Right Behind," www.tpmcafe.com/blog/coffeehouse/2006/ aug/05/right_behind, accessed April 6, 2007. Rosenberg said that he was once an aide to Israeli prime minister Benjamin Netanyahu (www.joelrosenberg .blogspot.com, accessed April 6, 2007).

30. Judy Keen, "Strain of Iraq War Showing on Bush, Those Who Know Him Say," *USA Today*, April 1, 2003, p. 1A, available at www.usatoday.com/news/ washington/2003-04-01-bush-cover_x.htm, accessed April 6, 2007. Evans was one of the oilmen who recruited Bush for Bible study in Midland in the

mid-1980s; see "Midland's Community Bible Study," www.pbs.org/wgbh/pages/frontline/shows/jesus/president/cbs.html, accessed April 6, 2007.

31. Michael Gerson, "The Danger for America Is Not Theocracy," beliefnet.com, December 2004, www.beliefnet.com/story/159/story_15943_3.html, accessed April 6, 2007. "It's not a strategy," Gerson protested. "It comes from my own background and my own reading of the history of American rhetoric." But, of course, Bush was well aware of Gerson's background, and let his religious language stand because he felt it expressed him well. Gerson went on to maintain that Bush's biblical references were squarely in an American presidential tradition that included Franklin D. Roosevelt and Bill Clinton, the latter of whom, he said, "referred to Jesus or Jesus Christ more than the president does." If Gerson's claim about Clinton is in fact accurate, the important difference is less in the word-by-word text of Bush's remarks and more in the nature of the transaction between Bush and his audience.

32. Suskind, "Without a Doubt," p. 51.

33. This is, of course, the language of the famous "Downing Street Memo," the record of the July 23, 2002, meeting of Tony Blair, with his top advisers, at which the head of Britain's MI6, Sir Richard Dearlove, used these words to describe what high-level officials in Washington with whom he had just consulted, including CIA director George Tenet, were saying about the Bush administration's thrust toward war with Saddam's Iraq. The memo was first published in the *Times of London* on May 1, 2005.

34. Bob Woodward, *Bush at War* (New York: Simon & Schuster, 2002), p. 34.

35. After trying to avoid testifying to the 9/11 Commission in 2004, Condoleezza Rice, then the national security adviser, told the commission that she and Bush considered the PDB a "historical document," not a "warning"; see Online NewsHour, "Report Warned of Possible Al-Qaida Attacks in United States," April 12, 2004, www.pbs.org/newshour/updates/pdb_04-12-04.html.html, accessed April 6, 2007.

36. Condoleezza Rice, "Campaign 2000—Promoting the National Interest," *Foreign Affairs* (January–February 2000), www.foreignpolicy2000.org/library/issuebriefs/readingnotes/fa_rice.html, accessed April 6, 2007. Cited in Frum, *The Right Man*, p. 226.

37. See my *Media Unlimited: How the Torrent of Images and Sounds Overwhelms Our Lives* (New York: Metropolitan, 2002).

38. See the White House's Web site, "President Addresses Nation, Discusses Iraq, War on Terror," www.whitehouse.gov/news/releases/2005/06/20050628-7.html, accessed April 6, 2007.

39. Richard W. Stevenson and Alan Cowell, "Bush Arrives at Summit Session, Ready to Stand Alone," *New York Times*, July 7, 2005, p. A14.

40. Frum, *The Right Man*, p. 89.

41. Ibid., p. 91.

42. Cheney's defense was: "If you look at what the dictionary says about '*throes*,' it can be a violent period, the *throes* of a revolution." (Quoted in William Safire, "No Free Throes," *New York Times Magazine*, August 7, 2005, p. 16.) Even the loyalist Safire could not find it in himself to give Cheney a lexicographical pass for the "last," though he worded his demurral as a chiding of Cheney's defender, Donald Rumsfeld, not of Cheney himself. It is also worthy of note that Cheney

said on September 17, 2003, "Our military is confronting the terrorists, along with our allies, in Iraq and Afghanistan so that innocent civilians will not have to confront terrorist violence in Washington or London or anywhere else in the world." See "Remarks by Vice-President Dick Cheney at the 2003 Air Force Association National Convention, Washington, DC, 17 September 2003," www .mtholyoke.edu/acad/intrel/bush/air.htm, accessed April 6, 2007.

43. Ruy Teixeira, "It's the White Working Class, Stupid," February 8, 2005, www.emergingdemocraticmajorityweblog.com/donkeyrising/archives/001042 .php, accessed October 14, 2006. The 2004 data are from National Election Pool exit poll, the 2000 data from its precursor, the Voter News Service.

44. Steve Holland, "Bush, at 60, Showing No Signs of Slowing," Reuters, August 7, 2006, http://go.reuters.co.uk/newsArticle.jhtml?type=reutersEdgeNews&story ID=1389442&section=finance&src=rss/uk/featuresNews, accessed August 16, 2006.

4. "The Un-Sixties"

1. Fred Barnes, *Rebel-in-Chief: Inside the Bold and Controversial Presidency of George W. Bush* (New York: Crown Forum, 2006), p. 14.

2. CBS News online, "Bush Disses Global Warming Report," June 4, 2002, www.cbsnews.com/stories/2002/06/03/tech/main510920.shtml, accessed May 31, 2006.

3. On Kennedy as guerrilla in power, see Garry Wills, *The Kennedy Imprisonment* (Boston: Little, Brown, 1981).

4. Jerome Karabel, *The Chosen: The Hidden History of Admission and Exclusion at Harvard, Yale, and Princeton* (Boston: Houghton Mifflin, 2005), pp. 344, 345.

5. Bill Minutaglio, *First Son: George W. Bush and the Bush Family Dynasty* (New York: Times Books, 1999), pp. 87–88; Kevin Phillips, *American Dynasty: Aristocracy, Fortune, and the Politics of Deceit in the House of Bush* (New York: Viking, 2004), p. 44.

6. Karabel, *The Chosen*, p. 331.

7. Ibid., pp. 357, 358.

8. Ibid., pp. 359, 364.

9. J. P. Goldsmith, quoted in Minutaglio, *First Son*, p. 110.

10. Minutaglio, *First Son*, p. 91.

11. Ibid., p. 96.

12. Ibid., p. 97.

13. Elsie Walker, quoted in Minutaglio, *First Son*, p. 107–108.

14. Minutaglio, *First Son*, pp. 89–90.

15. Ibid., p. 85.

16. Ibid., p. 105.

17. Ibid., p. 85. Years later, Coffin wrote to George W. to say that he didn't remember speaking those words. Whether he did or not, the important thing is that Bush thought he heard them—heard them speak to him through the symbolic instrument of Coffin's voice.

18. Phillips, *American Dynasty*, pp. 46–47.

19. David Brooks, "Ends without Means," *New York Times*, September 14, 2006, http://select.nytimes.com/2006/09/14/opinion/14brooks.html?n=Top%2f

Opinion%2fEditorials%20and%20Op%2dEd%2fOp%2dEd%2fColumnists, accessed September 15, 2006.

20. Myron Magnet, *The Dream and the Nightmare: The Sixties' Legacy to the Underclass* (San Francisco: Encounter Books, 2000), p. 8.

21. Typical tributes are these from Fred Barnes, *Rebel-in-Chief*, pp. 166, 169, 170, 171: "[O]n taxes, Bush is Reagan redux. . . . On Social Security, Bush is Reagan's rightful heir. . . . On national security, Bush is indisputably Reagan's successor."

22. Magnet, *The Dream and the Nightmare*, pp. 8–9.

23. Steve Bridges on NBC's *Meet the Press*, May 7, 2006.

24. Michael Beschloss, *Taking Charge: The Johnson White House Tapes, 1963–1964* (New York: Simon and Schuster, 1997). On Johnson's intricate duplicities as majority leader, see Robert Caro, *Master of the Senate* (New York: Knopf, 2002), pp. 519–655.

25. On Johnson and the Tonkin Gulf, see Eric Alterman, *When Presidents Lie: A History of Official Deception and Its Consequences* (New York: Viking, 2004), chap. 4, esp. pp. 194, 196, 202, 204, and 213.

26. For examples, see John F. Harris, *The Survivor* (New York: Random House, 2005), pp. 270–272.

27. Ibid., p. 410.

28. See Joe Conason, *Big Lies: The Right-Wing Propaganda Machine and How It Distorts the Truth* (New York: St. Martin's Griffin, 2004), pp. 62-66, and David Corn, *The Lies of George W. Bush* (New York: Three Rivers Press, 2004).

29. Alterman, *When Presidents Lie*, pp. 297–302; Conason, *Big Lies*, passim; and Corn, *The Lies of George W. Bush*, passim.

30. James Moore and Wayne Slater, *Bush's Brain: How Karl Rove Made George W. Bush Presidential* (Hoboken, NJ: John Wiley & Sons, 2003), p. 277.

31. Jake Tapper, "Spin Room: Spinning the Third Presidential Debate," CNN, October 18, 2000, and Charles Lane, "A 'Flip-Flop' on Patients' Right to Sue?" *Washington Post*, April 5, 2004, p. A15.

32. Sam Donaldson and Cokie Roberts, *This Week*, ABC News, October 22, 2000.

33. "While Washington politicians deadlocked, I delivered a patients' bill of rights," said Bush in a campaign ad run in South Carolina against John McCain. Stuart Stevens, *The Big Enchilada: Campaign Adventures with the Cockeyed Optimists from Texas Who Won the Biggest Prize in Politics* (New York: Free Press, 2001), p. 144.

34. CNN's Candy Crowley reported that then Governor Bush said, "In Texas, we don't do nuance." CNN, April 25, 2001, http://archives.cnn.com/TRAN SCRIPTS/0104/25/lt.01.html, accessed October 14, 2006.

35. Quoted in David Frum, *The Right Man: An Inside Account of the Bush White House* (New York: Random House, 2003), p. 203.

36. Scott Shane, "Since 2001, Sharp Increase in the Number of Documents Classified by the Government," *New York Times*, July 3, 2005, p. A14.

37. Mary Jacoby, "Swaggering toward Election Day," Salon.com, September 3, 2004, www.salon.com/news/feature/2004/09/03/bush, accessed April 6, 2007.

38. Bob Woodward, *Bush at War* (New York: Simon & Schuster, 2002), pp. 145–146.

39. Dan Froomkin, "Bush Backs Rove, Palmeiro, 'Intelligent Design,'" August 2, 2005, www.washingtonpost.com/wp-dyn/content/blog/2005/08/02/BL200508 0201070.html, accessed April 7, 2007.

40. On Bush's nicknames for Rove, see Julian Borger, "Boy Genius or Turd Blossom?" *The Guardian*, October 2, 2003. On Bush's nickname for Lay, see CBS News, "Bush Edges Away from 'Kenny Boy,'" July 8, 2004, www.cbsnews.com/stories/2004/07/08/politics/main628320.shtml, accessed April 6, 2007.

41. Frum, *The Right Man*, p. 15.

42. Woodward, *Bush at War*, p. 144.

43. Frum, *The Right Man*, p. 272

44. Wead interview, www.pbs.org/wgbh/pages/frontline/shows/jesus/interviews/wead.html, accessed April 7, 2007. Wead went on to say that Bush's religion doesn't heighten his dogmatic tendencies, but on the contrary, "His faith has been a real tempering effect on who he is and his personality. 'You may not know everything, big shot. Slow down. Listen to the other side.' People ought to be thankful that he has a faith; [it's] not something to fear."

45. Moore and Slater, *Bush's Brain*, p. 317, quoting Rove in an interview with the authors.

46. Gelb quoted in Sidney Blumenthal, "Empty Words," Salon.com, June 29, 2005, www.salon.com/opinion/blumenthal/2005/06/30/bush_speech/index.html, accessed April 7, 2007. Emphasis added.

5. Men Riding out of the West on White Horses

1. Interview with Mark Leaverton, www.pbs.org/wgbh/pages/frontline/shows/jesus/president/cbs.html, accessed April 7, 2007.

2. Stuart Stevens, *The Big Enchilada: Campaign Adventures with the Cockeyed Optimists from Texas Who Won the Biggest Prize in Politics* (New York: Free Press, 2001), p. 236.

3. This is Patricia Nelson Limerick's phrase for the pioneer ideal—an ideal that, as she points out, bears "little resemblance to the events of the Western past." *The Legacy of Conquest: The Unbroken Past of the American West* (New York: Norton, 1987), p. 323.

4. Ibid., p. 78.

5. Barry Goldwater, *The Conscience of a Conservative* (New York: Macfadden, 1960).

6. Interestingly, the fourth conservative politician to play a leading part in the politics of the last half-century, the gentleman from Georgia, Newt Gingrich, is the only one who does not evoke saddles and Stetsons and, not coincidentally, is also the only one who failed to inspire personal affection that extends beyond his ideological base.

7. Debate transcript, October 5, 2000, www.debates.org/pages/trans2000d.html, accessed August 18, 2006.

8. See, in particular, Limerick, *The Legacy of Conquest*.

9. Frederick Jackson Turner, *The Frontier in American History* (New York: Henry Holt, 1920), chap. 1. The 1921 edition is reproduced at http://xroads.virginia.edu/~HYPER/TURNER, accessed April 6, 2007, from which I draw my quotations.

10. Turner, *The Frontier*, chap. 7.

11. A good introduction to some of the more recent contributions to the voluminous Turner literature is Thomas C. McClintock, "The Turner Thesis: After Ninety Years It Still 'Lives On,'" *Journal of the American West* 25 (July 1986): 75–82, http://xroads.virginia.edu/~DRBR/mclintok.html, accessed April 6, 2007.

12. Limerick, *Legacy of Conquest*, pp. 28, 23.

13. Turner, *Frontier*, chap. 7.

14. The term *American dream* did not crop up abundantly until the 1930s, when it was taken up by the popular historian James Truslow Adams. See Jim Cullen, *The American Dream: A Short History of an Idea That Shaped a Nation* (New York: Oxford University Press, 2004), and my own discussion in *The Twilight of Common Dreams: Why America Is Wracked by Culture Wars* (New York: Metropolitan, 1995), pp. 46–47, 57–58.

15. Turner, *Frontier*, chap. 7.

16. Turner, *Frontier*, chap. 1. Emphasis added.

17. Warren Vieth, "Burnishing an Image at the USA Corral," *Los Angeles Times*, August 29, 2005, p. A1.

18. Michael Lind, *Made in Texas: George W. Bush and the Southern Takeover of American Politics* (New York: Basic Books, 2003), p. 24.

19. This lesson has been learned chiefly from Pierre Bourdieu's *Distinction* (Cambridge, MA: Harvard University Press, 1984).

20. On the "good man" in Bush's world, see Bill Minutaglio, *First Son: George W. Bush and the Bush Family Dynasty* (New York: Times Books, 1999), p. 24.

21. Bush interviewed by Brian Williams, August 30, 2006, www.huffingtonpost .com/2006/08/30/video-bush-explains-his-_n_28367.html, accessed October 17, 2006.

22. Walter Prescott Webb, *The Texas Rangers: A Century of Frontier Defense* (Austin: University of Texas Press, 1965 [1935]), p. v, quoted in Limerick, *The Legacy of Conquest*, p. 257.

23. Ron Suskind, *The One Percent Doctrine: Deep Inside America's Pursuit of Its Enemies since 9/11* (New York: Simon & Schuster, 2006), p. 219.

24. Ibid., p. 225.

25. Ibid., p. 309.

26. Ibid., pp. 173–174.

27. The next seven paragraphs borrow from my "Europe? Frankly, America Doesn't Give a Damn . . . ," *Guardian*, February 3, 2003, p. 20.

28. Bart Barnes, "Barry Goldwater, GOP Hero, Dies," *Washington Post*, May 30, 1998, p. A01.

29. William Faulkner, *Requiem for a Nun: A Play from the Novel by William Faulkner* (New York: Random House, 1959), p. 33.

6. Pulpits of Bullies

1. Patrick D. Healy, "Rove Criticizes Liberals on 9/11," *New York Times*, June 23, 2005, p. A13.

2. From my own hypothesis at tpmcafe.com, June 23, 2005.

3. James Moore and Wayne Slater, *Bush's Brain: How Karl Rove Made George W. Bush Presidential* (Hoboken, NJ: John Wiley and Sons, 2003), p. 205.

4. Green went on to say, "Having studied what happens when Karl Rove is cornered, I came away with two overriding impressions. One was a new appreciation for his mastery of campaigning. The other was astonishment at the degree to which, despite all that's been written about him, Rove's fiercest tendencies have been elided in national media coverage." Green, "Karl Rove in a Corner," *Atlantic*, November 2004, www.theatlantic.com/doc/200411/green, accessed April 7, 2007. But it could be at least equally well argued that a good deal of Rove's reputation for mastery was overstated, circular, and self-fulfilling. A reputation for fearlessness and indefatigability might leave opponents cowering.

5. Ron Suskind, "Why Are These Men Laughing?" *Esquire*, January 2003, www.ronsuskind.com/newsite/articles/archives/000032.html, accessed August 19, 2006.

6. Richard A. Viguerie and David Franke, *America's Right Turn: How Conservatives Used New and Alternative Media to Take Power* (Chicago and Los Angeles: Bonus Books, 2004), p. 340.

7. This discussion draws on my "We Disport. We Deride," *American Prospect*, February 2003, pp. 43–44. See also Eric Boehlert, *Lapdogs: How the Press Rolled Over for Bush* (New York: Free Press, 2006); Michael Massing, *Now They Tell Us: The American Press and Iraq* (New York: New York Review Books, 2004); and Eric Alterman, *What Liberal Media?* (New York: Basic Books, 2003).

8. Noam Scheiber, "The Apostle," *New Republic*, December 18, 2006, p. 20.

9. Mariah Blake, "Stations of the Cross," *Columbia Journalism Review*, May–June 2005, www.cjr.org/issues/2005/3/blake-evangelist.asp, accessed April 5, 2007.

10. According to former FCC chairman Reed Hundt (personal communication, November 2002), Murdoch's Australian-owned News Corporation should not have been permitted to buy an American television network in the first place, even though Murdoch himself had become an American citizen in order to circumvent another legal restriction. An FCC investigation conducted at the behest of NBC in the Nineties confirmed as much. But having reached this conclusion, Hundt decided it was too late to revoke Murdoch's privileges.

11. Air America Radio, a weak echo of Fox News, was launched only in 2004 and also picks up about 1.2 percent of market share where it has affiliates. See http://en.wikipedia.org/wiki/Air_America_Radio, accessed April 7, 2007.

12. Dani Dodge, "Busby on Defense, Says She Misspoke," *San Diego Union-Tribune*, June 3, 2006, p. NC1.

13. Interview with Francine Busby, August 17, 2006.

14. Philip J. LaVelle and Dani Dodge, "Bilbray Edges Out Busby," *San Diego Union-Tribune*, June 7, 2006, www.signonsandiego.com/news/politics/20060607-0052-7n7duke.html, accessed August 22, 2006.

15. "How the County Voted," *San Diego Union-Tribune*, June 8, 2006, p. A12.

16. See Sinclair Broadcast Group's Web site, www.sbgi.net and the entry on Sinclair on the Daily Kos's dKosopedia, www.dkosopedia.com/wiki/Sinclair_Broad cast_Group, accessed April 7, 2007.

17. Todd Gitlin, "The Pro-War *Post*," *American Prospect*, April 1, 2003, www.pros pect.org/web/printfriendly-view.ww?id=6751, accessed April 19, 2006. Subsequently, the *Post* added a weekly liberal column by Harold Meyerson.

18. Michael Tomasky, "Whispers and Screams: The Partisan Natures of Editorial Pages," Research Paper R-25, Shorenstein Center, Kennedy School of Government,

Harvard University, July 2003, www.ksg.harvard.edu/presspol/Research_Publica
tions/Papers/Research_Papers/R25.pdf, accessed August 20, 2006.

19. See Michael Dolny, "Right, Center Think Tanks Still Most Quoted," Fairness &
Accuracy In Reporting's Web site, May/June 2005, www.fair.org/index.php?
page=2534, accessed April 7, 2007.

20. Paul Waldman, "John Fund Again?" *Washington Monthly*, March 2006, available at www.washingtonmonthly.com/features/2006/0603.waldman.html/,
accessed April 6, 2007.

21. For mountains of chapter and verse, see Boehlert, *Lapdogs*, and Alterman, *What
Liberal Media?* My review of *Lapdogs*, "All the President's Pets," appeared
in *American Prospect*, July 2006, www.prospect.org/web/print-friendly-view
.ww?id=11658, accessed August 19, 2006.

22. See Gene Roberts and Hank Klibanoff, *The Race Beat: The Press, the Civil Rights
Struggle, and the Awakening of a Nation* (New York: Knopf, 2006).

23. Rob Corddry, *The Daily Show*, Comedy Central, August 23, 2004.

24. On Miller, see Michael Massing, "Now They Tell Us," *New York Review of
Books*, February 26, 2004, www.nybooks.com/articles/16922, accessed April 7,
2007. On Miller and Woodward, see my "All the President's Friends," *American
Prospect*, May 2006, www.prospect.org/web/printfriendly-view.ww?id=10745,
accessed August 19, 2006.

25. The point about access was made to me forcefully by the former CBS political
chief Dotty Lynch in conversation, March–April 2006.

26. Thomas B. Edsall, lecture, Graduate School of Journalism, Columbia University,
October 26, 2006.

27. John F. Harris, "Mr. Bush Catches a Washington Break," *Washington Post*,
Outlook Section, May 6, 2001, p. B1.

28. Telephone interview, Max Frankel, May 2004, quoted in my "Media: It Was
a Very Bad Year," *American Prospect*, July 2004, www.prospect.org/web/
printfriendly-view.ww?id=7873, accessed August 19, 2006.

29. Some of this paragraph is taken from my "From the Left," commissioned by
Public Editor Daniel Okrent for "Political Bias at the *Times*? Two Counter-
arguments," *New York Times*, Week in Review, October 17, 2004, p. 2. For an
example of successful dot-connecting, see Anne C. Mulkern, "Watchdogs or
Lap Dogs? When Advocates Become Regulators," *Denver Post*, May 23, 2004,
p. A1.

30. See my "Times Out of Joint," *American Prospect*, www.prospect.org/web/page
.ww?section=root&name=ViewPrint&articleId=12238, accessed April 7,
2007.

31. On social tilt, see Alterman pp. 104–118.

32. Leon V. Sigal, *Reporters and Officials: The Organization and Politics of News-
making* (Lexington, MA: D. C. Heath, 1973). On the particular servility of the press
toward Ronald Reagan, see my book, "Media as Message: Campaign '80," *Socialist
Review*, March/April 1981; and Mark Hertsgaard, *On Bended Knee: The Press and
the Reagan Presidency* (New York: Farrar, Straus and Giroux, 1988).

33. On the media as a legitimating force, see my book *The Whole World Is Watching:
Mass Media in the Making and Unmaking of the New Left* (Berkeley: University
of California Press, 1980), part 3; and Daniel C. Hallin, *The "Uncensored War":
The Media and Vietnam* (New York: Oxford University Press, 1986), pp. 23–25,

50, and *We Keep America on Top of the World: Television Journalism and the Public Sphere* (New York: Routledge, 1994), pp. 54–55.

Part Two. Wilderness: Fits and Starts

The epigraph to this part is drawn from *American Prospect* online, www.prospect. org/web/page.ww?section=root&name=ViewWeb&articleId=11562, accessed May 27, 2006.

7. Parties and Movements: A Brief Excursus on Democratic Dilemmas

1. Mancur Olson, *The Logic of Collective Action: Public Goods and the Theory of Groups* (Cambridge, MA: Harvard University Press, 1965), pp. 163–164.
2. This story has been told many times in some detail in Rick Perlstein, *Before the Storm: Barry Goldwater and the Unmaking of the American Consensus* (New York: Hill & Wang, 2001), and in John Micklethwait and Adrian Wooldridge, *The Right Nation: Conservative Power in America* (New York: Penguin, 2004), and skeletally in my *Letters to a Young Activist* (New York: Basic, 2003), pp. 113–114.
3. Calculated from Campaign Finance Institute, "House and Senate Winners' Receipts, 1998–2006," November 10, 2006, Table 1, www.cfinst.org/congress, and "Presidential Candidates' Total Receipts, Individual Contributions, and Matching Funds, 1976–2004," www.cfinst.org/president/CandHist.aspx/, accessed, May 15, 2007.
4. Richard A. Viguerie and David Franke, *America's Right Turn: How Conservatives Used New and Alternative Media to Take Power* (Chicago: Bonus Books, 2004) p. 349.
5. Richard A. Viguerie, "Bush's Base Betrayal," *Washington Post*, Outlook Section, May 21, 2006, p. B1.
6. Dick Armey, "Where We Went Wrong," *Washington Post*, Outlook Section, October 20, 2006, p. B1.
7. Ken Connor, "Christian Conservatives Deserve Blame for Corrupt Republicans," *Human Events* online, November 13, 2006, www.humanevents.com/article.php?print=yes&id=18019, accessed November 17, 2006.
8. Quoted in Richard John Neuhaus, "The Public Square," *First Things*, June–July 1999, www.firstthings.com/ftissues/ft9906/public.html#text3, accessed November 17, 2006.
9. Ronald Reagan, *A Time for Choosing: The Speeches of Ronald Reagan, 1961–1982* (Chicago: Regnery Gateway, 1983), pp. 184–185, as quoted in my book *The Twilight of Common Dreams: Why America Is Wracked by Culture Wars* (New York: Metropolitan, 1995), p. 76.
10. Lisa McGirr, *Suburban Warriors* (Princeton, NJ: Princeton University Press, 2002), p. 113.
11. Thomas B. Edsall, *Building Red America: The New Conservative Coalition and the Drive for Permanent Power* (New York: Basic, 2006), pp. 15–16.
12. Sidney M. Milkis and Jesse H. Rhodes, "George W. Bush, the Republican Party, and the 'New' American Party System," unpublished paper, June 2006.

13. Joel H. Silbey, *The American Political Nation, 1838–1893* (Stanford, CA: Stanford University Press, 1991), p. 243.

14. David R. Mayhew, *Placing Parties in American Politics: Organization, Electoral Settings, and Government Activity in the Twentieth Century* (Princeton, NJ: Princeton University Press, 1986), p. 325.

15. Dominic Sandbrook, *Eugene McCarthy and the Rise and Fall of Postwar American Liberalism* (New York: Anchor, 2004), p. 164.

16. Sidney M. Milkis, "The Modern Presidency, Social Movements, and the Administrative State: Lyndon Johnson and the Civil Rights Movement," paper for Conference on Race and American Political Development, May 2006, pp. 56, 36.

17. Mayhew, *Placing Parties in American Politics*, p. 330.

18. Milkis and Rhodes, "George W. Bush, the Republican Party, and the 'New' American Party System," citing Larry J. Sabato, *The Party's Just Begun: Shaping Political Parties for America's Future* (Glenview, IL: Scott Foresman, 1988), on Reagan.

19. Ari Berman, "Where's the Plan, Democrats?" *Nation*, July 17, 2006: 18–20. In 2006, Dean's fifty-state strategy put him at odds with DCCC head Rahm Emanuel, who wanted party funds channeled toward the most promising congressional candidates. For a sample of the debate over Emanuel's choices, see Rick Perlstein, "Plan of Attack," *New Republic* Online, November 8, 2006, www.tnr.com/doc.mhtml?i=w061106&s=perlstein110806, accessed November 10, 2006; and Ryan Lizza, "Bloggers v. Rahm," *New Republic* Online, November 8, 2006, www.tnr.com/blog/theplank?pid=56035, accessed November 19, 2006.

20. Farewell speech at West Point, May 12, 1962, www.nationalcenter.org/MacArthurFarewell.html, accessed June 14, 2006.

8. Movements versus Party: 1964–1980

1. Ruy A. Teixeira and Joel Rogers, *America's Forgotten Majority: Why the White Working Class Still Matters* (New York: Basic Books, 2000), p. 32.

2. David Maraniss, *First in His Class: The Biography of Bill Clinton* (New York: Simon & Schuster, 1995), p. 285.

3. Ibid., p. 240.

4. Ibid., pp. 281–282. Maraniss wrote:

> The key to Clinton's success, according to [Taylor] Branch [with whom Clinton shared Texas coordinator duties during the 1972 McGovern campaign], was his ability to study the personalities of the people he was dealing with and determine what it took to get along with them, where their weak spots were, who was lazy, who was committed. He was Johnsonian in that sense—knowing how to read personalities.

(p. 282). The question may well be asked how Clinton's style of personal knowledge—and Johnson's, for that matter—differed from George W. Bush's. Clinton and Johnson were not only far more articulate about what they understood about other players, but demonstrably far more successful in inventorying the strengths and weaknesses around them in order to accomplish their own goals. It is worth noting, however, that Clinton and Johnson do in a certain way qualify as frontier personalities of the sort described by Frederick Jackson Turner.

5. Michael Waldman, *POTUS Speaks: Finding the Words That Defined the Clinton Presidency* (New York: Simon & Schuster, 2000), p. 30.

6. Telephone interview with Michael Waldman, July 24, 2006. Waldman went on to say that "it could be awful to live through it, because you didn't know where he really stood."

7. John Keats, letter to George and Thomas Keats, December 21, 1817. Quoted in Andres Rodriguez, *Book of the Heart: The Poetics, Letters, and Life of John Keats* (Great Barrington, MA: Lindisfarne Books, 1993), p. 40.

8. Another writer to conjure a similar recommendation was not thinking of politics either. F. Scott Fitzgerald wrote, "The test of a first-rate intelligence is the ability to hold two opposed ideas in the mind at the same time, and still retain the ability to function." Fitzgerald, *The Crack Up* (New York: New Directions, 1956), p. 69.

9. Waldman, *POTUS Speaks*, p. 31.

10. *Bureau of Labor Statistics' Directory of Labor Unions*; *Directory of National Unions and Employee Associations*; and *BNA's Directory of U.S. Labor Organizations*, as well as assorted Web sources.

11. Kevin Boyle, *The UAW and the Heyday of American Liberalism, 1945–1968* (Ithaca, NY: Cornell University Press, 1995), p. 158.

12. Boyle, *The UAW*, pp. 158–160. In his biography of Walter Reuther, Nelson Lichtenstein wrote, "[F]or this brief moment in the history of American liberalism [1964] the UAW and SDS shared an equally radical agenda. . . . Reuther saw these young people as a bridge through which the labor movement could rewin the loyalty and appreciation of young intellectuals and then energize its white-collar organizing campaigns." *Walter Reuther: The Most Dangerous Man in Detroit* (Urbana: University of Illinois Press, 1995), pp. 390–391. The liberal journalist Harold Meyerson, who follows labor closely, noted that in its sympathy for the civil rights, student, and other sixties movements, "the UAW was an exception: most unions were uncomfortable with the struggles and the styles of the movements of the 1960s." Harold Meyerson, "'50s Hip," *American Prospect*, November 30, 2005, www.prospect.org/web/page.ww?section=root &name=ViewWeb&articleId=10669, accessed July 8, 2006.

13. See my discussion of movement radicalism versus managerial liberalism in *The Sixties: Years of Hope, Days of Rage* (New York: Bantam, 1987), pp. 133–135.

14. Ibid., p. 162.

15. Interview with Miles Rapoport, November 14, 2005.

16. See my book with Nanci Hollander, *Uptown: Poor Whites in Chicago* (New York: Harper and Row, 1970).

17. See the helpful discussion by Craig Anderson, "The GOP Dynasty," *East Bay Express*, Express Books Section, March 1992, pp. 8–9.

18. In two auto worker strongholds, Macomb County (Detroit's blue-collar suburbs) and Genessee County (Flint), the Democratic vote for Humphrey averaged about 20 points lower than the 1964 Johnson vote. Boyle, *The UAW*, pp. 255–256. By 1980, white working-class flight from the Democrats had reached such

proportions that Macomb voted 2–1 for Reagan over Carter, exactly reversing the 1960 vote for Kennedy over Nixon. Thomas Byrne Edsall with Mary D. Edsall, *Chain Reaction: The Impact of Race, Rights, and Taxes on American Politics* (New York: Norton, 1991), pp. 181–182.

19. Edsall and Edsall, *Chain Reaction*, pp. 79–80.

20. *Bureau of Labor Statistics' Directory of Labor Unions*; *Directory of National Unions and Employee Associations*; and *BNA's Directory of U.S. Labor Organizations*, as well as assorted Web sources.

21. Boyle, *The UAW*, p. 258.

22. See Tom Engelhardt, *The End of Victory Culture: Cold War America and the Disillusioning of a Generation* (New York: Basic Books, 1995).

23. James Fallows, "The Passionless Presidency," *Atlantic*, May 1979, www.theatlantic.com/unbound/flashbks/pres/fallpass.htm, accessed May 22, 2006.

24. Waldman, *POTUS Speaks*, p. 23.

25. Calculated from the results of polls conducted by NORC (March 1978), Gallup/*Newsweek* (February 1976), the *Washington Post* (September 1978, July 1979), and CBS News/*New York Times* (February 1976, June 1976, August 1976, May 1977, October 1977, October 1979, March 1980, November 1980), all available courtesy of the Roper Public Opinion Research Center.

26. Joseph Nye et al., *Why People Don't Trust Government* (Cambridge, MA: Harvard University Press, 2002), p. 1.

27. Miles S. Rapoport, "Winning with Tax Reform: The Connecticut Story," *American Prospect*, January 1, 1993, www.prospect.org/web/print-friendly-view.ww?id=5182, accessed July 5, 2006.

28. Interview with Miles Rapoport, November 14, 2005.

29. Calculated from the results of polls conducted by the *New York Times* (June 1983, April 1990), CBS News/*New York Times* (November 1984, November 1985, January 1986, February 1987), ABC News/*Washington Post* (March 1985, September 1986, January 1988), *Time*/CNN/Yankelovich Clancy Shulman (October 1989), and the *Los Angeles Times* (January 1991, March 1992), all available courtesy of the Roper Public Opinion Center.

30. Survey conducted for *Time* by Yankelovich Clancy Shulman. Courtesy of the Roper Public Opinion Center.

9. An Unlikely Steward: Bill Clinton and Liberalism in the Nineties

1. Thomas B. Edsall, *Building Red America: The New Conservative Coalition and the Drive for Permanent Power* (New York: Basic, 2006), pp. 16–18.

2. David Maraniss, *First in His Class: The Biography of Bill Clinton* (New York: Simon & Schuster, 1995), p. 361.

3. Ibid., p. 360.

4. Ibid., p. 400, and Hillary Rodham Clinton, *Living History* (New York: Simon & Schuster, 2003), p. 93.

5. Bill Clinton, *My Life* (New York: Knopf, 2004), p. 287.

6. Kenneth S. Baer, *Reinventing Democrats: The Politics of Liberalism from Reagan to Clinton* (Lawrence: University Press of Kansas, 2000), pp. 192, 163–165.

7. Ibid., p. 164.

8. Ibid., p. 191.
9. Ibid., p. 195.
10. Ibid., pp. 195–196, 198.
11. Quoted in Sidney Blumenthal, "The Anointed," *New Republic*, February 3, 1992, p. 27.
12. Baer, *Reinventing Democrats*, p. 198.
13. Blumenthal, "Anointed."
14. Michael Waldman, *POTUS Speaks: Finding the Words That Defined the Clinton Presidency* (New York: Simon & Schuster, 2000), p. 269.
15. The case for Clinton's progressive achievements is made by his former special assistant, Sidney Blumenthal, in *The Clinton Wars* (New York: Farrar, Straus & Giroux, 2003), pp. 771–772. See also Maurice Isserman and Michael Kazin, "As Bill Goes, So Do We," *Nation*, May 30, 1994, p. 744.
16. Dan Levy, "Castro Crowd Toasts Clinton: Election Hailed at Giant Street Party as Victory for Gays and Lesbians," *San Francisco Chronicle*, November 4, 1992, p. A19.
17. Joe Conason and Gene Lyons, *The Hunting of the President: The Ten-Year Campaign to Destroy Bill and Hillary Clinton* (New York: St. Martin's Griffin, 2001) , pp. 68–72, and Blumenthal, *Clinton Wars*, pp. 72–76.
18. Lars-Erik Nelson, "Despite Mauling, Clinton Still on Feet," *New York Daily News*, February 10, 1992, quoted in Blumenthal, *Clinton Wars*, p. 39.
19. Blumenthal, *Clinton Wars*, p. 66.
20. George Stephanopoulos, *All Too Human: A Political Education* (Boston: Little Brown, 2000 [1999]), p. 140. This note was recorded by Stephanopoulos on April 14, 1993.
21. Telephone interview with Michael Waldman, July 24, 2006.
22. On the base-building motivation of faith-based programs, see Ron Suskind, "Why Are These Men Laughing?" *Esquire*, January 1, 2003, www.ronsuskind .com/articles/000032.html, accessed April 7, 2007, and Tom Hamburger and Peter Wallsten, *One Party Country: The Republican Plan for Dominance in the 21st Century* (Hoboken, NJ: John Wiley & Sons, 2006), p. 124.
23. See Bennett Roth, "GOP Seeks Way to Heal the Split over Health Care," *Houston Chronicle*, January 2, 1994, p. A1.
24. Richard Lowry, "The Lost Crusade?" *National Review*, September 12, 1994, p. 22.
25. Quoted in Hamburger and Wallsten, *One Party Country*, p. 174.
26. William Greider, "The Education of David Stockman," *Atlantic*, December 1981, www.theatlantic.com/doc/198112/david-stockman, accessed April 7, 2007.
27. Quoted in John Cassidy, "The Ringleader: How Grover Norquist Keeps the Conservative Movement Together," *New Yorker*, August 1, 2005, p. 43, and Hamburger and Wallsten, *One Party Country*, p. 24.
28. Bob Woodward, *The Agenda: Inside the Clinton White House* (New York: Simon & Schuster, 1994), pp. 161–162.
29. John F. Harris, "Mr. Bush Catches a Washington Break," *Washington Post*, Outlook Section, May 6, 2001, p. B1.
30. Richard Rothstein, "The Left's Obsessive Opposition," *American Prospect*, Fall 1993, available at www.prospect.org/web/page.ww?section=root&

name=ViewPrint&articleId=5113, accessed July 26, 2006. Rothstein trenchantly argued as follows:

> When economists at Clinton's economic summit last December proposed a $60 billion stimulus package, liberals cheered. When Clinton suggested that $30 billion might be viable, they began to suspect the clarity of the president-elect's vision. When the president concluded that he couldn't get more than $16 billion through Congress, liberals groaned at the tokenness of it all. Then Republican leader Bob Dole organized a filibuster to defeat even that small program. Liberal critics complained implausibly that the program failed because it wasn't big enough to inspire support.

31. Isserman and Kazin, "As Bill Goes, So Do We," p. 744.
32. See the indignant letters published June 13 and July 25, 1994.
33. Telephone interview with Michael Waldman, July 24, 2006.
34. Waldman, *POTUS Speaks*, pp. 75–76.
35. Telephone interview with Michael Waldman, July 24, 2006.
36. See again Thomas Byrne Edsall with Mary D. Edsall, *Chain Reaction: The Impact of Race, Rights, and Taxes on American Politics* (New York: Norton, 1992). The Republicans' continuing reliance on Wallace's 1968 themes is noted by Thomas Byrne Edsall's important successor study, *Building Red America*, p. 9.
37. Waldman, *POTUS Speaks*, p. 128.
38. Ibid., pp. 75–76.
39. See Todd S. Purdum, "Facets of Clinton," *New York Times Magazine*, May 19, 1996, p. 36.
40. Waldman, *POTUS Speaks*, p. 147.
41. Ibid., pp. 188–189.
42. *Los Angeles Times* (April 1994), Henry J. Kaiser Family Foundation/Harvard/ *Washington Post* (November 1995), CBS News/*New York Times* (October 1996), ABC News/*Washington Post* (January 1998), CBS News (January 1999), Gallup/CNN/*USA Today* (July 2000).
43. John Hawkins, "Bill Clinton Is Every Bit as Advanced a Witch as Was Adolf Hitler, *Right Wing News*, www.rightwingnews.com/crackpots/clintonwitch. php, accessed June 14, 2006.
44. Quoted in Stanley Renshon, *High Hopes: The Clinton Presidency and the Politics of Ambition* (London: Routledge, 1998), p. 277.
45. Toni Morrison, "Talk of the Town," *New Yorker*, October 5, 1998, pp. 31–32.
46. Lorelei Kelly, "Progressive Organizing Bears Fruit," *Democracy Arsenal*, www.democracyarsenal.org/2006/05/progressive_org.html, accessed May 25, 2006.
47. See Waldman, *POTUS Speaks*, p. 22. Clinton did not use the phrase again before a large audience for two and a half years, in his 1995 State of the Union message (p. 78).
48. In three polls taken just before Clinton left office, the questions about approval were asked slightly differently, but the numbers were remarkably similar: 68 percent approval in two instances, 66 percent in the third. Princeton Survey Research Associates/*Newsweek* poll of January 18–19, 2001, CBS News poll of January 15–17, 2001, NBC News/*Wall Street Journal* poll of January 13–15,

2001, data provided by the Roper Center for Public Opinion Research, University of Connecticut, http://roperweb.ropercenter.uconn.edu/cgi-bin/hsrun.exe/Roper web/iPOLL/StateId/R30crAg6zfg1to7XtgjEHHToZGBOE-U3Lq/HAHT page/SelectedQs_Link, accessed June 2, 2006.

49. Telephone interview with Michael Waldman, July 24, 2006.

10. The Party as Movement, 2004 and After: The Deaniacs, the Purple States, and the Netroots

1. See "Scranton's Lackawanna Station," http://lackawanna.railfan.net/scrantn3. htm, accessed April 7, 2007.

2. See http://en.wikipedia.org/wiki/Scranton%2C_Pennsylvania, accessed April 7, 2007.

3. Telephone interview with Steve and Jackie Grumbacher, June 25, 2005.

4. See Jake Tapper, *Down and Dirty: The Plot to Steal the Presidency* (Boston: Little, Brown, 2001), chap. 3, and my review in the *Chicago Tribune*, Books Section, April 15, 2001, p. 1.

5. "Just Another Netroots Monday," Scott Winship's review of the Pew Research Center for the People and the Press survey, "The Dean Activists: Their Profile and Prospects," http://people-press.org/reports/display.php3?ReportID=240, accessed July 20, 2006 at www.thedemocraticstrategist.org/strategist/2006/07/ just_another_netroots_monday.php. Winship points out that the response rate to Pew's survey of Dean supporters was extremely low—13 percent. It seems to have included the older, more educated, and more engaged.

6. Scott Winship, "Netroots . . . Revealed!" www.thedemocraticstrategist.org/ strategist/2006/07/netrootsrevealed.php, accessed July 20, 2006.

7. Winship, "Netroots . . . Revealed!"

8. Credit to Diane Sawyer, who on ABC News's *World News Tonight* demonstrated that Dean's intense appeal to his troops to go on fighting only sounded like a wild scream because he thought he needed to shout over the crowd noise, not realizing that his microphone was perfectly capable of distinguishing his voice from the buzz surrounding it.

9. See "The Dean Activists: Their Profile and Prospects," a survey conducted by the Pew Research Center for the People and the Press, April 6, 2005, http://people-press.org/reports/display.php3?PageID=932, accessed April 9, 2007. A full 90 percent of another Pew netroots sample (a small one, admittedly) also called themselves liberal. "Data," www.pewinternet.org/data.asp, accessed April 10, 2007, as reported in Scott Winship, "How Influential Is the Netroots? or, You Want Links?" www.thedemocraticstrategist.org/strategist/2006/07/how_ influential_is_the_netroot.php, accessed April 10, 2007.

10. See Scott Winship's computation from data gathered by the Pew Internet & American Life Project, " How Influential Is the Netroots?" Winship defined "the Democratic netroots" as those adults who "regularly" get "news or information" from "online columns or blogs such as Talking Points Memo, the Daily Kos, or Instapundit" and who are either self-identified Democrats or liberals. About two-thirds of these "either attended a campaign rally, donated money to a campaign, knocked on doors, or worked a phone bank" in 2004, for a total of 1.6 million adults (0.7 percent of the adult population of the United States). Either the

2.24 million or the 1.6 million activists among them contrasts favorably with the following numbers of interest group members:

- NOW: 500,000 contributing members
- NARAL Pro-Choice America: 900,000 members of their Choice Action Network
- Sierra Club: 750,000 members
- National Resources Defense Council: more than 1 million members
- ACLU: more than 500,000 members
- Human Rights Campaign: nearly 600,000 members.

But the larger number for the Democratic netroots is only about one-seventh of the number of union members, a total of 15.7 million.

In a follow-up post (www.thedemocraticstrategist.org/strategist/2006/07/netroots_continued.php, accessed July 12, 2006), Winship noted that the sampling error in this survey is large, that most surveys of net visitors are poor, and that a survey of Daily Kos readers in April 2005 recorded only 212,000 unique visitors during the month.

11. Jerome Armstrong and Markos Moulitsas Zúniga, *Crashing the Gates: Netroots, Grassroots, and the Rise of People-Powered Politics* (White River Junction, VT: Chelsea Green, 2006), p. 169.
12. Interview with Eli Pariser, April 13, 2005.
13. George Packer, "Smart-Mobbing the War," *New York Times Magazine*, March 9, 2003, p. 46.
14. See Mark Schmitt, "Who's Responsible for the Lieberman Meltdown?" *TPM Café*, www.tpmcafe.com/blog/coffeehouse/2006/jul/13/whos_responsible_for_the_lieberman_meltdown, accessed April 7, 2007.
15. Henry Farrell, "Bloggers and Parties," *Boston Review*, September–October 2006, bostonreview.net/BR31.5/farrel.html, accessed October 6, 2006.
16. Matt Stoller, "The New New Left," posted August 14, 2006, www.mydd.com/story/2006/8/14/42110/6232, accessed April 7, 2007.
17. Farrell, "Bloggers and Parties."
18. Chait, "Purely Foolish Democrats," *Los Angeles Times*, available at www.latimes.com/news/opinion/la-oe-chait9jul09,0,9464,print.column?coll=la-utilop-ed, accessed July 12, 2006. Chait elaborated (including the second quotation) "More—Far More!—on Lieberman/Lamont" *New Republic* online, www.tnr.com/blog/theplank?pid=24141, accessed July 12, 2006.
19. Digby's Hullaballoo, "Norquistian Bogeyman," http://digbysblog.blogspot.com, accessed July 12, 2006.
20. See Armstrong and Moulitsas, *Crashing the Gates*, pp. 169, 173. Actually, the dig at the "activism establishment" is a new element.
21. Quoted in Armstrong and Moulitsas, *Crashing the Gates*, p. 148.
22. On the Hackett campaign, see Armstrong and Moulitsas, *Crashing the Gates*, pp. 161–62.
23. See Miles S. Rapoport, "Winning with Tax Reform: The Connecticut Story," *American Prospect*, January 1, 1993, www.prospect.org/web/printfriendly-view.ww?id=5182, accessed July 5, 2006.

24. Commenters pbg, olvlzl, fauxreal, at http://digbysblog.blogspot.com/2006_07_01_archive.html; see comment section pursuant to the post of July 11, 2006, titled "Norquistian Boogeyman," about halfway down the page.

25. Compare Ryan Lizza, "Wag the Blog," *New Republic*, June 26, 2006, available at www.tnr.com/doc.mhtml?i=20060626&s=lizza062606, accessed April 9, 2007.

26. See Markos Moulitsas Zúniga, "AFSCME's Bottom-Up Revolution," *Daily Kos*, August 4, 2006, www.dailykos.com/storyonly/2006/8/4/133743/7622, accessed April 9, 2007.

27. See Armstrong and Moulitsas, *Crashing the Gates*, chap. 1.

28. Ibid., pp. 146, 174.

29. The argument about a division of labor is made by Kaja Tretjak, "Why U.S. Liberalism Must Change or Die," *Critical Sense*, Spring 2005, pp. 155–168. It is to the advantage of movement activists to emphasize the movement's importance as it is to the advantage of party activists to emphasize the party's. Consider this no-doubt self-serving statement from the longtime movement's conservative figure Richard A. Viguerie and his collaborator David Franke (*America's Right Turn: How Conservatives Used New and Alternative Media to Take Power* [Chicago and Los Angeles: Bonus Books, 2004], p. 346), writing about the period of rapid conservative growth:

> [T]he New Right leaders thought of *themselves*—not the Republican Party—as the alternative to the Left and the Democrats. And thanks to the independence provided by direct mail fundraising, none of the New Right's organizations depended upon the Republic Party for their existence. The great majority of these leaders did not hold public office, and had never held public office. Conservatives did not look to elected officials for their leadership. The politicians were necessary to organize votes for or against something, of course, but generally they did not provide the leadership on key issues. That came from the New Right leaders, utilizing alternative media.

Viguerie and Franke are reluctant to acknowledge that their movement moved to a new level of significance when it swept into the Republican Party and made its political home there.

30. See Michael Tomasky, "Whispers and Screams: The Partisan Nature of Editorial Pages," Joan Shorenstein Center on the Press, Politics and Public Policy's Web site, www.ksg.harvard.edu/presspol/research_publications/papers/research_papers/R25.pdf, accessed April 7, 2007. See also David Brock, *The Republican Noise Machine: Right-Wing Media and How It Corrupts Democracy* (New York: Crown, 2004).

31. Interview with Miles Rapoport, November 14, 2005.

32. William A. Galston and Elaine C. Kamarck, "The Politics of Polarization," the Third Way Middle Class Project, October 2005, p. 7; and John Halpin and Ruy Teixeira, "The Politics of Definition: The Real Third Way," *American Prospect Online*, www.prospect.org/web/page.ww?section=root&name=ViewWeb&articleId=11435, accessed April 7, 2007. According to Galston and Kamarck, Kerry, the first major party Catholic candidate for president since 1960, lost Catholics by 5 points.

33. Telephone interview with Steve and Jackie Grumbacher, June 25, 2005.

34. According to "11/2004 Pennsylvania Voter Registration Analysis—Advantage Bush," freerepublic.com, www.freerepublic.com/focus/f-news/1259047/posts, accessed on July 2, 2005.

35. For 2004, see "Pennsylvania's 2004 Presidential Vote and 2002 Gubernatorial Vote by County," http://politicspa.com/FEATURES/votehistory.htm, accessed July 2, 2005. For 2000, see www.seventy.org/67seventy/LebanonCounty.html, accessed July 2, 2005.

36. Halpin and Teixeira, "The Politics of Definition." The 52 percent figure comes from 2004 Current Population Survey Voter Supplement data cited there.

37. Fred Barnes, *Rebel-in-Chief: Inside the Bold and Controversial Presidency of George W. Bush* (New York: Crown Forum, 2006), p. 196.

38. Ibid., pp. 181–184.

39. Halpin and Teixeira, "The Politics of Definition."

40. Steve Rosenthal, "Okay, We Lost Ohio. The Question Is, Why?" *Washington Post*, Outlook Section, December 5, 2004, p. B3.

41. For more on Blackwell's political maneuvers in 2004, see Andrew Gumbel, *Steal This Vote: Dirty Elections and the Rotten History of Democracy in America* (New York: Nation Books, 2005), pp. 281–282.

42. See John Conyers, *What Went Wrong in Ohio: The Conyers Report on the 2004 Presidential Election* (Chicago: Academy, 2005); Mark Crispin Miller, "None Dare Call It Stolen," *Harper's*, August 2005, http://harpers.org/archive/2005/08/0080696, accessed April 8, 2007; and Robert F. Kennedy Jr., "Was the 2004 Election Stolen?" *Rolling Stone*, June 1, 2006, www.rollingstone.com/news/story/10432334/was_the_2004_election_stolen/1, accessed April 8, 2007.

43. Rosenthal, "Okay, We Lost Ohio."

44. Spiro Agnew, address at Pennsylvania Republican Dinner, Harrisburg, October 30, 1969, http://wps.prenhall.com/wps/media/objects/108/111235/ch29_a4_d2.pdf, accessed April 6, 2007.

45. Gary C. Jacobson, *A Divider, Not a Uniter: George W. Bush and the American People* (New York: Pearson Longman, 2007).

46. Thomas B. Edsall, *Building Red America: The New Conservative Coalition and the Drive for Permanent Power* (New York: Basic, 2006), p. 70.

47. Ibid., p. 71.

48. On the missing 4 million, see interview with Christine Todd Whitman, *Frontline*, www.pbs.org/wgbh/pages/frontline/shows/architect/interviews/whitman.html, accessed April 7, 2007.

49. Tom Hamburger and Peter Wallsten, *One Party Country: The Republican Plan for Dominance in the 21st Century* (Hoboken, NJ: John Wiley & Sons, 2006), pp. 138, 139. For details of the Republican tactics, see pp. 141–147.

50. Thomas B. Edsall and James V. Grimaldi, "On Nov. 2, GOP Got More Bang for Its Billion and James V. Grimald; Analysis Shows," *Washington Post*, December 30, 2004, p. A1.

51. Hamburger and Wallsten, *One Party Country*, p. 140. On Republican tactics for tapping the anger of their most devoted followers, see Edsall, *Building Red America*, chap. 2.

52. Edsall, *Building Red America*, p. 77.

53. Edsall and Grimaldi, "GOP Got More Bang."

54. Hamburger and Wallsten, *One Party Country*, p. 151.

55. Edsall and Grimaldi, "GOP Got More Bang."

56. Hamburger and Wallsten, *One Party Country*, p. 152.

57. Philip A. Klinkner, "Mr. Bush's War: Foreign Policy in the 2004 Election," *Presidential Studies Quarterly* 36, no. 2 (June 2006): 283.

58. Klinkner, "Mr. Bush's War," p. 282, citing Alan Abramowitz, "Did Gay Marriage Referenda Help Bush Get Reelected?" www.emergingdemocraticma jorityweblog.com/donkeyrising/archives/000934.php, accessed April 6, 2007. "Similarly," Klinkner added, "Daniel Smith shows that the gay marriage referendum did not help Bush in the pivotal state of Ohio." Daniel A. Smith, "Was Rove Right? The Partisan Wedge and Turnout Effects of Issue 1, Ohio's 2004 Ballot Initiative to Ban Gay Marriage," paper presented at the University of California Center for the Study of Democracy/USC-Caltech Center for the Study of Law and Politics/Initiative and Referendum Institute Conference, January 14 to 15, 2005, in Newport Beach, California, http://lawweb.usc.edu/cslp/conferences/ direct_democracy_05/documents/smith.pdf, accessed April 6, 2007.

59. Klinkner, "Mr. Bush's War," pp. 284, 285.

60. Ibid., p. 286.

61. The software came from Sage, a Massachusetts company, where Dave White, the 2004 Scranton field coordinator, later went to work.

62. Telephone interview with Howard Thomas, November 27, 2006.

63. *Pittsburgh Tribune-Review*, November 28, 2006, http://hosted.ap.org/dynamic/ files/elections/2006/general/by_county/us_sen/PA.html?SITE=PAGREELN& SECTION=POLITICS, accessed November 30, 2006.

64. Robert W. Snyder, "Good Man, Bad War," *Newark Star-Ledger*, May 30, 2005, p. 15.

65. See Patrick Murphy, "Real Leaders Must Have a Plan for Iraq," on Murphy's Web site, www.murphy06.net/planforiraq.html, accessed November 30, 2006.

66. Christine Schiavo, "Murphy Proud of His Pounding of Pavement," *Philadelphia Inquirer*, November 9, 2006, www.philly.com/mld/philly/news/15965214.htm, accessed November 30, 2006.

67. Interview with Robert W. Snyder, November 15, 2006.

68. MoveOn.org, "Election 2006: People Powered Politics," November 2006, http://pol.moveon.org/2006report, accessed November 20, 2006.

69. John Latimer, e-mail to author, July 11, 2006.

70. Steve Grumbacher, e-mail to author July 10, 2006; telephone interview with Steve and Jackie Grumbacher, July 15, 2006.

71. John Latimer, e-mail to author, July 11, 2006.

72. *Pittsburgh Tribune-Review*, November 28, 2006, http://hosted.ap.org/dynamic/ files/elections/2006/general/by_county/us_sen/PA.html?SITE=PAGREELN& SECTION=POLITICS, accessed November 30, 2006.

73. An uncommonly interesting, though not altogether successful, attempt to account for political activism as a function of the declining pleasures of consumer goods is Albert O. Hirschman's *Shifting Involvements: Private Interest and Public Action* (Princeton, NJ: Princeton University Press, 1982).

74. Sidney Blumenthal, "Generation Dem," Salon.com, November 30, 2006, www.salon.com/opinion/blumenthal/2006/11/30/006_election_trends/print .html, accessed November 30, 2006, citing Charlie Cook in the *National Journal*.

75. Jill Lawrence, "Public Expects the Dems to Deliver," *USA Today*, November 14, 2006, p. 1A, available at www.usatoday.com/printedition/news/20061114/1a_lede14_dom.art.htm, accessed November 14, 2006.

76. Blumenthal, "Generation Dem."

77. "Trends in Political Values and Core Attitudes: 1987–2007," Pew Research Center for the People and the Press, http://people-press.org/reports/display.php3?ReportID-312, accessed April 2, 2007.

11. Frames, Demons, and No-Longer-Silent Majorities

1. The point is underscored in a book by a more subtle linguist, Geoffrey Nunberg, *Talking Right; How Conservatives Turned Liberalism into a Tax-Raising, Latte-Drinking, Sushi-Eating, Volvo-Driving, New York Times–Reading, Body-Piercing, Hollywood-Loving, Left-Wing Freak Show* (New York: Public Affairs, 2006), especially p. 8. Nunberg's trenchant critique of Lakoff's theory that fundamental differences about the family underlie political differences is at pp. 98–104.

2. Geoffrey Nunberg makes a similar argument about Lakoff's reductiveness and determinism in "Frame Game," Open University/*New Republic* online, November 4, 2006, www.tnr.com/blog/openuniversity?pid=54417, accessed December 9, 2006.

3. I am, I believe, the first American professor to use the term *frame* in talking about what media do. I do not mean to boast, but this is a fact. I analyzed media frames in detail in my book *The Whole World Is Watching: Mass Media in the Making and Unmaking of the New Left* (Berkeley: University of California Press, 1980), which originated as my dissertation in 1977. In my defense, though, I was usually careful there to examine the interaction of media with other social forces and not to exaggerate the impact of media as forces in themselves.

4. See Jerome Armstrong and Markos Moulitsas Zúniga, *Crashing the Gates: Netroots, Grassroots, and the Rise of People-Powered Politics* (White River Junction, VT: Chelsea Green, 2006), p. 169.

5. Benjamin Weyl, "A Republican Revolution," *American Prospect* online, August 3, 2006, www.prospect.org/web/page.ww?section=root&name=ViewWeb&articleId=11804, accessed August 3, 2006.

6. Paul Harris, "Democrats Dare to Dream of Recapturing the Bush Heartland," *Observer* (London), June 25, 2006, http://observer.guardian.co.uk/world/story/0,,1805330,00.html, accessed July 24, 2006.

7. Quoted in E. J. Dionne Jr., "Reed and the End of a Road," *Washington Post*, July 21, 2006, p. A17.

8. Jeffrey M. Jones, "Four in 10 Republicans Would Not Find McCain an 'Acceptable' Nominee," http://poll.gallup.com/content/?ci=23764, accessed July 21, 2006.

9. David Ignatius, "Hagel's Moment," *Washington Post*, November 29, 2006, p. A23.

10. Myron Magnet, *The Dream and the Nightmare: The Sixties' Legacy to the Underclass* (San Francisco: Encounter Books, 2000), p. 1.

11. Barry Goldwater, *The Conscience of a Conservative* (New York: Macfadden Books, 1960), p. 2.

12. Magnet, *The Dream and the Nightmare*, p. 1.

13. See Jared Bernstein's blog, *No Yo Yo Economics*, www.noyoyoeconomics.com, accessed August 5, 2006.

14. Gary C. Jacobson, *A Divider, Not a Uniter: George W. Bush and the American People* (New York: Pearson Longman, 2007), p. 261.

15. James Carney, "General Karl Rove, Reporting for Duty," CNN.com, September 30, 2002, http://archives.cnn.com/2002/ALLPOLITICS/09/30/timep.rove.tm/index.html, accessed August 5, 2006.

16. Karl Rove, speech to the New York Conservative Party, June 23, 2005, www.freerepublic.com/focus/f-news/1429250/posts, July 26, 2006.

17. Dan Balz, "Rove Offers Republicans a Battle Plan for Elections," *Washington Post*, January 21, 2006, p. A1.

18. For putting this point sharply, I am indebted to Thomas B. Edsall, in a talk to the Ph.D. program in communications, Columbia University, October 26, 2006.

12. Is the Tent Big Enough?

1. Barry Goldwater, *The Conscience of a Conservative* (New York: Macfadden Books, 1960), p. 1. Goldwater's capital C. It is worth noting that during much of his career, Goldwater had little to no sympathy for the social-conservative ideal of a society whose morals would be policed by the government, though he was willing to make use of moral panic themes during his 1964 presidential campaign.

2. Richard Hofstadter, *The American Political Tradition and the Men Who Made It* (New York: Vintage, 1955), p. vii.

3. William A. Galston and Elaine C. Kamarck, "The Politics of Polarization," the Third Way Middle Class Project, October 2005, www.third-way.com, p. 25.

4. Galston and Kamarck, "Politics of Polarization," Table 15, p. 42.

5. Winship started by observing, in accord with the Galston-Kamarck summary, that there is considerable consistency among various surveys in the percentages of self-identified liberals and conservatives. Scott Winship, "How Many Liberals and Conservatives?" thedemocraticstrategist.org, July 10, 2006, www.thedem ocraticstrategist.org/strategist/2006/07/how_many_liberals_and_conserva.php, accessed August 2, 2006. I am indebted to Winship for making his calculations available to me and for helpful correspondence about his research.

6. When the NES prompted self-proclaimed "moderates" to choose "liberal" or "conservative," "liberals" rose to 33 percent, "conservatives" to 56 percent. A Pew poll of adults around the same time came up with 19 percent liberal, 39 percent conservative, and the rest moderate. In January 2006, the Democracy Corps found 19 percent calling themselves liberal and 36 percent conservative.

7. Paul Waldman, "The Hippie Era Just Won't Die," TomPaine.com, December 13, 2006, www.tompaine.com/articles/2006/12/13/the_hippie_era_just_wont_die.php, accessed December 16, 2006.

8. Winship's second set of data is in a personal communication, December 9, 2006.

9. "President Addresses Nation, Discusses Iraq, War on Terror," June 28, 2005, www.whitehouse.gov/news/releases/2005/06/20050628-7.html, accessed December 8, 2006.

10. Harold Meyerson, "Southern Exposure," *American Prospect* online, December 8, 2006, www.prospect.org/web/page.ww?section=root&name=View Web& articleId=12283, accessed December 8, 2006.

13. Narratives and Values

1. Newt Gingrich, "The Republicans Must Get Their Act Together," *Time*, March 27, 2006, available at www.time.com/time/nation/article/0,8599,1177137,00 .html, accessed December 12, 2006.
2. Fred Barnes, "Revenge of the Squares," *New Republic*, March 13, 1995, p. 23.
3. Thomas B. Edsall, *Building Red America: The New Conservative Coalition and the Drive for Permanent Power* (New York: Basic, 2006), pp. 16–17.
4. William A. Galston and Elaine C. Kamarck, "The Politics of Polarization," The Third Way Middle Class Project, October 2005, p. 42.
5. John Halpin and Ruy Teixeira, "The Politics of Definition," *American Prospect* online, April 20, 2006, www.prospect.org/web/page.ww?section=root& name=ViewWeb&articleId=11435, accessed August 5, 2006.
6. Michael Tomasky, "Party in Search of a Notion," *American Prospect* online, May 2006, www.prospect.org/web/printfriendly-view.ww?id=11424, accessed August 5, 2006.
7. In fact, as Ira Katznelson has pointed out, Social Security was *not* universal: it left out domestic and farm workers, disproportionately African American. Ira Katznelson, *When Affirmative Action Was White* (New York: W.W. Norton & Company, 2005).
8. S. R. Collins, K. Davis, M. M. Doty, J. L. Kriss, and A. L. Holmgren, "Gaps in Health Insurance: An All-American Problem," Commonwealth Fund, April 2006, www.cmwf.org/publications/publications_show.htm?doc_id=367876, accessed August 6, 2006.
9. David U. Himmelstein, Elizabeth Warren, Deborah Thorne, and Steffie Wool- handler, "Illness and Injury as Contributors to Bankruptcy," www.demos.org/ pubs/Harvard_MedDebtFeb05.pdf, accessed August 6, 2006.
10. Catherine Arnst, "The Best Medical Care in the U.S.," *Business Week*, July 17, 2006, p. 50.
11. Washington Post-ABC News Poll: Health Care, October 20, 2003, www .washingtonpost.com/wp-srv/politics/polls/vault/stories/data102003.html, question 47, accessed April 9, 2007.
12. David Sirota, "Addressing America's Health Care Taboo," www.examiner.com/ a-206490~David_Sirota__Addressing_the_country_s_health_care_taboo.html, accessed August 7, 2006.
13. See the Apollo Alliance's Web site, www.apolloalliance.org, accessed August 4, 2006.
14. Dukakis's July 21, 1988, nomination acceptance speech can be read online at www.geocities.com/Wellesley/1116/dukakis88.html, accessed August 5, 2006.
15. Ron Suskind, *The One Percent Doctrine: Deep Inside America's Pursuit of Its Enemies since 9/11* (New York: Simon & Schuster, 2006), p. 2.

14. Enemies, Bogeyman, and the Limits of American Power

1. I wrote these words two days before a *Washington Post* columnist declared that in denying the priority of law enforcement in fighting terrorists, a certain anon- ymous Bush administration official committed a "farrago of caricature and non sequitur" and showed the administration "eager to repel all but the delusional."

In his article, titled "The Triumph of Unrealism," the columnist noted that John Kerry "had a point" when he said in 2004 "that although the war on terror will be 'occasionally military,' it is 'primarily an intelligence and law enforcement operation that requires cooperation around the world.'" This was the dean of America's conservative pundits, George Will ("The Triumph of Unrealism," *Washington Post*, August 15, 2006, p. A13, www.washingtonpost .com/wp-dyn/ content/article/2006/08/14/AR2006081401163.html, accessed April 6, 2007).

2. On the National Security Strategy of 2002, see my "America's Age of Empire: The Bush Doctrine," *Mother Jones*, January–February 2003, pp. 35–39.
3. George W. Bush, speech at Fort Bragg, North Carolina, June 28, 2005, www .whitehouse.gov/news/releases/2005/06/20050628-7.html, accessed August 13, 2006.
4. Mark Mazzetti, "Qaeda Is Seen as Restoring Leadership," *New York Times*, April 2, 2007, p. 1.
5. Fallows, "The Fifty-First State?" *Atlantic*, November 2002, www.theatlantic .com/doc/200211/fallows, accessed April 6, 2007.
6. James Fallows, "Declaring Victory," *Atlantic*, September 2006, www.theatlan tic.com/doc/200609/fallows_victory, accessed April 7, 2007.
7. Fred Kaplan, "Cold Comfort," *Washington Monthly*, July/August 2006, p. 43.

15. The Human Face

1. James McGregor Burns, *The Power to Lead: The Crisis of the American Presidency* (New York: Simon & Schuster, 1984), p. 140. Cited in Joel H. Silbey, *The American Political Nation, 1838–1893* (Stanford, CA: Stanford University Press, 1991), p. 315, n. 5.
2. I elaborate on the meaning and consequence of media saturation in *Media Unlimited: How the Torrent of Images and Sounds Overwhelms Our Lives* (New York: Metropolitan, 2002).
3. Richard Hofstadter, *The American Political Tradition and the Men Who Made It* (New York: Vintage, 1955), p. 331.
4. Bill Clinton to Colonel Eugene Holmes, December 3, 1969, American Presidents Web site, http://americanpresidents.org/letters/41.asp, accessed December 16, 2006.
5. I have adapted some of the following discussion from my *Letters to a Young Activist* (New York: Basic, 2003), pp. 105–123. I wrote about New Left ambivalence toward its own leaders in *The Whole World Is Watching: Mass Media in the Making and Unmaking of the New Left* (Berkeley, CA: University of California Press, 2003), chap. 5.
6. George Stephanopoulos, *All Too Human: a Political Education* (New York: Little, Brown, 1999), pp. 150–152.
7. Interview with Miles Rapoport, November 14, 2005.
8. See the Progressive Majority's Web site, www.progressivemajority.org/candi dates, accessed August 10, 2006.
9. Ibid., accessed December 16, 2006.
10. Interview with Dean Nielsen, June 3, 2005, and Progressive Majority's Web site www.progressivemajority.org/recruit, accessed August 10, 2006.

11. Joann Loviglio, "Democrats Win Control of Pa. House after 12 Years in Minority," Philly.com, www.philly.com/mld/philly/16115775.htm, accessed December 16, 2006.

12. Here and further on I have borrowed some phrases from a liberal manifesto written in the fall of 2006 by Bruce Ackerman and myself, "We Answer to the Name of Liberals," *American Prospect*, November 2006, pp. 23–24, www.prospect.org/web/page.ww?section=root&name=ViewWeb&articleId=12124, accessed April 6, 2007.

13. On Bush administration deployment of political chiefs for government bureaus, see David E. Lewis, "Testing Pendleton's Premise: Do Political Appointees Make Worse Bureaucrats?" Princeton University, Woodrow Wilson School, 2006, www.princeton.edu/~delewis/research.htm, accessed April 8, 2007. Lewis found that political appointees scored lower on performance tests than did career bureaucrats.

INDEX